T0127978

From Silicon Valley to Shenzhen

ASIA/PACIFIC/PERSPECTIVES
Series Editor: Mark Selden

From Silicon Valley to Shenzhen

Global Production and Work in the IT Industry

Boy Lüthje, Stefanie Hürtgen, Peter Pawlicki, and Martina Sproll

ROWMAN & LITTLEFIELD
Lanham • Boulder • New York • Toronto • Plymouth, UK

Published by Rowman & Littlefield
4501 Forbes Boulevard, Suite 200, Lanham, Maryland 20706
www.rowman.com

10 Thornbury Road, Plymouth PL6 7PP, United Kingdom

British Library Cataloguing in Publication Information Available

Library of Congress Cataloging-in-Publication Data

Lüthje, Boy.
From Silicon Valley to Shenzhen : global production and work in the IT industry / Boy Lüthje, Stefanie Hürtgen, Peter Pawlicki, and Martina Sproll.
pages cm. — (Asia/Pacific/Perspectives)
Revised English translation of: Von Silicon Valley nach Shenzhen : globale Produktion und Arbeit in der IT-Industrie / Stefanie Hürtgen ... [et al.].
Includes bibliographical references and index.
ISBN 978-0-7425-5588-4 (cloth : alk. paper) — ISBN 978-0-7425-6849-5 (electronic)
1. High technology industries. 2. High technology industries—Location. 3. International division of labor. 4. Offshore assembly industry. 5. Offshore assembly industry—Employees—Social conditions. 6. Globalization—Economic aspects. I. Hürtgen, Stefanie. II. Title.
HC79.H53L88 2013
338.4'7004—dc23
2013018558

∞ ™ The paper used in this publication meets the minimum requirements of American National Standard for Information Sciences Permanence of Paper for Printed Library Materials, ANSI/NISO Z39.48-1992.

Printed in the United States of America

We dedicate this book to Wilhelm Schumm.

Contents

Acknowledgments

The present volume is the result of the work of a project group at the Frankfurt Institute of Social Research from 2001 to 2010 that developed long-term research on various aspects of global electronics contract manufacturing and its specific locations. The research was carried out under a major grant from the German Research Foundation (DFG) during the years 2001–2005 under the title "Neue Produktionsmodelle und internationale Arbeitsteilung in der Elektronikindustrie" (New Models of Production and International Division of Labor in the Electronics Industry). The research drew on the findings of a previous project sponsored by DFG on the electronics contract manufacturing industry in the United States and Germany (see Lüthje, Schumm, and Sproll 2002).

Important insights on the relocation of engineering and product development in the IT industry were generated from another major research project funded by the Volkswagen Foundation, which carried the title "Why Is Chip Design Moving to Asia?" This project was carried out in cooperation with our colleague Dieter Ernst at the East-West Center in Honolulu, Hawaii, between 2004 and 2008. Research on Mexico was supported by a grant from the Hans Böckler Foundation. Martina Sproll's PhD dissertation, derived from this research, was published in German under the title "High Tech für Niedriglohn: Neotayloristische Produktionsregimes in der IT-Industrie in Brasilien und Mexiko" (High Tech, Low Wage: Neo-Taylorist Regimes of Production in the IT Industry in Brazil and Mexico) at Verlag Westfälisches Dampfboot in Münster. The Hans Böckler Foundation has supported a major research project by our institute and the School of Labor Relations at Renmin University in Beijing on socioeconomic transformation and industrial relations in China, which also produced important insights for this book. The

Friedrich Ebert Foundation supported discussion of our research results with academics and labor experts in a workshop in Penang, Malaysia, in 2005.

The research supported by DFG was carried out in two phases. During the first phase, we focused on the organization of manufacturing and work in contract manufacturing facilities in low-cost locations in Eastern Europe, Mexico, Malaysia, Singapore, and China, and on the competition between such factories and those in developed industrial countries. The research was based on factory visits and extensive interviews with managers (usually general managers, human resources managers, and purchasing managers) along semistandardized sets of questions. In some of these factories, detailed data on the organization of work in particular areas or divisions could be gathered. In addition, interviews were conducted with local experts from academia, government, trade unions, research organizations, and NGOs in order to explore the local economic and political environment. Such interviews with external experts also helped us to control information on the particular factories, since at most sites trade unions or independent employee representations do not exist.

In Eastern Europe, we visited ten locations with fifteen factories in Hungary, one in Romania, two in Poland, and one in Estonia. In Asia, twenty large- and medium-sized facilities were visited (ten in China and ten in Malaysia and Singapore) as well as five smaller suppliers of nonelectronic components and four factories of major brand-name companies. The research in those locations was complemented by visits to selected production sites of IT-contract manufacturers in Germany and the United States (four in each region), in order to compare field data and insights from low-cost countries with the situation in developed industrial economies. In Hungary, China, and Malaysia, about half of the sites were visited twice or several times, which helped us observe the often rapid changes in the particular facilities.

During the second phase of this research, our focus became the restructuring of global production networks in the wake of the global recession of 2001–2002 and the increasing competition among low-cost locations. We tried to develop an integrated perspective directed at three interrelated levels: (1) the division of labor between brand-name companies and contract manufacturers, (2) the division of labor among locations within major contract manufacturers, and (3) organization of work and labor policies at the local level. This research resulted in three detailed case studies on the PC and server, the mobile phone handset, and the game console industries. They were based on thirty interviews with managers in the supply-chain organizations of the relevant brand-name firms in Europe, the United States, Taiwan, Singapore, Hong Kong, and China. This was supported by additional visits to four major factories of these companies in order to study interfaces between in-house and outsourced manufacturing.

During this phase of the research, we also conducted special studies on the production model of original design manufacturing with seven interviews and two factory visits at relevant contract manufacturers in Taiwan. Furthermore, extensive interviews were conducted in thirteen factories in Poland, Hungary, and Romania and in Western Europe (Scotland, Germany, France) in order to explore the impact of ongoing processes of relocation. Research in Mexico focused on Guadalajara. During field visits of several weeks in 2002, 2003, and 2005, sixty-five interviews were conducted with managers, workers, supervisors, engineers, temporary labor agencies, trade unionists, and labor experts from academia and government.

An additional set of research activities in 2009 and 2010 focused on the impact of the global financial and economic crisis on contract manufacturing factories and workers in low-cost locations, in China and Mexico in particular. During this phase, six major contract manufacturing facilities were visited in China in 2009, with extensive interviews with internal and external experts. In Mexico, a set of interviews with academic and NGO experts in Guadalajara was conducted in 2009.

This book would not have been possible without the cooperation of many companies and their representatives, government agencies, trade unions, and NGOs in the respective regions. We are not able to name them all, but we express our gratitude to these organizations and the individuals within them. Literally hundreds of people in more than a dozen countries contributed to this effort. Their willingness to accept our visits and engage in often lengthy discussions on strategy and organization as well as on practical questions of shop-floor operations has been invaluable for our work. In the course of this process, we have learned that this gigantic industry is made up of many individuals who are constantly raising questions about the nature of their organizations, their work, and their values and who are seriously trying to improve their environments. We are grateful to all of them.

The present text is a joint product by the authors. It is based on an earlier version of this book, published in 2009 by VSA Verlag in Hamburg under the title *Von Silicon Valley nach Shenzhen. Globale Produktion und Arbeit in der IT-Industrie*. We are grateful to VSA's generous handling of copyrights.

Our empirical research was divided among the members of our research team. Research in Eastern Europe at the beginning was conducted by Martina Sproll; later, Stefanie Hürtgen took over this field. Boy Lüthje was in charge of field research in Asia, and Martina Sproll conducted our activities in Mexico. Our study greatly benefitted from the research for Martina's PhD dissertation on contract manufacturing in Brazil and Mexico. Peter Pawlicki provided excellent research assistance during the entire duration of this project. He particularly contributed research on the transformation of engineering work in the chip design industry, which also resulted in a PhD dissertation.

He and Pamela Passano at the Frankfurt Institute of Social Research provided invaluable support in editing and proofreading this manuscript. The English version of this text was edited by our friend David Bacon. He was not only an excellent editor but also a source of productive criticism and inspiration, based on his previous experience as a union organizer in the electronics industry in Silicon Valley.

The Institute of Social Research, Frankfurt, is the home base for our research team. Our work also received invaluable institutional support from a number of universities and research organizations in the United States and China. We have to name in particular the East-West Center Research Program in Honolulu, Hawaii, where our friend Dieter Ernst was a collaborator over many years, the School of Labor Relations at Renmin University of China, and the Joint Center for Comparative Labor Research at Sun Yat-sen University in Guangzhou, China, under its codirectors Prof. He Gaochao of Sun Yat-sen University and Katie Quan of the University of California, Berkeley Labor Center.

Finally, the authors express their thanks to Wilhelm Schumm, who directed this project in his capacity as a member of the board of directors of the Frankfurt Institute of Social Research. He was a coauthor of the German version of this book but decided to abstain from further writing activities on this subject after his retirement. In appreciation of his support and friendship, this volume is dedicated to him.

Frankfurt, Guangzhou, Honolulu

Introduction

Like no other industry, information technology symbolizes the innovative potential of modern capitalism. Not only has the industry been at the core of the technological revolutions of recent decades, the IT sector also has been a hotbed for the creation of new forms of companies, production networks, and work. During the 1990s, those were often portrayed as ingredients of a new form of capitalism, in which the permanent growth of new technologies, start-up companies, and high-paying jobs would put an end to the cycles of recession and stagnation prevalent in most industrialized countries since the 1970s. Economists called this the "New Economy," and sociologists predicted the rise of the "network society" (Castells 1996).

Since the bursting of the Internet bubble in the global financial markets and the massive downturn in the IT sector in 2001 and 2002, many aspects of this development were seen more soberly. The wave of bankruptcies, plant closures, and relocations of production in the centers of the world high-tech industry—particularly in Silicon Valley, but also in older industrial regions in the US East and South as well as in Europe—revived doubts about the IT industry's potential as a growth engine for new jobs. At the same time, large new complexes of IT production grew in low-cost regions such as Mexico, Southeast Asia, Eastern Europe, India, and, most notably, China. Not only manufacturing was moved from industrial centers, but also product development and design of chips and software. Industry experts began to talk of "innovation offshoring" (Ernst 2006a) to describe the increasingly integrated character of high-tech production in emerging economies.

The global financial crisis of 2008–2009 so far has only accelerated this development. At the same time, the development of the IT industry mirrors the fundamental changes in the capitalist world economy following the demise of the finance-driven mode of capital accumulation of recent decades.

1

In the aftermath of the crisis, major emerging economies, in Asia in particular, are not only the principal locations for production, they also have become the main engines for market growth in IT, as the debt-financed growth path of the United States and other major developed economies has faded.

One of the key elements of the restructuring of production in the information technology industry has been the emergence of a new brand of global subcontractors that since the 1990s has taken over the entire process of assembly of IT systems and their main components, printed circuit boards. These multibillion-dollar companies provide manufacturing and the related engineering, procurement of parts and components, distribution logistics, and after-sales functions such as product repair as an integrated "service." Thus, contract manufacturing of this kind is often termed electronics manufacturing services (EMS).

The major companies in this industry are mostly based in the United States and Taiwan, with some in Europe, Canada, and Singapore. Since the 1990s, they have taken over numerous factories from well-known electronics companies such as IBM, Lucent, Siemens, and Ericsson. At the same time, they have built massive production sites in Mexico, Eastern Europe, Malaysia, and, especially, China to provide modern mass production while paying the lowest wages possible. These factories often employ several thousand or tens of thousands of workers. The largest of them in the Chinese city of Shenzhen has more than three hundred thousand workers.

In spite of the fact that this model of production has transformed the entire manufacturing base of the electronics industry, little is known about this phenomenon. The major contract manufacturers hide their names from the public on behalf of their brand-name customers. In contrast to famous brand-name companies such as Intel, Microsoft, and Apple, they do not put their names "inside" the product they manufacture. The *Los Angeles Times*, therefore, aptly called this "stealth manufacturing." Only on very rare occasions, for instance, in the wake of the tragic wave of suicides among young Chinese migrant workers in early 2010 at Taiwan-owned Foxconn, the world's largest contract manufacturer, do the realities of workers' lives inside the factories surface in public media.

The Foxconn incidents, however, have raised basic issues of transparency and public scrutiny over subcontracting relations and labor standards in the IT industry in unprecedented ways. Massive publicity was also directed at Apple, the corporate superstar in the post–financial crisis US information technology industry. Not only has negative news about working conditions at Apple suppliers in China become a source of daily headlines, but in a more fundamental way, the Apple-Foxconn affair raised deep questions about the continuing shift of manufacturing jobs to China and the hollowing out of the innovative base of the US economy. The issue was publicly raised by President Obama in a conversation with Apple's late CEO Steve Jobs (*NYT*, January 21, 2012).

DIGGING DEEPER: GLOBAL PRODUCTION NETWORKS AND THE RESHAPING OF MANUFACTURING WORK

The structure, the forms of work organization, and the labor policies of the electronics contract manufacturing industry in its low-cost locations are the subject of this book. A deeper understanding of this model of production not only requires extensive empirical analysis of the shape of production networks in the IT industry and of the labor process in the factories, but also of the profound systemic changes in capitalist production relations that have been largely ignored in mainstream economics and social science literature. We have to take account of the systemic instabilities of network-based production and of the specific potential for crisis resulting from the "outsourcing" of entire production systems to contract manufacturers, as well as the changing power relationships between global brand names and their "manufacturing service partners." In particular, we have to understand the massive reintegration of production resources in the obscure but pivotal arena of contract manufacturing networks and factories, which are reminiscent of models of vertically integrated mass production, Fordism in particular, common in earlier periods of modern capitalism.

A thorough analysis of the political economy of what can be called network-based mass production has to include the resulting changes in the global economy. On the one hand, one has to understand the consequences of the massive shifting of technology resources and manufacturing know-how to contract manufacturers. We have to ask whether this will result in an increasing "hollowing out" among IT brand-name firms of their technological and organizational knowledge and their ability to control global production networks. On the other hand, we have to analyze the consequences for the development of productive resources in emerging economies. The growth of cutting-edge production complexes in these countries, however, does not necessarily translate into sustainable economic and social development. We therefore have to analyze the contradictory nature and the limits and shortcomings of industrial upgrading, especially in the field of labor. In particular, we have to ask in what ways the older forms of direct control of branch factories in developing countries through multinational corporations is being replaced by other, more indirect forms of control over work and socioeconomic development.

All this calls for an integrated view of the simultaneous changes in industry organization, production models, outsourcing relationships, and work. Such a perspective, however, is often missing in contemporary analyses of global production systems and networks. Older theories of the international division of labor have extensively analyzed the relationship between the global shifting of production and the emergence of highly segmented work in developing countries. Their vision of the global assembly line, however, did not fully consider the potentials of industrial development and the related formation of new workforces and their struggles for better working conditions and democratic representation at the shop floor. Conversely, in today's theories of "global production networks," "global commodity chains," or "global value chains," the opportunities and strategies for successful upgrading under global production are discussed extensively, but systematic perspectives on the changing nature of production, work, and labor relations remain underdeveloped. Therefore, it has been a key goal of our research on electronics contract manufacturing to bring the labor process back in and to integrate perspectives of critical political economy and labor sociology.

Our analysis focuses on tracing the development of the new networks of globalized mass production in the IT industry and the reorganization of work since the 1990s, trying to capture the systemic nature of industry-wide restructuring of production and work in the global context. We thereby hope to make a theoretical contribution to ongoing academic and political debates on globalization of production, especially by taking these debates beyond narrow perspectives of determining criteria of "success" for participation in global production networks. Rather, we emphasize the changing nature of work, employment relations, and labor policies and their implications for the possibilities of sustainable economic and social development.

Since shop-floor relations develop under the specific social, political, and cultural conditions of the respective regions and countries, our study includes analysis of the complex relationship among "global," "national," and "local" factors in the development of global production networks. Such an analysis leads to fundamental questions concerning control of labor standards in IT manufacturing, and also of public scrutiny over global production networks and their political regulation. These questions clearly reach beyond today's dominant discourse of sustainability through voluntary self-control by multinational brand-name companies and their stakeholders to limit illegal and unethical practices.

The title of this book relates to two places which have become central to the development of global production networks in the IT industry: Silicon Valley in California and the city of Shenzhen in South China's Guangdong Province, which during the last decade has emerged as the location of the largest electronics contract manufacturing factories in the world. Our research, however, includes many other traditionally important locations of the IT industry in the United States and Western Europe, as well as new locations of mass manufacturing in Eastern Europe, Mexico, and Southeast Asia. From the study of the simultaneous transformations taking place in the various locations of the IT industry's global production networks we hope to generate specific insights on the nature of this development.

OUTLINE

In this volume, the presentation of the extensive empirical material from our studies and of our theoretical reflections is organized as follows.

In chapter 1, major threads of the theoretical discussion on capitalist restructuring, transnational production, and the changing international division of labor are inspected and discussed regarding their relevance to the subject of this study, electronics contract manufacturing. We refer to theories of the "new international division of labor" from the 1970s and 1980s, recent theories of global commodity chains, value chains and production networks, and newer labor process theories analyzing the impact of modular or network-based production and the related rationalization of work "along the chain." We then explain the basic categories of our own analysis, which derives from French regulation theory and the concept of regimes of production, going back to the works of Michael Burawoy in the 1970s and 1980s. On this basis, we develop our major proposals for the interpretation of our empirical data.

In the following chapters, the empirical material is presented under three distinctive perspectives. Chapter 2 focuses on the far-reaching changes in the production systems of the IT industry since the 1990s, the rapid development of contract-based production during that period, and its crisis and restructuring in the wake of the bursting of the Internet bubble in the years 2001 and 2002 and the global financial and economic crisis in 2008. We particularly analyze the emergence of two competing models of production in electronics contract manufacturing, known as electronics manufacturing services (EMS) and original design manufacturing (ODM). We also look at the contradictory tendencies of vertical specialization of production systems at their top end (i.e., the model of "ultralean" technology companies focusing on highly specialized products or components), and the vertical reintegration of manufacturing at the bottom (i.e., at the level of contract manufacturers). We analyze the instability of the norms of production governing capital accumulation and production in the IT industry and the implications for the restructuring of manufacturing.

In chapter 3, we analyze the locational strategies of the electronics contract manufacturing industry, the resulting changes in the international division of labor, and the emergence of new locations of large-scale, low-cost manufacturing in East Asia, Eastern Europe and North America. This includes a closer look at the diverging shape of global production systems between EMS and ODM contract manufacturers and the influence of specific economic, social, and political conditions in the respective locations. Our analysis focuses on the question of whether and to what extent there is a global division of labor based on the location of the more complex functions of production in industrialized and of standardized mass production in developing economies. We demonstrate how the massive vertical reintegration of production and technologies among contract manufacturers is reshaping the international division of labor by placing highly integrated factories and manufacturing clusters in low-cost locations.

Chapter 4 presents in detail our research on the changing organization of work and its sociopolitical regulation in contract manufacturing in low-cost locations. We trace how the global standardization of production processes and work patterns is leading to highly uniform models of work organization around the globe and how these models are being implemented in various locations. We particularly ask how this globalized model of work is being implemented into various sociopolitical contexts and how the corporations are trying to integrate and take advantage of the uneven conditions of development among the respective countries and regions. The emerging formations of work in contract manufacturing are analyzed as a manifestation of neo-Taylorism, its amalgamations with national- and regional-specific forms of control and political regulation as regimes of production. Since the workforce in most of the countries investigated is made up predominantly of women and migrant workers, the analysis of gender, ethnic, and social discrimination against such groups of workers forms a key element in our conception of regimes of production.

In chapter 5, we return to our theoretical reflections at the beginning of this book and discuss the theoretical and political implications of our empirical analysis. We discuss some general conclusions with regard to the changing structure of contemporary capitalism and assess the implications for further research on global production networks. Finally, we explain our conclusions concerning labor standards in the IT industry, worker representation and union organizing, and problems of social control and political regulation over global production networks in a key sector of modern capitalism, which have thus far remained largely unaddressed by policy makers and academia.

Chapter One

Bringing the Labor Process Back In

Global Production Networks and Work

People say, "Oh you are so smart." And I say, "What, because we're doing what Henry Ford did in 1927 at River Rouge?" This is not genius. It's about being in the right place at the right time, and it's about execution.
—Michael Marks, ex-CEO, Flextronics International,
quoted in *Wired* magazine, November 2001

As the globalization of production has become a political and household issue throughout the developed and less developed world, the changing shape of work in the context of global production networks remains obscure. Critical social sciences focus on the global movement of money, financial markets, and the military and geopolitical aspects of capital's unfettered dominance in the global arena. Theoretically based empirical analysis of the changing shape of work within global production networks and systems, however, remains hard to find. In particular, the massive industrial development in countries such as China or Mexico and the changing shape of work within the highly modern factories in those countries are poorly understood. So too are the social and political implications of the global recomposition of the workforce in core industries and the working classes in the respective regions and countries.

The ongoing restructuring of the former core enterprises of Fordist capitalism through outsourcing and the internal reorganization of capitalist corporations designed to foster competition among business units, factories, and their workers is accompanied by the emergence of new forms of vertically integrated mass production in the new centers of globalized manufacturing in the former Third World. A new brand of transnational subcontractors, suppliers, or outsourcing partners is organizing this reintegration of production on a

worldwide scale. The reemergence of transnational networks of mass production is the downside of the ongoing fragmentation of global brand-name
and technology companies, a process often analyzed by economists as vertical specialization, flexible specialization, or modularization. In the information technology industry, the term "electronics contract manufacturing" has
become a shorthand name for this change.

The simultaneous movement of *vertical disintegration* and *reintegration*
is the hidden agenda of so-called network capitalism, seen as a global empire
of disintegrated economic actors involved in mutual "high-trust" relationships in a post-Fordist and postsocialist world. A more dialectical view reveals that the new mass-production factories are modeled after the principles
of vertical integration, those associated with Henry Ford in an earlier period
of capitalism. At the same time, these factories in newly industrializing countries are reinstituting the highly segmented assembly-line work designed by
Ford's co-genius, Frederick Winslow Taylor. The result is not only pressure
on manufacturing and increasingly on nonmanufacturing jobs in developed
capitalist countries but also a profound restructuring of the international division of labor. This change is at the core of the development of new centers of
capital accumulation in a number of large developing countries such as China, Mexico, Brazil, and India. These countries increasingly challenge the
supremacy of the United States and other established core economies of the
triad of world capitalism in manufacturing, organizational, and technological
innovation.

In this chapter we review some key debates in recent political economy
and industrial sociology on corporate restructuring, transnational production
networks, and the changing international division of labor and relate this to
contract manufacturing in the electronics industry. Starting from a short
introduction to electronics contract manufacturing as a relatively new model
of mass production following the demise of the dominant models of the
post–World War II era in the tradition of Henry Ford, we take a closer look at
current research on the development of production systems in the IT industry. We examine these changes in the wake of the global recession in the
years 2001–2002 and the inherent crisis of network-based production established during the boom of the so-called New Economy. We then refer to the
approaches that have guided most critical research on global production in
recent decades. These include theories of the international division of labor,
global commodity chains (GCC), and global production networks. We discuss some of their implications and their shortcomings with regard to the
institutional regulation of production systems and work. From there, we explain our own analytical framework, which is based in French regulation
theory and the concept of regimes of production as developed by Michael
Burawoy and his school. Finally, an outline of our main propositions guides
the reader into the empirical chapters of this book.

MASS PRODUCTION IN THE AGE OF NETWORK CAPITALISM

Electronics contract manufacturing emerged from the massive restructuring of the US information technology industry that began in the 1980s and was centered in Silicon Valley and other high-tech districts in the western and southern parts of the United States (Sturgeon 1997). In those regions, which became the hotbeds of the so-called New Economy of the 1990s, profound changes in the forms of capitalist competition and the organization of production and work occurred. In the context of this development, an industrial structure took shape that was no longer dominated by vertically integrated giant corporations such as IBM but rather was shaped along horizontal lines of specialized suppliers of key components such as computer chips, software, hard disk drives, and graphics cards (Grove 1996). In the PC industry, the epicenter of this industrial revolution, the suppliers of the core chips (Intel) and the operating software (Microsoft) gained quasi-monopolistic control over the entire ecosystem of supply and innovation in this field. Referring to the brand logos of these companies, political economists described the new system of industrial organization as "Wintelism," a concept derived from combining Windows and Intel, two pivots of the emerging system (Borrus and Zysman 1997; for critical adaptations, see Lüthje 2001; Jürgens and Sablowski 2004).

The hallmark of this restructuring was a new strategic approach to externalize, or "outsource," production and work. In the Wintelist computer industry, new companies without factories of their own (dubbed as "fabless") emerged. They allocated most or all of their manufacturing and, to an increasing extent, their routine work in product development to external contract manufacturers, which rapidly grew in size. This system of contract-based production was linked to new forms of global production networks, characterized by "the disintegration of the industry's value-chain into constituent functions that can be contracted out to independent producers wherever those companies are located in the global economy" (Borrus and Zysman 1997, 2; see Borrus, Ernst, and Haggard 2000, 4ff.).

The terms "Wintelism" and "global production networks" refer not only to a new form of "modular" manufacturing but to a historically new model of innovation, encompassing the established forms of product development and the generation of technology (Ernst 2005a; Lüthje 2007a). In an earlier study, Dieter Ernst and David O'Connor (1992) described the dynamics of this restructuring as a double-edged or dialectical process of "fragmentation" and "centralization." According to this argument, the vertically disintegrated elements of the IT industry, initially led by the relatively small and specialized flag bearers of the "PC revolution" from Silicon Valley, have created their own production networks, characterized by a distinctive openness as opposed to the vertical integration prevalent in Fordist mass-production industries.

This new model of production emerged from the profound transformation of the international division of labor engendered by the proliferation of relatively integrated supply infrastructures in the emerging economies of low-cost regions such as Southeast Asia, Mexico, Eastern Europe, and China. At the same time, large-scale electronics contract manufacturing marked a deep change in the organization of industry that went far beyond the use of outside suppliers for component or part manufacturing. Rather, contract manufacturers themselves took over entire chains of production, supply, and logistics for complex products such as PCs, laptop computers, and cell phones. Compared with other technology-based manufacturing industries, this marked an almost complete break with the idea of integrated manufacturing by the brand-owning company and a radically new structure of globally dispersed manufacturing based on contractual relationships.

This dualism between fabless brand-name firms and highly integrated contract manufacturers differs markedly from the outsourcing strategies of other industries. The automobile industry, for instance, also has substantially reduced the scope of in-house manufacturing through outsourcing. Parts and components are produced by outside suppliers, led by highly integrated "system suppliers" with far-flung networks of subsuppliers. However, the emergence of these supply pyramids has not fundamentally changed the traditional model of production, which is still based on quality and market control by the corporations manufacturing and developing the automobiles (Borrus and Zysman 1997; Jürgens and Rehbehn 2006).

These changes are taking place during a period of crisis and the restructuring of the Fordist production system and its model for work organization, Taylorism. As has been widely analyzed by political economists and industrial sociologists, standardized mass production linked to national markets lost its clout in the 1970s (Aglietta 1979). Restructuring was increasingly dominated by the expanding control of financial markets over manufacturing industries under the banner of shareholder value. Short-term profit expectations drove market-type evaluation and control of the internal functions of corporations and factories. At the same time, the focus of rationalization expanded from individual workplaces and processes to production chains and permanent measuring of the comparative advantages of "inside" and "outside" suppliers (Sauer and Döhl 1994, 103ff.). In a certain way, full-scale outsourcing strategies such as electronics contract manufacturing represent an extreme consequence of this development, in which the finance-driven model of innovation and corporate restructuring of the US high-tech industry in the 1990s became the motor of a radical change in manufacturing practices (Sturgeon 1997).

However, the bursting of the high-tech bubble (Brenner 2002) and the subsequent decline of the US New Economy after 2001 have demonstrated the structural problems inherent in this kind of manufacturing revolution. We have learned the limits of Wintelism as a model of profitable capital accumulation, a model which was presented as a potential remedy to the declining fortunes of the United States as the undisputed global leader in manufacturing (Lüthje 2007b). Simultaneously, newly industrializing countries, in the "China Circle" (Naughton 1997) in particular, use highly competitive and advanced high-tech manufacturing. This has engendered another round of changes in the international division of labor. Some of the former low-cost assembly locations, such as South Korea, Taiwan, and Singapore, have significantly upgraded their technological and organizational skills. Together with India and China, today they challenge the global leadership of established high-tech economies. Current literature on global production networks in the IT industry, however, has only partially addressed this challenge and its economic, political, and social implications.

Tim Sturgeon's important analysis of electronics contract manufacturing as a "new American model of manufacturing" (1997) discusses the particular characteristics of this model shaped in Silicon Valley. Sturgeon's more recent work depicts contract manufacturing as a US version of modular production, an alternative configuration of outsourced manufacturing, or "lean production," initiated in Japan during the 1980s. He points to the political and social environment in the United States, which seems to permit more large-scale outsourcing of production because of fewer legal restrictions and the limited influence of trade unions (Sturgeon 2006).

With regard to recent debates on concepts of modularity (see Chesbrough 2003; Lester and Piore 2004; Ernst 2004) and their implications for the international division of labor, Sturgeon and Ji-Ren Lee (2005) developed the concept of "industrial coevolution." They describe relationships between brand-name firms and contract manufacturers and the respective locations in industrialized and developing countries as a systemic interaction of mutually dependent actors. There are high risks but potentially great benefits in terms of productivity, manufacturing quality, and economic development. Included in this analysis are not only the first-generation large-scale contract manufacturers, which emerged in the United States during the 1990s, but also their competitors from Taiwan. Taiwanese companies used a distinct model of modular manufacturing, which challenged their older US competitors in the wake of the recession of 2001–2002 and reversed the world order in this industry segment in recent years. Yet Sturgeon and Lee see the distinctive features of the manufacturing strategy of most Taiwanese contract manufacturers (see chapter 2) as a potential disadvantage compared with the older American model. From this perspective, the higher degree of product diversification in most US contract manufacturing firms seems to provide the potential for long-term dominance in the world of electronics manufacturing.

However, this proposition tends to neglect the consequences of the globalization of contract manufacturing and its dispersion throughout North

America and Europe and their related low-cost locations. Japanese electronics companies, who have been relatively reluctant to adapt US-style contract manufacturing (see chapter 3), are implicitly criticized for not having understood the lessons of radical modularization and the related strategies of platform leadership (Cusumano and Gawer 2002). The massive crisis of electronics contract manufacturing in 2001–2002 is treated as a cyclical downturn rather than a structural problem of production and innovation in the IT industry and its social division of labor (Sayer and Walker 1992). The concept of industrial coevolution also does not help in understanding the competition between various models of contract manufacturing, the protracted struggles between brand-name firms and contract manufacturers over the boundaries of knowledge and profit making between them, and recent tendencies to relocate important parts of production back from contract manufacturers to brand-name firms (see chapter 2).

Greg Linden, Clair Brown, and Melissa Appleyard (2004) take a sharper look at the structural elements of the crisis of the Wintel model. Their analysis points to the high costs and limited applicability of the model of innovation and market control generated in the PC industry. This model is based on relatively "open" technological standards controlled by lead firms such as Microsoft or Intel ("open-but-owned standards"; Borrus and Zysman 1997). Especially in markets such as mobile telecommunications, which are heavily dependent on monopolistic network operators, or in traditional consumer goods turned digital (such as televisions), models of vertically disintegrated mass production have proved less effective than in PCs or Internet-related equipment. The concept of the new "Net world order" is proposed as an alternative paradigm to Wintelism in order to gain a better understanding of the diversity of production systems governing the IT industry of the early twenty-first century. The authors do not expect a return to the Fordist model of vertical integration, however. Platform leadership is based on a much broader portfolio of technology resources, company networks, and long-term alliances than in the Wintel model. Vertically integrated high-tech companies such as Nokia may offer better examples of successful market control than the models of Silicon Valley focused on market segmentation and short-term monopoly status in "hip" product markets (Linden, Brown, and Appleyard 2004).

This analysis seems to offer a better understanding of the variety of innovation strategies in today's IT industry. But it remains vague in its implications for the organization of production and the related changes in the international division of labor. In particular, the ongoing vertical reintegration of manufacturing in newly industrializing countries, embodied in the emergence of large-scale factories with a comprehensive combination of production functions, and the related processes of deindustrialization in older high-tech regions of the developed world are not taken into consideration. These shortcomings are symptomatic of most current literature on production networks in the IT industry and in manufacturing industries in general. We lack concepts that expose the dynamics of fragmentation and centralization in new production systems, that is, of vertical specialization on the one hand and the often massive reintegration of manufacturing on the other. Concepts of industrial coevolution imply a relatively harmonious division of labor along the chain, neglecting the often hierarchical nature of global production networks (Ernst 2003a). At the same time, the vision of a more or less complementary division of labor (Berger et al. 2001, 69) underestimates the massive changes in the organization of production that make global relocation possible (for a recent critical discussion, see Voskamp and Wittke 2008a, 2008b). Such a division exists between industrializing countries, which keep development and higher ends of manufacturing, and newly industrializing countries, who concentrate on mass manufacturing and standard products.

Understanding the contradictory nature of these processes in a globalized capitalist economy requires an integrated view of the complex changes in the social division of labor (Sayer and Walker 1992) in the IT industry. This view has to integrate (a) the changing international geography of manufacturing location, (b) production models and firm strategies, and (c) the organization of work and its political regulation in the particular locations. Such a perspective can hardly be developed without an extensive analysis of their human elements. Those elements include the labor process in the various sections of global production systems and the organization of work and social control over labor at the shop-floor level and in the politics of the respective societies. In particular, the notion of "industrial upgrading" of newly developing industrial districts and economies requires that we systematically examine the complex issues of human resource development in the respective regions. That should include the methods by which large and diverse workforces are mobilized and integrated into the far-flung and complex production systems of global capitalism. The recombination of the labor force at the various levels, their respecialization along the chain, and the complex social, cultural, and political implications of these processes is the most neglected, but perhaps the most complex, part of the analysis of global production networks, especially in high-tech industries.

THEORIES OF INTERNATIONAL DIVISION OF LABOR AND GLOBAL COMMODITY CHAINS

Theories based on a comprehensive notion of labor and production as a social process in the traditions of Marx's critique of political economy have extensively analyzed the connections between the internationalization of production and the changes in the labor process.

The "classical" approach in this field was developed by Folker Fröbel, Jürgen Heinrichs, and Otto Kreye (1977), with their theory of the *new international division of labor* (NIDL). This inspired a vast body of literature on the relocation of production to low-cost countries in the periphery in the wake of the mid-1970s crisis of the Fordist model of accumulation. In these authors' view, the new element of what they called "worldwide sourcing" was the creation of new mechanisms by multinational corporations to segment and relocate production. This resulted in the simultaneous transformations of the location and the form of organization of particular segments of the production process (Fröbel, Heinrichs, and Kreye 1977, 37ff.). The preconditions were set by institutional innovations in surplus-value production and the accumulation of capital, mainly the liberalization of capital markets and foreign investment. From the so-called free production zones created in a number of developing countries, a world market for labor of relatively low skill and "world-market factories" emerged, allowing the transfer of labor-intensive mass manufacturing at a fraction of its cost in developed industrial countries (ibid., 479ff.).

Central to these strategies of global relocation were highly segmented processes of production and work in many manufacturing industries, such as textile and garment. The fact that productivity in such industries could no longer be raised by further segmentation provided the major incentive for relocation. Thus, the crisis of the Taylor paradigm of rationalization and the tapping of the often large industrial reserve armies in developing countries put the workforces in the developed countries in direct competition with newly recruited workers. Workers in developed countries often had union-negotiated wages, working conditions, and benefits while newly recruited workers received "Third-World wages" and had no collective representation and few benefits. Fröbel, Heinrichs, and Kreye and their followers gave ample documentation of the implementation of Taylorist patterns of work organization and control in newly industrializing countries, leading to problems of speed-up, overlong working hours, and violations of basic health and safety standards, based on recruitment of workforces overwhelmingly composed of young women (ibid.).

The relocation of relatively low-skilled labor along the global assembly line, for which the electronics industry became a prime example, was the key phenomenon of that period, characterized by the global crisis of the postwar mode of capitalist accumulation and growth. The NIDL concept described an initial stage of change in the international division of labor in which highly integrated industrial companies relocated specific steps of production and outsourced them to third-party suppliers. This was still linked to a static concept of complementary specialization based on the relocation of lower-skilled elements of the production process. The strategy of relocating more complex production activities, and finally research and development, had not yet appeared. The rapid move of multinational capital toward more complex strategies of relocation, as well as the resulting industrial upgrading in developing countries, could not be captured sufficiently with the NIDL concept. That led to extensive debates about the viability of the underlying concepts of dependency created through trade and unequal exchange (Lipietz 1987; Henderson 1989) and a gradual shift of theoretical debate toward concepts of production networks or global commodity chains.

The strength of the older theories of the NIDL unquestionably lay in the inclusion of the labor process and the forms of work organization. These were treated as a key element of the theoretical and empirical analysis of globalization. Departing from Fröbel, Heinrichs, and Kreye's pioneering work, a broad spectrum of literature emerged that analyzed the conditions of work in the low-wage factories of the global assembly lines of late Fordism. For the electronics industry, the studies of Ernst (1983) and Jeffrey Henderson (1989) in the emerging field of microelectronics were very important. The labor process was analyzed in the most detail by Terence McGee's (1986) and Aihwa Ong's (1987) empirical studies of work and women workers' lives in the electronics factories of Malaysia's free trade zones. Ong's analysis of the semirural conditions of reproduction for the newly emerging mass workforce of young Muslim women is a model for the integration of gender and cultural-religious segmentation into sociological studies of work organization. However, the schematic assumption of a continuing divide between center and periphery along the lines of skilled and unskilled production had its impact on the analysis of the changing labor process in factories in developing countries. The vision of global Taylorism could hardly capture the upgrading of working processes and the increasing differentiation of the working class in the relocation of integrated factories and production chains (see Harley Shaiken's 1994 pioneering work on the auto industry in Mexico). Yet due to a lack of viable theories in this field, visions of the global assembly line are still alive in many critical discourses on globalization today.

Since the 1980s, NIDL theories were particularly challenged by two developments. On the one hand, the rise of developing countries such as Brazil, Mexico, and the "four Asian tigers"—South Korea, Taiwan, Hong Kong, and Singapore—ran counter to the basic assumptions of the NIDL concept of a continuing exclusion of the periphery from higher-end industrial development. The notion of export-led industrialization increasingly dominated the agenda of international debates on development and industrial upgrading (see Amsden 2001). This shift became particularly apparent in the wake of the breakup of the Soviet Union, after which successful integration into a capitalist world economy dominated by neoliberalist policies and ideologies appeared as the only remaining alternative to developing countries for industrial upgrading. On the other hand, the changes in the social organization of capitalist corporations and production led to an increasing fragmentation of production systems along chains and networks of suppliers and subsuppliers. This also implied a relative decline in the role of vertically integrated corporations of the Fordist period and the rise of new fabless brand-name firms or retail companies as leaders of global production systems and networks.

These seminal shifts were reflected in concepts of *global commodity chains* (GCC), most prominently developed by Gary Gereffi and his colleagues (Gereffi and Korzeniewiczs 1994). These scholars analyze the international division of labor based on the reconstruction of complex chains of product generation, often departing from changes in the trade and retail systems or consumer behavior in the particular markets. The concept is based on Terence Hopkins and Immanuel Wallerstein's (1986) idea of global commodity chains constituted mainly through trade relations between national economies at different levels of economic development. The GCC approach of the more recent years focuses on networks between companies at various levels of global production systems and their respective locations. Two basic types of GCC are distinguished. Those dominated by retail and brand-name companies without manufacturing (such as Walmart or Nike) are called *buyer-driven* chains. Those dominated by big manufacturing companies that outsource parts and components products (e.g., the auto industry) are called *producer-driven* chains. In the course of its broad reception and application in empirical studies, various interpretations of the GCC approach have been developed (Bair 2005, 2009). Some of them relate to concepts of global value chains, and others focus on the governance and politics of GCC, exploring the linkages and cross-linkages between local manufacturing and scenarios of global production relations in specific industries and their subsegments.

From the perspective of industrial sociology, the GCC approach seems attractive. It can be related to "marketization" of the internal and external production relationships and workplaces as well as the continued optimization of production and value chains based on strict control of comparative cost and efficiency advantages. It examines the search for certain strategies of cost optimization—the struggles and alliances between management and workers in various enterprises along the chain and the limits of company-based strategies among the respective actors. It places them in a broader global perspective (Schumm 2003, 200). However, the application of the GCC approach to technology-intensive industries, with frequent changes in the sector-wide patterns of innovation and production, is difficult.

For the IT industry in particular, the distinction between buyer- and producer-driven commodity chains is too schematic. In the Wintelist segments of the industry, the lead firms can be classified neither as retailers or fashion designers nor as manufacturers. As mentioned above, both the factory-owning and the fabless flagship companies in the IT sector are highly innovative developers of complex technologies operating under extreme constraints of profitability and time. The lead firms themselves are often component suppliers; some have extremely capital-intensive manufacturing operations—for example, Intel and other major chipmakers—while some have no interest in manufacturing at all—for example, Microsoft (Lüthje, Schumm, and Sproll 2002). Concepts of global commodity chains do not capture the enormous dynamics of innovation in the respective industry segments (Ernst and Lüthje 2003) nor the complex dynamics of vertical reintegration of manufacturing. Electronics contract manufacturing provides the case in point (Lüthje 2006). As we will discuss in further detail, GCC concepts also tend to neglect complex institutional, social, and political regulation underlying the development of global production networks in different locations, a weakness shared with NIDL theories.

TRANSNATIONAL PRODUCTION AND INSTITUTIONAL FORMS OF REGULATION

Since the 1980s, transnational production networks developed in response to the crisis of the model of the hierarchic-bureaucratic corporation with vertically integrated mass production, based on internal economies of scale. Decentralization and marketization (Sauer and Döhl 1994) start from outsourcing and the formation of supplier networks and create a vertical disintegration of business processes. The change toward "external economics" (Sturgeon 2000) and fragmentation of value chains (Faust, Voskamp, and Wittke 2004, 24) is further driven by changes in information technology. Although the global distribution of network-based business activities appears highly dispersed in comparison to older forms of vertical-divisional organization, new elements of central coordination and control based on advanced information technology can be used to secure the optimization of value chains. Therefore, transnational production networks do not typically entail fragmentation in the sense of decentralized, market-based self-control of individual units.

The theoretical concept of the global production network thus must be distinguished from the concept of the "network society" popularized in recent theories of contemporary capitalism and its transformations. These theories are based on the notion of the "information society," in which information becomes the key driver of social change and IT-based knowledge networks form the dominant medium of social interaction and power. In Manuel Castells's view, this proposition includes the assumption that "for the first time in history, the capitalist mode of production shapes social relationships over the entire planet" (1996, 471). This generates a new kind of capitalism, centered on networks of global financial flows and a new organizational form of enterprise called the network enterprise. According to this theory, productivity is primarily generated by informational networking, and the process of production is mostly examined from the perspective of the way information technologies reshape work (ibid., 274ff.). Industrial production systems in the traditional sense are of minor significance.

Obviously, Castells disregards the contradictory dynamics of what is called the new network capitalism. For an adequate understanding of the socioeconomic functions of transnational production networks, one needs to take a sharper view of the interplay of economics and politics underlying the development of global capital. Under existing conditions, companies establish their production systems in specific locations with distinctive institutional settings. Governments and capital in these regions, with their respective policies and strategies, become competitors in a global race between locations. Competition between regions is usually explained by two approaches. Mainstream economics follows Williamson's theory of transaction costs. It analyzes institutional regulations as alternative sets of decision making between internal hierarchy and external competition. On the other hand, political and social science theories have gained importance. They call into question neoliberal market orthodoxy and explicitly include political regulations and cultural orientations as factors *sui generis*. Such theories consider companies and corporations as social institutions whose organization is decisively influenced by politics, in terms of both the legal and ideological framework of business organization as well as labor laws and industrial relations. These debates regularly refer to the notion of "varieties of capitalisms," helping explain the spectrum of institutional constraints and opportunities that must be taken into account by strategies of multinational companies and networks (Miller 2005).

The sources of these theories can be found in the work of Karl Polanyi (1944, 1978), whose studies of the emergence of capitalism in nineteenth-century England for the first time established basic institutionalist perspectives in modern social sciences. His characterization of capitalist development as a double-edged movement between market and regulation (ibid., 185) is still viable today. For dynamic economic development, a self-regulating market environment must exist. On the other hand, the organization of capitalist production itself has to be protected from the destructive consequences of market competition. According to Polanyi's widely accepted concept of "embeddedness," corporate strategies cannot be established along a unified global pattern. Rather, they have to take account of regional and local forms of regulation that govern the political, social, and cultural framework of economic development. These strategies always include elements of economic globalization, but they also shape the specific faces of globalization in the respective regions, resulting in diverse global-local configurations of production, competition, and social regulation.

Transnational production networks can be analyzed within such a framework. Such analysis focuses on the way links between developed and less developed industrial regions are created and which specific resources are being transferred between them. Answers to these questions are sought through concepts of *industrial upgrading*, which exist in great variety today (with regard to the relevant locations in Asia, see Jomo, Felker, and Rasiah 1999; Best 1999; Amsden 2001; Ernst 2003a; Berger and Lester 2005; for Mexico, see Dussel Peters 2004, 2005; Palacios 2001; for Eastern Europe, see Bohle and Greskovitz 2004; Havas 1998; Radosevic 2004). In recent debates, Ernst (2002b) proposes that vertical specialization of global production networks enables the change to products with higher value added by newly industrializing countries. Sturgeon and Richard Lester (2002) maintain that transnational contract manufacturing in developing countries will enhance the flow of knowledge, capabilities, and technologies to such locations and point in a similar direction. However, the question remains as to what extent the transfer of practices and knowledge from industrialized countries really will spill over beyond firm boundaries, that is, to local suppliers or into product and organizational innovations in the respective regions. As we explain in the course of this book, electronics contract manufacturing, with its tendency to internalize knowledge in large, vertically integrated factories and industrial parks, is a case in point.

Answers to this problem can hardly be found through purely economic theories. More elaborate concepts of production networks, however, also tend to omit work, labor, and industrial relations. The relationship between institutional forms of national capitalisms and their respective regulation of work and the wage relationship is a core issue in newer debates on varieties of capitalism and their competitiveness. But this relationship is rarely discussed in relation to newly industrializing countries. Relevant approaches in this field refer to the concept of regimes of production to determine patterns of institutional regulation and resulting path dependencies in the development and transformation of the respective capitalist economies. Soskice (1999, 106ff.) distinguishes two basic regimes of production among developed industrialized economies. The main difference lies between countries where the state determines the institutional framework and a considerable degree of coordination exists between companies, called business-coordinated market economies, and countries without such mechanisms, dubbed uncoordinated market economies. A regime of production in a particular country is made up of the existing system of industrial relations, intercompany relations, finance and investment, and education and skill development.

Certainly, these concepts offer much better insight into the differences between various types of capitalism, especially those with corporatist systems versus those dubbed market economies. However, the labor process and the organization of work and production are absent from these debates, too. The discourse remains limited to industrial relations and their regulations. The contested terrain of the organization of work at the shop floor and within the particular societies in general remains uncharted (Bohle 1999). Under such perspectives, the notion of industrial upgrading is largely confined to, and misunderstood as, institutional upgrading in the field of labor laws, collective bargaining, and workers' representation—designed to develop the right mix of "institutional supply" for comparative cost advantages in the global race between locations.

Again, concepts of the social division of labor following Andrew Sayer and Richard Walker (1992) help in seeing the social shaping of work and the control over labor in the context of varying national and also regional regimes of production. Based on the above-mentioned perspectives on technology and social control in Marx's analysis of the capitalist process of production, the social division of labor can be seen as a constitutive element of what Burawoy (1985) calls the "politics of production," referring to implicit and explicit patterns and practices of competition and class behavior. At the same time, the social division of labor can be related to the generic forms of economic organization as well as cross-company cooperation and dependency, designed to ensure integration and control, and of workers' representation and self-organizing under the auspices of competition in globalized production systems.

In the face of the often massive processes of industrialization in the context of global production networks, such a perspective is of particular interest with regard to developing economies. Such approaches have remained rare in recent years. One of the few examples is C. K. Lee's studies of the politics of production in China, which, to an important extent, are based on detailed sociological investigation of the labor process in electronics assembly firms in the Pearl River Delta in South China (Lee 1998). From these studies, a comparative perspective has been developed on other industrial sectors and regions in China, resulting in a characterization of Chinese labor relations in the period of market transformation as a system of "disorganized despotism" (Lee 2002, 2007; see also chapter 4). Lee's analysis provides a compelling view of the often chaotic changes in the political system in one of the most important newly industrializing countries. It links the changes to the social contours of factory control and the underlying social, ethnic, and gender divisions in a workforce overwhelmingly composed of migrant workers from rural areas. However, the empirical base of her studies is confined to the situation of workers in smaller and medium-sized enterprises at the lowest end of the global assembly line. The enormous transformation generated by the recent surge of large-scale industrial investment, with often highly modern labor processes (such as in electronics contract manufacturing), may require a fresh look at this extremely rapid process of social transformation.

CAPITALIST RESTRUCTURING AND THE GLOBALIZATION OF NORMS OF PRODUCTION

An integrated view of restructuring of capitalist accumulation, models of production, and work is offered by regulation theory, initially developed in France by Michel Aglietta, Alain Lipietz, and their colleagues. The central proposition of the regulation school is that the internal contradictions of the capitalist mode of production are regulated through distinctive institutional forms within historical formations of capitalist development (Aglietta 1979, 179, 291). Such formations are based on specific regimes of accumulation and modes of regulation, characterized by certain interrelationships between politics and economics. A regime of accumulation is shaped in the context of competition and conflicts over social standards of technology and productivity, capitalist organization, and labor policies. These standards decisively determine the logic of capital valorization. The historical forms of production cannot be deduced from the capitalist law of value *in abstracto*.

The dominant mode of capitalist growth in the golden age of capitalism after World War II has been characterized by regulation theorists as *Fordism*. This concept refers not only to the typical organization of standardized mass production during that period. Rather, regulation theory places the inherent model of work organization of the Taylorist assembly line into the broader context of a macroeconomic growth model based on the simultaneous development of productivity, wages, and purchasing power. The resulting virtuous circle of continuously rising productivity, full employment, and growth during the postwar era created a period of previously unseen economic growth and stability in the developed industrial world, with a high degree of regulation of labor relations and social policies. Fordist accumulation was centered on relatively stable national markets on the one hand and free trade within the nonsocialist world on the other. Production primarily served these national markets and was organized mostly within the respective countries under the control of vertically integrated corporations (Lipietz 1985).

Regulation theory has widely analyzed the crisis of the Fordist mode of growth since the 1970s and its causes and consequences among various national regimes of accumulation and modes of regulation, particularly in developed industrial countries in the Western Hemisphere. However, the theoretical perspectives remained largely confined to national formations of capitalism and their competitiveness. With a few exceptions (Lipietz 1987), systematic reflections on the changing global division of labor and the globalization of production and technology are absent (Esser, Lüthje, and Noppe

1997; Ten Brink 2008). In particular, the newer debates on transnational production networks and global commodity chains have not been integrated into basic theoretical concepts of regulation theory (Lüthje 2001, 58). The question has not been answered: In global production networks, can norms of production and technology be generated at the transnational level? How are socioeconomic standards of technological innovation, production, and work shaped, defining industries and industry-specific modes of accumulation, in such arenas lacking the relatively coherent regulatory framework of national states? The emergence of highly uniform global production systems, such as electronics contract manufacturing, highlight the importance of this problem. These systems establish standards of work organization, quality, and productivity throughout their worldwide operations, often under very different political and social conditions.

Empirical studies of global production networks and the underlying restructuring of the social division of labor within key industries of contemporary capitalism could be one important avenue of conceptual progress. For instance, the model of innovation and competition referred to as Wintelism can be conceived as a sector-specific model of accumulation and competition involving complex sets of new norms of production and technology (Lüthje 2001). Aglietta's proposition, coined in the mass-production industries of Fordism, that specific norms of production define industries by establishing relatively uniform spaces of surplus-value production, offers an important insight into the nature of the Wintelist model of competition. As discussed earlier, this revolves around the permanent definition of industries and their subsegments through an extremely accelerated generation of new technologies and "breakthrough innovations" (Florida and Kenney 1990). Contract manufacturing, on the other hand, provides the global infrastructure of production for the Wintelist model of accumulation in the IT industry. It results in the emergence of subcontracted manufacturing as an industry segment of its own, with large and highly complex companies that reintegrate and recentralize mass production disconnected from the often fabless designers and producers of new product architectures. At the same time, the differences along the chain between brand-name technology firms and their manufacturers can be interpreted in the context of intrasectoral hierarchies and different conditions of profit generation (Lüthje 2001). The competition between various models of modern contract manufacturing, with different philosophies concerning the integration of product development and with different places of origin (such as the United States and Taiwan), can also be conceived as an internal capitalist struggle over competing norms of production.

The other field for a thorough understanding of the relationship between "global" and "local" in the construction of new norms of production is certainly the restructuring of work and labor policies. The emergence of large-scale manufacturing service providers, with tightly interwoven global networks of factories, global standards of work organization, and a huge workforce of low-skilled, newly recruited workers in developing countries, is another step away from strategies of the reintegration and reprofessionalization (Kern and Schumann 1984) of work developed in industrialized countries during the 1980s in response to the crisis of the Fordist-Taylorist model. The return to more restrictive forms of work organization, increased speedup, management by stress (Parker and Slaughter 1993), and the related conservative rollback in labor policies (Dörre 2003) in the core industries of capitalism is accompanied by the emergence of a new mass workforce in some countries of the former periphery, toiling under neo-Taylorist methods of control in often highly authoritarian forms. This development does more than reinvoke former visions of the global assembly line, coupled with the ongoing vertical reintegration of production resources "at the bottom" of global production networks. It also raises the more general question of whether we are facing a historical return of Fordism under the disguise of network-based forms of capitalist production (Lüthje 2004a).

Both elements point to the viability of new norms of production that are essentially constructed in the transnational arena and constitute global models of capital accumulation in the respective industries (driven by the financial markets). The challenge, however, is to avoid the pitfalls of universalism. It is certainly true that Wintelism, with its underlying global production networks, has been an extremely successful model that revolutionized the norms of production in the IT industry. It created a relatively coherent mode of accumulation based on vertical specialization and the segmentation of key technology markets. However, the limits of this norm of production appeared in the wake of the global recession in the IT industry of 2001–2002 under the impact of the bursting Internet bubble in the financial markets. Those limits show that the Wintel model is not the "one best way" of restructuring in the IT industry. Equally, the global reorganization of work entailed in the production systems of electronics contract manufacturers has to operate through a highly differentiated set of divergent institutional, social, and cultural traditions in the respective locations. These conditions not only produce enormous difficulties, risks, and costs in such globalized production systems. The potential of social conflict associated with the recruitment of the new mass workforces, as well as the aspirations of the political elites of the respective countries and regions for industrial upgrading, could soon demonstrate the limits of such neo-Taylorist models. It would accelerate the search for more sustainable models of manufacturing based on more highly skilled, betterpaid, and more stable workforces.

NEO-TAYLORISM AND THE COMPLEXITY OF
PRODUCTION REGIMES

Our analysis of the organization and politics of work in the electronics contract manufacturing industry is centered on the term "neo-Taylorism." As pointed out in previous studies (Lüthje, Schumm, and Sproll 2002), this concept refers to the combination of segmented assembly-line work in highly automated factories with extreme flexibility of working and employment conditions and specific strategies for motivating workers in companies with no brand-name products and cultures of their own. This is typical for contract manufacturing plants in developed industrial countries in North America and Europe. The term "neo-Taylorism" has been used in industrial sociology and political economy in various connotations in order to characterize strategies to reform the Taylorist model of work without giving up on its basic elements of work segmentation and control (for an early discussion, see Aglietta 1979). In our context, this terminology should underline our view that the emergence of standardized mass manufacturing in global production networks does not imply a simple return to Fordism or the global assembly line of older NIDL theories. Rather, the labor process is shaped by its distinctively global character and the problems of regulating the economic and social conditions of factory work under highly diverse institutional and cultural settings in different countries and locations (for a detailed discussion, see Sproll 2010).

As we explain in the following chapters, the organization of work in electronics contract manufacturing is shaped by the specific position of the manufacturing service companies within the sector-wide global production networks. Contract manufacturing combines diverse and often massive resources in manufacturing, product design, and logistics into transnational production systems. These systems have to coordinate economies of global mass production with the flexibility requirements generated by localized production in facilities in low-cost locations as well as end-user markets in or near developed industrial countries. Contract manufacturers are basically facing similar challenges and dilemmas of balancing volume with quality and flexibility, familiar in more traditional assembly industries. However, they have to deal with the particular requirements set by the production needs and marketing strategies of the brand-name companies. Contract manufacturers have to stay away from and protect the intellectual property of technology-owning brand-name firms. On the other hand, they have to offer an environment of seamless cooperation with their customers, define standardized and transparent interfaces with customer organizations, and develop the potential to change production volumes and processes frequently and quickly (Lüthje, Schumm, and Sproll 2002, 112ff.). Contract manufacturers coordinate complex resources and exert considerable purchasing power within global production networks, but they lack the technological competence as well as the financial and political leverage of established brand-name firms. With their huge supplier networks, the largest contract manufacturers exert the function of "flagship firms" in global production networks (Ernst 2003a). However, due to the lack of brand-name power, it might be more accurate to qualify them as "secondary flagships."

Contract manufacturers try to secure efficiency and profitability through global strategies aiming at a strict standardization of central elements of corporate, factory, and work organization and implementation of these strategies throughout their facilities. In the newly emerging centers of globalized mass manufacturing, such as China, Malaysia, and Mexico, the local units often have to operate under extremely difficult conditions that challenge the implementation of globally standardized operating procedures. Thus, the companies and their local factory management have to balance global standardization with local flexibility under conditions of extremely short and often disruptive market and product cycles. The technological and organizational standards of production and logistics, supply-chain management, quality management, and some elements of the compensation system are defined at the global level. Control is highly centralized and hierarchic. Employment policies, wages, working hours, and related issues are usually determined locally. The result is a sort of "flexible standardization" which combines elements of neo-Taylorist work organization with market-based coordination and control. The boundaries between global and local decision making are often contested under the impact of immediate demands by brand-name customers concerning the configuration and allocation of products and manufacturing processes.

Work organization and control at the shop floor are essentially shaped by labor policies and the regulation of the wage relation practiced and institutionalized in specific countries and locations. The complex interactions between corporate control over labor processes and workers and their political, social, and cultural environments, sanctioned by certain forms of state power over and in the workplace, create complex *politics of production*. These result in specific *regimes of production* in different factories and regions across global production systems. Following Burawoy's theoretical trajectory from the 1970s and 1980s, shop-floor organization can be seen as a highly politicized relationship shaped by specific sets of rules and institutions, reproduced in the context of social conflict and formal or informal bargaining among workers, management, and sometimes government institutions. The contradictions and conflicts between the various actors are the medium through which social rules and norms of wage labor are institutionalized and a certain consensus reached between capital and workers over the day-to-day standards of capitalist exploitation (Burawoy 1979, 1985).

In contrast to many mainstream theories of industrial relations and also management theories of production networks, Burawoy's approach conceives the sociology of the modern workplace as a condensation of economic, social, and political power relations. These are produced and reproduced both through labor management conflicts over work, working conditions, and factory rules and through political regulations, for example, laws and government regulation of minimum wages, workers' representation, and trade union rights (Lüthje 1993, 2001). Such a perspective transcends distinctions between "internal" and "external" influences over workplace regimes and the underlying dichotomies of "hierarchy" versus "market" and "politics" versus "economics." In global production systems and networks, such an approach offers a more integrated view of production relations, which we identified as a major deficit in current theories of global production networks, commodity chains, and the NIDL concept. This approach does not separate internal criteria of organization, such as the allocation of production tasks, the work structures, or control, from external influences, such as legal status of employees, labor laws and regulations, education and professional training, relationships between trade unions and employers, and so on (see Whitley 1997). Instead, concepts of regimes of production focus on the making, shaping, and reproduction of the organizational and institutional forms in the context of complex social and political power relationships and workers' action contesting them (for an excellent application of Burawoy's approach to modern world-market factories, see Lee's studies on China, 1998, 2007).

Our interpretation of the concepts of production politics and regimes of production focuses on three distinct but interrelated dimensions of the social architecture of the workplace and control, which for the purposes of our empirical investigation can be defined as the regime of work, the regime of employment, and the regime of control.

- *Regime of work* is an analytical category used to describe the organization of work in its technological and managerial aspects and related strategies, rules, and conflicts within the factories and production networks. In our empirical analysis, the focus will be on the type of labor processes resulting from allocation of certain products to certain factories, the structure of work, and the related concepts of quality management in electronics manufacturing plants.
- *Regime of employment* describes employment, working conditions, and regulation of work, especially recruitment and wages, job assignment, working hours, skill development, and company-provided transport and social reproduction facilities, such as dormitories and cafeterias. Our empirical analysis is closely related to the underlying patterns of labor market segmentation caused by the massive use of migrant and female labor in

contract manufacturing factories in most low-cost locations, since the nature of this workforce decisively determines the regime of employment.

- *Regime of control* refers to the social norms of employment and work and the related forms of social and political control established and regulated through government and bargaining between workers and management, both on the shop floor and in regions and industries. In the absence of collective bargaining and trade unions in most contract manufacturing plants, we focus on labor laws and government regulation of minimum wages, working hours, benefits, and occupational health and safety, as well as on labor standards established under international laws, human resources (HR) policies of the particular companies, and codes of conduct and corporate social responsibility (CSR) sometimes monitored by public interest groups.

Such a conception of multiple elements and levels of politics and regimes of production is particularly aimed at a comparative perspective between different workplaces in different locations within globally unified production systems and networks. Its main purpose is to analyze the complex social environment created by the implementation of modern mass production with highly complex labor processes and factory organization. Since we are dealing with typically nontraditional workforces made up of migrant workers, women, and ethnic and cultural minorities, we have to identify the intrinsic links between factory regimes and gender, racial, and ethnic discrimination engendered in labor-market policies and in the regimes of labor migration. Following Aihwa Ong (1987), Lee (1998), and many other authors, gender, migration, and racial-ethnic discrimination have to be considered as constitutive elements of production regimes, creating massive barriers but also new dynamics of social organization among the new workforces in global production networks.

PROPOSITIONS AND OUTLINE

Our study summarizes and synthesizes the observations of a long-term empirical investigation of the electronics contract manufacturing industry and of major factories and industrial parks in the industry's low-cost locations in Mexico, Eastern Europe, Malaysia, and China carried out between 2001 and 2009. The empirical data is analyzed in three major aspects: the development of electronics contract manufacturing as a key industry segment within the IT sector and its production networks; the changing international division of labor shaped through the production systems of major contract manufacturers and their strategies of geographical allocation; and the transformation of the labor process in the context of global production networks and the emergence of a new mass workforce in low-cost locations in North America, Asia, and Europe.

In chapter 2, we trace the structure and development of electronics contract manufacturing within the global production *networks* of the IT sector, focusing on the impact of the global IT industry crisis (and the so-called New Economy) in 2001–2002. We explain and discuss the proposition developed above that production networks in the IT industry follow a distinctive logic of vertical de- and reintegration. The massive outsourcing of production among brand-name firms, initiated under various company strategies and mechanisms of control, goes along with a buildup of highly integrated global production systems of unseen scale by electronics contract manufacturers. The logic of vertical reintegration is shaped by the different strategies among contract manufacturers regarding the integration of product design and development into their operations, resulting in the emergence of two competing models of contract manufacturing dubbed electronics manufacturing services (EMS) and original design manufacturing (ODM; see chapters 2 and 4). At the same time, this development is integrated into a broader process of triangular restructuring of the "upper ends" of the sector-wide technology chains, engendering a far-flung recombination of product development activities among brand-name systems firms, chipmakers, and contract manufacturers (see chapter 2).

Chapter 3 focuses on the global production *systems* of electronics contract manufacturers, examining three interrelated sets of questions.

First, we trace the changes in the international division of labor engendered by the buildup of global infrastructures of outsourced electronics manufacturing. We ask to what extent a complementary specialization has developed between lead factories in developed industrial countries, with strategic concentration on product development, "ramp-up" of new manufacturing processes, and manufacturing of more specialized and complex products, and low-cost locations as centers for standardized high-volume manufacturing. We discuss this in the context of changing production models, leading to the conclusion that the international division of labor between high-end and low-end production has become increasingly blurred, especially under the impact of the increasing "offshoring" of innovative product development.

Second, we take a closer look at the locational strategies of major contract manufacturers in the global context and within the economic zones of the triad of North America, Europe, and Asia and the resulting patterns of relocation between industrialized centers and low-cost locations. We ask whether different strategies of production and outsourcing among the major brand-name firms in different regions might result in intraregional divisions of labor related to dominant models of production in North America, Europe, and Asia. We show that the international division of labor is shaped by a complex set of factors in which cluster dynamics resulting from relocation of older segments of the electronics industry, the opening up of new areas of low-wage production such as Mexico under NAFTA, and industrial development policies in emerging economies go along with the intensifying search for cheap labor in manufacturing and, increasingly, engineering. The combination of these factors creates highly uneven conditions of surplus value production, which can be identified as the main drivers for the geographical architecture of global production systems. These diverging constellations form the basis for intensified competition between the various low-cost locations, in which Asia, with its highly diversified intraregional division of labor between low-cost and high-cost economies, has accumulated significant strategic advantages.

The third set of questions relates to the impact of large-scale investment in contract manufacturing facilities and networks on industrial development in local economies. We assume that the massive vertical reintegration of production and the related internal concentration of resources within large factories and industrial parks limit external upgrading effects on indigenous regional supplier and service networks, especially in science and development-related support functions. As our case studies show, contract manufacturing engenders significant potential for industrial upgrading within the respective facilities and their manufacturing capabilities. However, such developments are often limited by the centralized global decision making on product allocation by contract manufacturers and their brand-name customers, as well as by the dominant pattern of neo-Taylorist organization of work and the related deskilling of the industrial workforce. Industrial upgrading remains highly precarious under these conditions.

In chapter 4, we analyze the diverging regimes of production in the major low-cost locations of electronics contract manufacturing. Our proposition is that forms of neo-Taylorist work organization are emerging in these factories on an unprecedented scale, with a much greater dominance of segmentation, hierarchical control, and deskilling than in industrialized countries with some history of reintegration of assembly-line work. In all regions, production regimes are characterized by authoritarian forms of control on the shop floor, embedded in certain regimes of labor migration and ethnic and gender discrimination, as well as government policies to secure favorable investment climates for global companies in employment conditions, health and safety, and environmental regulations. However, the social forms of control vary greatly between countries and regions, causing very different conditions for shop-floor management and control, enforcing a considerable degree of "flexibility" and "decentralization" in the globally standardized work organization and human resource strategies of contract manufacturers.

Following our distinction of regimes of work, regimes of employment, and regimes of control, we assume that the variations between production regimes appear in different ways in the various fields.

- *Regimes of work* may be relatively similar across countries and regions, since production technologies, work organization, and models of quality management are subject to heavy standardization at the corporate level. The question has to be asked, however: To what extent might the existing social and political conditions in the respective locations, especially the availability of skilled workers, favor or enforce modifications in work organization (e.g., in Eastern Europe, where relatively skilled and experienced industrial workforces exist)?
- *Regimes of employment* may vary to a much greater degree, since workers' recruitment and employment conditions are strongly linked to the structure of local labor markets and the governing patterns of labor migration and gender and ethnic discrimination. Again, we may assume huge differences between the older locations of offshore assembly in the electronics industry, such as Malaysia, the more recent ones, such as Mexico and China, and the newcomers with an established history of industrial work, such as Hungary, Poland, and the Czech Republic. However, the rapid upgrading of the newer locations and the potential downgrading of older ones under the impact of the permanent competition between regions may produce a greater uniformity in this area.
- *Regimes of control*, naturally, should also be highly different across countries and regions, since the politics of production are generated in the context of the institutional and political systems of different countries and their very different conditions and histories of labor policies and working-class organization. In addition, our comparison includes countries with established capitalist market economies (such as Malaysia and Mexico) and those that have been transformed from a socialist, planned economy to market capitalism with very different trajectories of transition (such as Eastern Europe and China). However, we have to ask whether some elements of the labor policies of contract manufacturers, such as their hostility to trade unions or the widespread use of corporate social responsibility schemes, may be considered as globally unifying elements of control regimes.

In chapter 5, we return to the broader theoretical and political aspects of our study and summarize our results and their implications for current debates on transnational production networks. We relate the development of transnational production networks in the IT industry to the ongoing changes in the capitalist world system and the shifting economic and power relationships between regions in offshoring production and innovation from older capitalist countries and the emergence of new economies from the former periphery. We want to link the problem of industrial upgrading, widely discussed among elites in newly industrializing countries as well as in international expert communities, with the problem of neo-Taylorist regimes of production and the related authoritarian and undemocratic form of labor policies in these countries. We hope to bring the labor process back into political debates from which it is absent too often.

Chapter Two

Beyond the New Economy

*The Global Restructuring of Production Models in
the IT Industry*

We know that the degree of vertical integration tends to be cyclical.
—Terence Hopkins and Immanuel Wallerstein, 1986

Electronics contract manufacturing provides a particularly striking example of the restructuring of the information technology industry related to the so-called New Economy during the 1990s and its subsequent crisis. Although this model of production has been around for more than a decade now, the inner workings of the electronics contract manufacturing industry are not very well known. This is mostly a result of the policies of the major IT brand-name companies, which seek to hide their suppliers and their manufacturing power and working conditions. Dramatic changes also took place in the forms of cooperation between brand-name companies and contract manufacturers, the related competition among different models of contract manufacturing, and the continuing outsourcing of production and product development in traditional "core competencies." During the 1990s, restructuring focused on comprehensive outsourcing of complex manufacturing activities (including the sale of traditional brand-name factories around the world to contract manufacturers). The more recent development, following the crisis of 2001–2002, increasingly shifted product development and engineering to contract manufacturers that had growing engineering workforces in low-cost regions, a development aptly named *innovation outsourcing* (Ernst 2006a).

In this chapter, we take a closer look at the complex changes in the IT industry's production system. First, we retrace the short but multifaceted development of large-scale contract manufacturing and its different models

33

since the beginning of the 1990s. We follow with an analysis of the impact that the 2001–2002 crisis had on the global IT industry and the subsequent consolidation among both contract manufacturers and brand-name firms. This shaped the existing pattern of production and industry development today. Of special interest here are the changes in the production networks of global brand-name firms in some key segments of the IT industry, particularly the manufacturing of PCs, server and notebook computers, mobile phones, and game consoles. The latter became a significant mass product of contemporary consumer electronics. Before providing this background, we analyze the emergence of two competing models of contract manufacturing: *electronics manufacturing services (EMS)*, created mainly by US contract manufacturers during the 1990s, and *original design manufacturing (ODM)*, which led to the rapid rise of a second generation of contract manufacturers headquartered in Taiwan during the past decade. Finally, we discuss the recent shift of key resources of technological innovation in the IT industry related to the increasing use of contract manufacturing and the emerging global design networks (Ernst 2003a; Ernst and Lüthje 2003; Lüthje 2007a) in other sectors of the IT industry, chip production in particular.

The focus of our analysis is on the contradictory tendencies of *vertical specialization* of production—mainly on the part of major brand-name and lead firms—and the *vertical reintegration* of manufacturing resources occurring among contract manufacturers. We examine this development in the context of seminal changes in the norms of production and capital valorization in the IT industry. This development took place in relation to the Wintel model of industry organization, which was particularly connected to the meteoric rise of US IT companies based in Silicon Valley, such as Intel, Apple, and Cisco. These changes in global production networks in the post-Fordist IT sector do not happen along the smooth paths predicted by business textbooks but in discontinuous ruptures and leaps, which often are related to the crises of major industrial corporations and entire regions.

CONTRACT MANUFACTURING: CAREER OF A POST-FORDIST MODEL OF PRODUCTION

The history of the IT industry of the past three decades reads like the chronicle of a permanent revolution. The 1990s were dominated by the pathbreaking innovations of the personal computer and the Internet and marked a period of dramatic changes caused by macroeconomic gains in productivity, rapid technological and organizational innovation, and the globalization of industrial structures. Those changes gave the period the label of the "New Economy." In this process, new forms of industrial organization emerged in the IT industry. The flag bearer was a new generation of specialized producers of hitherto unknown computer hardware and software products such as personal computers, network servers, and various types of mobile computers.

These enterprises emerged, beginning in the 1970s, in California's Silicon Valley and other high-tech regions of the US West. Especially prominent were the rising new manufacturers of microchips, such as Intel, National Semiconductor, and AMD, and the PC-industry pioneers, led by Apple and followed by Microsoft and Compaq. These companies differed from older, vertically integrated computer and electronics companies that had emerged during the middle and later stages of Fordism, such as IBM, Digital Equipment, Fujitsu, and Siemens. The young companies in Silicon Valley did not produce entire computer systems; rather, they focused on certain key components, such as microprocessors or software operating systems. These products were developed and manufactured for the open market, not for in-house use in computer systems with proprietary brand names and architectures. The new manufacturers of microchips and products such as hard disk drives were called merchant producers (Ferguson and Morris 1993).

The break with traditional industry structures brought about a radically new model of innovation and market control, giving rise to an accelerating trend of modularization of production systems in the computer industry and later in telecommunications and consumer electronics manufacturing. In the new world of vertically disintegrated, network-based mass production (see chapter 1), the final products such as computers, servers, and Internet routers were assembled mostly from standard components, particularly microprocessors, memory chips, disk drives, graphics cards, modems, and displays. All these components could be purchased from specialized vendors on the open market and combined and configured in different ways by competing producers (Lüthje 2001, 189ff.).

The production systems of the "horizontal computer industry" (Grove 1996) reversed the organizational logic of Taylorist-Fordist mass production and even the concept of lean production as developed by Japanese carmakers such as Toyota. Although the latter is usually seen as the epitome of modular production, the Silicon Valley model of network-based mass production entailed a much more fundamental change in production philosophy. Outsourcing is not limited to certain components and subassemblies. Rather, the entire system is produced by external sourcing of key technologies and manufacturing. The term "Wintelism" (as opposed to "Fordism" and "Toyotism") became the academic paradigm used to describe this new form of technological innovation and market control and the resulting "fragmentation and centralization" (Ernst and O'Connor 1992) of markets and industry structures.

In the wake of the breakthrough of the PC as the paradigm setter for electronic data processing and the mass production of decentralized data systems, the flagship companies of the vertically specialized IT industry, such as Intel, Microsoft, Sun, and Cisco, became globally dominant corporations. At the same time, the outstanding economic success of such companies was hailed as the strategic answer of the US IT industry to the challenge from Japanese and later Korean electronics corporations during the 1980s. That challenge had seriously questioned US leadership in microelectronics (Borrus 1988). However, as part of the seminal shift to the Wintelism paradigm, many older computer companies in the United States and Europe, most notably IBM, had to move away from Fordist-type vertical integration toward network-centric models of organization.

The changes produced by Wintelist norms of technology and production can basically be characterized as follows (see Borrus and Zysman 1997; Lüthje 2001; Lüthje, Schumm, and Sproll 2002):

- Most electronics and IT products have become complex commodities, assembled from traded parts and components supplied by various industry segments. The control of the time cycle of new technologies and products has become the industry's chief problem of manufacturing organization.
- As market control has shifted from assemblers to "product definition companies," product innovation is increasingly separated from manufacturing. This also implies that brand-name companies have been losing interest in keeping manufacturing close to their headquarters in industrialized countries.
- In contrast to older industries, such as automobile manufacturing, today's electronics industry has no "focal corporations" (Sauer and Döhl 1994) that coordinate the value chain through their own manufacturing operations. The "supplier pyramid" governed by large-scale, final assemblers is replaced by networks of interacting industry segments. However, the resulting network formations are highly hierarchical. Hierarchy is defined by the flagships' ability to control technological development in key market segments as well as govern extensive networks of third-party manufacturers and suppliers.
- The production systems of the vertically disintegrated IT industry are essentially transnational. As opposed to Fordist and Toyotist models of manufacturing, which are fully or predominantly based on national manufacturing infrastructures, global production networks (GPN) are key elements of Wintelist mass production (Borrus, Ernst, and Haggard 2000; Ernst 2002a).

The emergence of Wintelist forms of production caused massive changes in the assembly segments of the IT industry. Historically, the electronics industry in general, and computer manufacturing in particular, relied on large numbers of suppliers and contract manufacturers. These were mostly small or medium-sized enterprises that specialized in the assembly of printed circuit boards and nondigital (often called "passive") components, such as resistors, coils, and cable assemblies. These enterprises existed in most centers of electronics manufacturing in the United States, Europe, and Japan. In Europe, Germany in particular, they were mostly family-owned, "Mittelstand" companies. In the new IT regions in the US West, especially Silicon Valley, they were increasingly low-wage sweatshops with a high proportion of immigrant entrepreneurs from Asian countries such as South Korea and Taiwan and workforces overwhelmingly composed of women immigrants from Mexico, Central America, and Asia (Lüthje 2001, 103ff.).

At the end of the 1980s, a new type of manufacturing emerged, called "electronics contract manufacturing." The companies in this segment developed a hitherto unknown model of integrated manufacturing services, which comprised all essential elements of the production, procurement, and logistics chains required to manufacture electronics products. The key concept behind this production model was providing outsourced manufacturing as a service (Lüthje and Sproll 2002). The service provider would coordinate all the functions of the manufacturing-related parts of the value chain. The new model therefore became known as *electronics manufacturing services (EMS)*. As opposed to the traditional subassembly of certain products or components, EMS contract manufacturers commanded comprehensive resources in production, technology, and logistics. They did this in all areas of electronics manufacturing, especially in the automatic and manual assembly of printed circuit boards (PCB), the final assembly and configuration of equipment and systems (also called *box build*), the production of nonelectronic supplies and components, such as plastic parts, metal enclosures, and cable assemblies, and even product development, materials procurement, distribution, and after-sales services (Sturgeon 1997, 1999).

EMS contract manufacturers rapidly emerged as important players within the IT industry. During the 1990s, the average growth rates of EMS production concerns were 25 percent or higher (see figure 2.1). The leading companies of the new industry segment, Flextronics, Solectron, Sanmina-SCI from Silicon Valley, Celestica from Toronto in Canada, and Florida-based Jabil Circuits, grew almost from scratch into corporations with annual revenues of around US$5 billion, sometimes over US$10 billion. The names of these companies, however, remain little known since it was a basic principle of the EMS business model that the manufacturer's name should not appear in connection with the product. Leading IT companies, such as Intel, aggressively promoted their brand as a key component "inside" the final product, but the names of the leaders of the global EMS industry remained hidden even to many experts. The *Los Angeles Times* therefore once aptly characterized EMS contract manufacturing as *stealth manufacturing* (*LAT* September 27, 1999).

The rapid growth of EMS companies was achieved particularly through mergers and acquisitions. Following the strategy of the lead firms in the

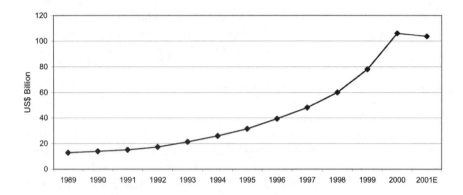

Figure 2.1.   Revenue of Electronics Manufacturing Services Industry, 1989–2001 (US$ billions) Technology Forecasters Inc.

expanding PC and networking equipment industry, major contract manufacturers broadened their know-how and technology by acquiring a broad spectrum of specialized technology and component suppliers. Flextronics, for example, took over Force, Fine Pitch, and Smart Technologies, with sophisticated capabilities in chip design, chip packaging, and electronic control modules. Flextronics created its own subsidiary for chip design, Flextronics Semiconductor, and funded start-up firms developing complex software systems for managing electronics manufacturing supply chains.

Still more important for the global expansion of electronics contract manufacturing, manufacturing facilities were acquired from leading electronics brand-name manufacturers. This process started in the mid-1990s with the purchase of major manufacturing plants of IBM, Texas Instruments, and Lucent by contract manufacturers such as Solectron and Flextronics in the United States. In 1997, Swedish telecommunications manufacturer Ericsson was the first major European brand-name company to sell full-fledged manufacturing facilities to EMS companies. Ericsson was followed by Germany's Siemens, the largest European electronics company, which sold to Flextronics a manufacturing facility formerly owned by Nixdorf in Germany and, later, facilities in other European countries. Expanding into electronics manufacturing formerly dominated by entrenched Fordist traditions, the EMS companies acquired world-class manufacturing know-how. Such knowledge transfer, however, came at the price of complex and difficult restructuring of the respective facilities. Integration into the "ultralean" and "no-frills" organization of contract manufacturers engendered vast changes in the work organization and working conditions in the affected plants and caused layoffs as well as considerable reductions to the existing level of wages, salaries, and benefits (for detailed analysis, see Lüthje, Schumm, and Sproll 2002). For brand-name firms, the sale of manufacturing facilities marked major steps in the transition to network-based mass production with extensive outsourcing, which became the globally dominant form of production in the IT industry.

This process was propelled by financial markets (see Jürgens and Sablowski 2004). Like many other new high-tech companies in the 1990s, the EMS firms were financed through institutional investors, particularly on the NASDAQ technology stock exchange in New York. EMS companies did not receive much venture capital from the well-known investors along Sandhill Road in Palo Alto, California, which had financed many successful technology firms in that region. Ample capital, however, flowed from investment banks, pension funds, and other financial organizations. The SEC listings of major investors in the EMS industry read like a *Who's Who?* of global finance. Under these circumstances, the EMS industry was ruled by the same financial speculation that resulted in the subsequent bursting of the Internet bubble in global financial markets in 2001–2002. In the case of the EMS industry, the overheating of profit expectations meant that while contract manufacturers made only very low profit margins from their manufacturing operations (around 3 percent on average), their stocks were among the fastest rising during the 1990s (Lüthje, Schumm, and Sproll 2002). Clearly, expectations were fueled by speculation over rapid gains in market share, creating the engine for the large-scale acquisitions and mergers among leading EMS firms during the second half of the 1990s.

FROM THE BELLE ÉPOQUE TO THE CRISIS OF WINTELISM

The massive restructuring of the manufacturing base of the IT industry represented one of the most striking examples of innovation in industrial organization during the 1990s. In 2000, barely ten years after the first contract manufacturers had appeared, EMS contract manufacturing had become an established segment of the electronics industry, accounting for about 15–20 percent of the value added in the manufacturing of electronics products (excluding chip production and software development). At the same time, this development indicated that the epicenter of organizational innovation in electronics manufacturing had shifted finally from the established centers of the industry, the US East Coast, Europe, and Japan, to the high-tech regions of the US West and the rapidly developing production bases around the Pacific Rim (Lüthje 2001). The dynamics of industry-wide structural crisis emerged, however, in the wake of this seminal shift in organization of the capitalist forces of production and their geographic dispersal.

The contradictions of Wintelist production models became apparent during the massive downturn of the IT industry in 2001 and 2002, caused by the end of the boom of the "dot-com" industries and the bursting of the related stock market bubbles (Brenner 2002). Most experts characterized this crisis as the deepest recession in the history of the IT industry. The industry's global production networks and the newly established model of large-scale contract manufacturing underwent massive restructuring. Structural overcapacity emerged in core industry segments rooted in Wintelist norms of production due to extremely short cycles of innovation and capital valorization.

This phenomenon became particularly visible in the production of PCs and servers, where the recession coincided with the fading of the "PC revolution" as a driving force of the Wintelist model of innovation. In other key growth markets of the 1990s, overcapacity emerged in even more dramatic ways, particularly in data networking equipment and mobile communications. In the latter case, capacity bubbles in manufacturing resulted directly from conflicts over the control of future network infrastructures fueled by financial speculation. Those conflicts were highlighted by the spectacular auction of licenses for third-generation mobile phone services in Germany and other European countries in 2000. The massive capital expenditures of telecom carriers in property rights drove up investment costs for such networks so much that the growth of this industry collapsed under the burden. At the same time, rapid expansion of advanced fiber-optics networks created huge unused network capacity. New telecommunication carriers collapsed, like US-based WorldCom and Global Crossing, which had been shaped by massive financial speculation.

The massive vertical disintegration of production systems achieved during the 1990s and the related policies of ultralean inventories and production flows created a massive domino effect along the IT industry's global value chain. It shifted the impact of the crisis onto the middle and lower tiers of the production networks, contract manufacturing in particular. These effects were also felt by the producers of key components of computer systems such as hard disk drives and storage equipment. In the hard disk drive industry, the slowdown triggered the collapse of the industry's lead companies that had emerged from Silicon Valley during the 1990s, such as Seagate. This resulted in the loss of tens of thousands of jobs in the highly sophisticated mass-production facilities of these companies in Singapore, Malaysia, and Thailand (see chapter 3).

The structural problem behind the more cyclical elements of the crisis is the long-term increase in the cost of innovation in the vertically specialized segments of the IT industry, particularly in the development and manufacturing of microchips. In core areas of chip production, this problem had been prevalent for many years. But it remained hidden behind the accelerated expansion of major product markets during the 1990s, such as PCs and mobile communications. In the production of complex chips used in consumer electronics, the cost explosion in manufacturing triggered the emergence of a new generation of chip firms operating without expensive factories.

These fabless chip companies transferred chip manufacturing to a new group of chip producers, mostly based in Taiwan and Southeast Asia, called "chip foundries" (Angel 1994).

The increasing cost of innovation in chip manufacturing resulted in a long-term slowdown in chip development productivity. This phenomenon became particularly visible in consumer electronics and mobile communications, where almost the entire system of key products such as cell phones were contained on one or a few microchips of enormous complexity and therefore called "system on chip," or SoC (Chang et al. 1999). The productivity gap in chip design was at the root of the accelerated outsourcing and relocation of increasingly sophisticated engineering work to Asia in recent years. The modularization of chip design promised cost efficiency through reuse of standard building blocks of complex chips; in cars, for instance, many elements are used in various models, not just in a single model. And cutting the design chain into pieces of relatively standardized engineering procedures opened new ways to relocate once-complex design lab operations to newly emerging low-cost locations (Ernst 2003a, 2003b; Lüthje 2007a).

Electronics contract manufacturing was at the center of industry-wide restructuring in the wake of the global recession, particularly in computer, data networking, and mobile communications equipment. The unexpected slowdown of these sectors caused a break in the phenomenal growth of contract manufacturing during the 1990s (see figure 2.1). An outright collapse of the contract manufacturing segment was avoided only because many vertically integrated electronics producers shifted manufacturing to contract manufacturers at an accelerated pace during the crisis. IBM provides a spectacular example. The company abandoned in-house manufacturing of PCs and sold its plants in the United States, Mexico, Asia, and Europe to Sanmina-SCI, one of the leading contract manufacturers (*WSJ*, January 11, 2002). Hewlett-Packard left PC manufacturing for the European market based in France to the same contract manufacturer (*FT*, January 19, 2002). Lucent (formerly Western Electric), the biggest US telecommunications manufacturer, transferred its most important manufacturing facilities to contract manufacturers Celestica and Solectron.

Contract manufacturing became a way to regulate industrial overcapacity. The leading US contract manufacturers therefore suffered the impact of speculation-driven expansion during the 1990s and the takeover of major manufacturing facilities at the request of their major customers during the crisis. The companies were hit by massive losses and shrinking revenues and had to write off billions of dollars as a result of plant closures, layoffs, excess inventory, and overpriced acquisitions. The once high-flying stock prices of contract manufacturers collapsed, and the companies' loans were downgraded to junk bond status. As we explain in more detail in the following chapters, workers in the industry had to face massive layoffs, particularly in the key locations of mass manufacturing in the US West and South, in Europe (Scotland and Ireland in particular), and in the newly established low-cost locations in Mexico, Malaysia, and Hungary. At the same time, a massive shift of manufacturing capacities to China began, which since then has shaped the industry's global production networks (see chapters 3 and 4).

Financial losses were caused particularly by the massive excess inventory EMS firms held on behalf of their customers. Huge supplies of parts and components had either been purchased directly by contract manufacturers to avoid shortages when markets were booming or were owned by brand-name companies and administered by their contract manufacturers. The complicated arrangements in this field produced chaotic relationships and conflicts between contract manufacturers and their brand-name customers. A leading market research firm, iSuppli, called this a "supply chain disaster" (*EN*, April 9, 2001). In many cases, when ownership of inventories could not be verified, EMS and brand-name companies pressured each other to accept financial responsibility. Of course, not much was publicly known about the woes of lean production and supply chain management. However, relevant market data demonstrate that the EMS companies finally had to bear the bulk of industry-wide excess inventories. According to iSuppli, at the peak of the crisis during the third quarter of 2001, the EMS industry held 49 percent of the global excess of microchips, with a total value of US$5.9 billion (*EB Asia*, March 2002). The image of contract manufacturers as organizers of highly efficient, low-cost chains of production and supply suffered greatly.

In the long term, the most serious impact of the crisis for North American EMS corporations was the shift of manufacturing orders to contract manufacturers in Taiwan. Taiwanese contract manufacturers up to the late 1990s were primarily low-cost providers of electronics components, even rather complex ones such as computer motherboards. Some contract manufacturers established EMS-style manufacturing services, which were particularly attractive because of their large-scale use of very cheap labor in China. This development was symbolized by the rapid rise of an almost unknown contract manufacturer, Foxconn, a subsidiary of Hon Hai, Taiwan's largest industrial conglomerate. During the crisis, Foxconn conquered global EMS markets with extremely low prices and a highly integrated manufacturing organization. It was reminiscent of the Ford Motor Company of the 1920s, rapidly acquiring orders from major US IT firms such as Cisco, Dell, Apple, and Hewlett-Packard. The rise of Foxconn, with double-digit revenue growth rates of up to 60 percent per year, fundamentally altered the global hierarchy among contract manufacturers, previously dominated by US companies. In 2005, Foxconn achieved the number one position among global contract manufacturers (see tables 2.1 and 2.2).

A second element of restructuring resulted from the shift of EMS production to the China Circle (Naughton 1997). *Original design manufacturing*

Table 2.1.   Top Ten EMS Contract Manufacturing, 2005 Compared to 2004

2005 Rank	2004 Rank	Company	2005 Revenue (US$ millions)	2004 Revenue (US$ millions)	Year-to-Year Change (%)
1	2	Foxconn	20,981	15,811	33
2	1	Flextronics	15,582	16,062	−3
3	3	Sanmina-SCI	11,343	12,484	−9
4	4	Solectron	10,207	11,630	−12
5	5	Celestica	8,471	8,839	−4
6	6	Jabil	8,057	6,575	23
7	7	Elcoteq	5,179	3,899	33
8	9	Venture	3,238	3,194	1
9	8	Benchmark	2,257	2,001	13
10	10	USI	1,621	1,613	1
		Total Top 10	86,936	82,108	9

Source: iSuppli Corp.

(ODM) emerged as a viable model of global electronics manufacturing services. As opposed to the EMS model developed by US contract manufacturers, ODM manufacturers also design the manufactured product on behalf of their brand-name customers, thereby developing substantial intellectual property rights, although the name of the manufacturer never appears in connection with the product. The ODM model initially became established in the production of notebook computers. Later it expanded rapidly into the production of PCs, cell phones, and a broad array of consumer electronics systems, such as MP3 players (for a more detailed explanation, see chapter 2). Contract manufacturing models became more differentiated, with an overarching trend of accelerated vertical integration of manufacturing and design in newly emerging low-cost locations. Thus, the global landscape of contract manufacturing at the beginning of the twenty-first century was shaped by global contract manufacturers from both the EMS and ODM field, listed in tables 2.1 and 2.2.

This order remained relatively stable until the world financial crisis began to appear at the end of 2007. Following the meltdown of the global financial system in the second half of 2008, a partial replay of the 2001–2002 situation occurred. Contract manufacturing facilities were idled or closed down around the globe on very short notice. This time, China was hit hardest, especially the very large facilities in South China. During the first quarter of 2009, the two biggest EMS factories in the region (and in the world) dismissed sixty thousand and twenty thousand production workers, respec-

Table 2.2.   Top Ten ODM Contract Manufacturing, 2005 Compared to 2004

2005 Rank	2004 Rank	Company	2005 Revenue ($US millions)	2004 Revenue ($US millions)	Year-to-Year Change (%)
1	1	Quanta	12,523	9,655	30
2	2	Asustek	10,737	7,826	37
3	3	Compal	6,860	6,433	7
4	5	Lite-On	5,054	4,959	2
5	6	Inventec	5,048	4,236	19
6	4	BenQ	5,043	5,016	1
7	7	Wistron	4,814	3,545	36
8	9	Inventec Appliance	3,577	2,454	46
9	8	Tatung	2,338	3,216	−27
10	11	Mitac Int'l	2,307	1,543	50
		Total Top 10	58,301	48,883	17

Source: iSuppli Corp.

tively—most of them migrant workers who returned to their villages to wait for better times after the end of the recession (2009 interview data; see chapter 4). However, the "supply chain disaster" of the 2001–2002 recession this time appeared less dramatic. Obviously, the centralization of control on the part of brand-name companies and contract manufacturers had its impact in this area. However, improved control over material and production flows did not prevent massive financial difficulties for some of the largest contract manufacturers.

The crisis resulted in a new wave of acquisitions and mergers in the industry. The most important one was the takeover of Solectron, the fastest-growing and largest EMS company during the 1990s, by Flextronics, announced late in 2007. Flextronics also purchased large factories from Taiwanese ODM company Arima in 2008, adding substantial ODM capabilities for notebook computers to its manufacturing portfolio. Also, a number of smaller takeovers and mergers occurred among Taiwanese EMS and ODM firms. This new round of mergers and acquisitions resulted in a new global hierarchy among contract manufacturers. As table 2.3 shows, the industry has become dominated by two "mega contract manufacturers," Foxconn and Flextronics, each with more than US$30 billion in revenues, and both with substantial EMS and ODM capabilities. Three companies in the range of US$10–15 billion in revenues (Quanta and Asustek on the ODM and Jabil on the EMS side) form the second layer, followed by a number of companies with US$5–10 billion in revenues, the majority of them from Taiwan. Thus, the role of the former North American "big five" has been reduced substantially, whereas Taiwanese companies dominate the industry by revenues and numbers.

Table 2.3. Top Ten EMS Contract Manufacturers, 2008 Compared to 2007

2008 Rank	2007 Rank	Company	2008 Revenue ($US millions)	2007 Revenue ($US millions)	Year-to-Year Change (%)
1	1	Foxconn	55,435	54,706	1
2	2	Flextronics	33,140	33,346	−0.6
3	3	Jabil Circuit	12,786	12,432	3
4	5	Celestica	7,677	8,069	−5
5	4	Sanmina-SCI	6,843	10,138	−32
6	6	Elcoteq	4,993	5,740	−13
7	8	Venture	2,692	2,617	2
8	7	Benchmark	2,589	2,915	−11
9	9	Universal Science	1,954	2,046	−4
10	10	Plexus	1,839	1,624	13
		Total Top 10	129,948	133,633	−3

Source: iSuppli Corp.

EMS VERSUS ODM: CONTRACT MANUFACTURING "WITH" AND "WITHOUT" PRODUCT DEVELOPMENT

The complex and often unintelligible restructuring of the global production networks of the IT industry in the early twenty-first century demonstrates that there are no simple pathways of vertical specialization, as suggested by mainstream theories of "market-based modularity" (Langlois 2001; for a critical discussion, see Ernst 2005a; see also chapter 1). On the one hand, vertically integrated models of production and innovation continue to be competitive in some areas of the electronics industry, such as the emerging multinational Asian corporations like Samsung, which achieved global leadership in areas such as communications and consumer electronics. On the other hand, the complex reintegration of production within global industry networks does not signal a return to the vertically integrated corporation in its "classical," that is, Fordist type. Today, the restructuring of production systems is part of global configurations of capital which are no longer controlled by traditional corporate champions with strong links to their respective domestic markets. Instead, the movement of capital is taking place within complex transnational production networks under the leadership of global flagship companies (Ernst 2002a).

After the end of the 1980s, industrial development in the IT industry was dominated by a dual logic of "fragmentation and centralization" of industry structures (Ernst and O'Connor 1992; Lüthje 2001), accelerated during the so-called New Economy. Production models were redefined in the face of slower growth rates and continuing problems of capital valorization during the recent decade. Certain elements of the production infrastructure were reformed as new industry segments with relatively distinct norms of production. Competition among contract manufacturers is not only about costs, prices, and profits but also about the definition of production models, comparable to the creation of market-defining products among the brand-name firms. Contract manufacturers do not compete to create new products and system architectures but to market and "package" distinctive portfolios of production, design, and logistics services. This implies accelerated vertical reintegration by contract manufacturers. However, the various models of contract production differ significantly—particularly in the degree to which contract manufacturers are involved in the design of products and production systems and the related definition of core competencies of the brand-name companies.

For a better understanding of these complex processes, a closer look at the acronyms used in electronics for various forms of contract manufacturing may be helpful. There are three basic models of external manufacturing: OEM (*original equipment manufacturing*), EMS (*electronics manufacturing services*), and ODM (*original design manufacturing*). In addition, there are a number of hybrids, such as *contract design manufacturing* (CDM). In-house production by brand-name companies is called *original brandname manufacturing* (OBM) (see table 2.4). The terminology is not always consistent. Especially confusing is the fact that brand-name firms are also called OEM (original equipment manufacturers)—common industry lingo, which for the sake of clarity will not be used in this book. The production portfolios of most major contract manufacturers contain all the major models of outsourced manufacturing. In this book, therefore, classification of particular firms as "EMS" or "ODM" companies will be based on the production model which is dominant among the manufacturing services of the particular company.

Original equipment manufacturing (OEM) is the oldest form of contract manufacturing in electronics, historically provided by medium-sized, often family-owned part suppliers or assembly firms. After the 1980s, this type of manufacturing took place increasingly in low-wage assembly shops in industrialized and developing countries such as Korea or Taiwan. In this form of contract assembly, the design of products and manufacturing processes rests entirely with the brand-name company, which often controls the details of assembly operations. Subassembly arrangements of this kind, also known as "board stuffing," are still widely used among multinational brand-name firms

Table 2.4.   Types of Production in Electronics Manufacturing

Name/Term	Abbreviation	Key Features
Original brand-name manufacturing	OBM	"Classic" own production: core capacities of product development, component purchasing, manufacturing, and logistics are in the hands of brand-name company
Original equipment manufacturing	OEM	"Classic" contract manufacturing: manufacturing of a brand-name product by contractor, product and manufacturing process developed and controlled by brand-name company, purchasing of supplier materials and components by brand-name company
Electronics manufacturing services	EMS	Production of brand-name products by contract manufacturers, product development by brand-name company, manufacturing processes and supply chains under the control of contract manufacturer, including production-related engineering, component purchasing, after-sales services (e.g., installation, repair), contract manufacturer as "manufacturing partner" with comprehensive, independent production know-how
Original design manufacturing	ODM	Like EMS, but also additional technical system development by contract manufacturer; own intellectual property of brand-name company is reduced to key elements of brand development (particularly product design, logos, user interface)

and their no-name suppliers, today mostly located in Asia. Major examples of contract manufacturing in OEM production includes the manufacturing of preassembled cell phone kits by Foxconn for Nokia. PCs are often made by no-name manufacturers in Taiwan or China for major retailers such as Walmart in the United States or Aldi in Europe, who then sell such systems under special trade names.

The transition from classical subassembly to comprehensive electronics manufacturing services dominated the agenda of the contract manufacturing industry throughout the 1990s. The transition was propelled by vertically specialized, "factoryless" technology companies using the Wintelist model.

This trend pushed contract manufacturers toward becoming manufacturing "partners," with substantial know-how in product development and the planning of production and logistics systems. This development also raised expectations that the new "American" model of full-service contract manufacturing would replace assembly shops in Asia and recover some ground for manufacturing in the United States and other developed economies (Lüthje 2002; Sturgeon and Lester 2002, 30–33).

These expectations were not realized. The crisis in 2001 not only demonstrated the limits of the EMS model of contract manufacturing, it also produced favorable conditions for the rise of *original design manufacturing*. Contract manufacturers from Taiwan initially produced notebook computers, followed by cell phones, PDAs, and other portable electronic devices. In contrast to the model of *electronics manufacturing services* (EMS), which focuses on manufacturing and logistics services, ODM production includes comprehensive services in product design. Often, the ODM provider offers a complete product design that will be adapted exclusively to the special requirements of the brand-name customer. With this strategy, ODM manufacturers reaped substantially higher profit margins than their US competitors during the 2001–2002 recession years while many EMS firms had to undergo massive restructuring.

The leading ODM manufacturers accumulated production know-how as suppliers to leading US mass producers in the PC industry, Dell, Compaq, and Apple in particular. During the 1990s, Taiwanese companies such as Mitac, FIC, Lite-On, and Tatung became important manufacturing partners of PC producers operating under the Wintel model. These relationships grew after the late 1980s, mostly on the basis of OEM contracts for motherboards and graphics cards (Dedrick and Kraemer 1998, 146ff.). ODM relationships emerged during the late 1990s, primarily in notebook computer manufacturing. Manufacturers received substantial support from the government of Taiwan, whose research and development programs opened access for local electronics producers to leading-edge technologies. During that period, Taiwanese contract manufacturers developed first-class know-how in customer-specific configuration of large-scale manufacturing orders and related logistics. They were supported by Taiwan's shipping companies, with their far-flung global customer relationships (Chen 2002). The rapid expansion of the ODM model into new areas, such as computer servers, cell phones, and consumer electronics, was accompanied by the development of massive vertically integrated manufacturing complexes on the Chinese mainland, particularly in the greater Shanghai area (see chapter 3).

Based on their first-class design and production capabilities, the leading ODM companies are fully integrated manufacturing firms with extensive resources at every level of "subarchitectural" product development. Their function and structure is similar to "system suppliers" in other manufacturing sectors. Large first-tier suppliers in the automobile industry, for instance, also integrate design and manufacturing of complex modules of end products with considerable autonomy in the development of the respective technologies. From the perspective of brand-name firms, the attraction of ODM (and its superiority over EMS) lies in the tight coordination of design and production, which eases the transition of new products into production. At the same time, brand-name firms can buy relatively complete product designs "off the shelf"—an easy way to fill design gaps in rapidly changing markets (2004 interview data).

However, the ODM model has inherent problems. ODM firms command a broader portfolio of manufacturing and design resources than EMS manufacturers, particularly at the interface between design and production. But they are focused on a considerably smaller spectrum of products and therefore are much more vulnerable to short-term fluctuations in the particular markets for those products (Sturgeon and Lester 2002, 63–66). ODM manufacturers have been trying to balance these risks by extending their product portfolios. However, with the extension of ODM into an increasing array of products, brand-name firms face the increasing loss of essential know-how to contract manufacturers—a severe limit to the ODM model.

This problem became particularly visible in mobile communications. A number of ODM firms from Taiwan, such as BenQ, DBTel, and HTC, entered the market with their own branded cell phone models. These were mostly sold in Taiwan, mainland China, and some emerging markets in Asia, India in particular. At the same time, these companies became important suppliers to big international telecom network operators for operator-branded cell phones. ODM manufactured phones therefore competed directly with the products of their major brand-name customers, such as Motorola or Nokia. This development not only put pressure on the profit margins of brand-name mobile phone producers, it also undermined their predominance over definition of core technologies and new concepts of telecommunications services. Telecom operators could create new alliances, circumventing their established brand-name suppliers. Deutsche Telekom, for instance, the dominant network operator in Germany, cooperated with Microsoft in the development of the operating system for future generations of mobile communications. This was directed against a global alliance led by Nokia named Symbian. Deutsche Telekom based its assault on the established market leaders on a manufacturing alliance with HTC, an ODM manufacturer from Taiwan (*Economist*, April 29, 2004), which later emerged as one of the leading suppliers of "smartphones" modeled after Apple's famous iPhone.

The increasing problems of the ODM model led to substantial restructuring among Taiwanese manufacturers. To bolster its quest to become a top brand name in the global PC market, Acer spun off its ODM business into a separate legal entity called Wistron 2001. In 2007, after its disastrous takeover of Siemens Mobile, BenQ took a similar step with the separation of ODM and brand-name businesses, forming Qisda as its manufacturing arm and retaining the BenQ brand for its brand-name business. In 2008 the Taiwanese electronics producer Asustek was split up into three entities, Asustek, Unihan, and Pegatron, focusing on three distinct fields. Asustek, renamed to Asus, now solely focuses on manufacturing Asus brand notebooks and PCs. Pegatron is responsible for component manufacturing as well as ODM business. Subcomponent and chassis manufacturing is done by Unihan.

EMS firms used the emerging intraindustry contradictions around ODM manufacturing to defend their position. One strategy was concentrating on the core competencies of EMS production in manufacturing and logistics, emphasizing the values of production as a service. The restructuring of Solectron, one of the pioneering EMS firms, in the wake of the 2001 recession followed this model. Severe financial problems forced the former world-market leader to abandon sophisticated resources in product development by selling its subsidiaries Force Computers and Zhone Technologies. The company focused its advertising on production services and started a highly publicized campaign promoting the lean manufacturing practices of Japanese car manufacturer Toyota. In the area of product design, Solectron introduced the concept of *contract design manufacturing* (CDM)—a "lite" version of ODM, limiting design activities of contract manufacturers to certain subcomponents of the manufactured products, which would leave the intellectual property rights for the system with the brand-name customer (Purvis 2004).

Other US contract manufacturers, namely Celestica and Jabil, followed suit by promising their customers "to protect their brand by not developing competitive intellectual property" (Jorgenson 2004). In contrast with these defensive strategies, Flextronics and Sanmina-SCI (the number one and number three EMS contract manufacturers during the first decade of the twenty-first century) actively tried to enhance vertical integration. They extended their production of nonelectronic components, in particular plastic and metal parts, and established new product design capabilities, bringing the companies closer to ODM-type integration of manufacturing and design services. In 2004, Flextronics took a major step in this direction by partnering with ARM, the world's leading supplier of standardized "development kits" for sophisticated chips. It acquired extensive capabilities in software development from Hughes, a former subsidiary of General Motors, and production capability for camera modules from Agilent. Finally, it added a new ODM service department specializing in the design of cell phones, with an engineering workforce based in Beijing and Shenzhen in China (2004 interview data).

In the ongoing struggle over defining norms of production, Taiwanese ODM companies are not immune from the sector-wide problems of the IT industry. Like their EMS competitors, ODM producers try to maintain low-cost contract manufacturing, even under continuous technological improvement, in order to compensate for the structural problems of capital profitability at the top of global production networks, that is, among brand-name companies.

These problems resulted in a protracted reduction of profit margins among ODM companies in recent years. Prior to this, during the 2001 recession, these companies had yielded higher profit margins than their EMS competitors. The profitability problems of established ODM manufacturers indicate growing problems in the "global factory" models created by the leading IT manufacturers from Taiwan (for a detailed analysis, see Ernst 2006b). They also show higher structural costs in vertically disintegrated innovation systems and an underlying slowdown in productivity of key technologies. Whether these contradictions will result in an increased convergence of ODM and EMS models of contract manufacturing (Pick 2004) or perhaps in accelerated attacks of ODM companies on brand-name product markets remains to be seen. However, the net effect of this competition is increased vertical integration of contract manufacturing resources and the shifting of the center of gravity of electronics manufacturing to East Asia, the China Circle in particular.

"TRUST IS GOOD, CONTROL IS BETTER": OVERACCUMULATION AND RECENTRALIZATION OF PRODUCTION RELATIONSHIPS

By the end of the 1990s, electronics manufacturing services had been established as a new type of production in the IT sector. It comprised a variety of outsourcing models which were all characterized by the complete or almost complete transfer of complex functions of production and logistics to contract manufacturers with a global scope of operation (Lüthje, Schumm, and Sproll 2002, 58ff.).

However, the comprehensive shift of manufacturing to contract manufacturers was debated among industry experts. Production managers of older vertically integrated corporations expressed concerns about abandoning complex production know-how, accumulated over years, at the expense of substantial investment. These experts warned that the transfer of entire factories and complex supply chains would cause the loss of their ability to rapidly and efficiently bring new technologies and products into mass production. Furthermore, they feared that in the long run, contract manufacturers would acquire their own know-how and compete directly with brand-name producers. They voiced similar concerns over the growing control by contract manufacturers of components purchasing and inventory management. EMS contract manufacturers advertised their capabilities in this field as one of their core competencies. They promised substantial cost savings through their purchasing power in global markets for key electronic components, such as chips, hard disk drives, and graphics cards. For contract manufacturers, smart calculation of component purchases and the related price margins were key elements ensuring profitability given the low profit margins in the assembly part of the business (Curran 1997).

Among most US and European electronics brand-name firms, such reservations rapidly lost ground as IT-product markets enjoyed seemingly limitless growth in the so-called New Economy and its related shortage of production capacity. In contrast, East Asian brand-name firms proved relatively immune to the promises of the new production model. Japanese electronics companies had already shifted production to contract manufacturers and relocated manufacturing to China in the wake of the stagnation of the Japanese economy during the 1990s (Ernst 2005b). They increasingly used outsourcing partners outside the traditional corporate "families," known as *keiretsu*, and their distinctive suppliers. Nevertheless, Japanese industry leaders such as Hitachi, Toshiba, and Sony retained the basics of their lean production models developed during the 1980s, giving preference to long-term relationships with outside suppliers. They tried to ensure that their company cultures were compatible with short-term cost calculations. Many of these companies set up supplier subsidiaries in China, mirroring the traditional model of intra-corporate supplier relations in new geographical area. The commodity character of the "American" model of contract manufacturing, however, is based on shorter-term contracts and massive manufacturing volumes, with EMS providers supplying similar manufacturing services (see Sturgeon 2006).

South Korean companies such as Samsung and LG have a long history as contract manufacturers themselves (Ernst 1994). They rose as preferred suppliers of manufacturing services to Japanese electronics companies, especially for mature products with standard components. Korean corporations started their own large-scale investment in developing key components, in particular memory chips and LCD screens. They became very conscious about controlling key competencies in design and manufacturing and therefore used contract manufacturers only to a limited extent. Korean companies built massive manufacturing complexes in China to perform low-cost in-house assembly (Kwon, Rhee, and Suh 2004, 428–29). Like their Japanese counterparts, Korean companies prefer Taiwanese contract manufacturers for their third-party manufacturing needs.

The limits of the EMS model became highly visible with the global slump in the IT industry in 2001. Contract manufacturers were relegated to the role of regulators of global overcapacity, bearing the burden of corporate restructuring. In the wake of this crisis, the IT industry underwent a classical cycle of reconcentration and recentralization of capital, which revealed the limits of vertical integration and industry-wide overaccumulation of capital. "Megamergers," such as the one between Hewlett-Packard and Compaq in 2002, were designed to take overcapacity out of computer markets and highlighted this development. Among contract manufacturers, major industry players disappeared or were taken over by competitors. The most prominent victim was SCI, the oldest EMS company and the industry leader of the mid-1990s. SCI was taken over by a much smaller contract manufacturer from Silicon Valley, Sanmina, and merged into a new company called Sanmina-SCI. Solectron, the fastest-growing contract manufacturer of the late 1990s, took over Singapore-based NatSteel, the flagship of the EMS industry in Asia at that time. As we explain in chapter 3, this merger also had a massive impact on major low-cost locations of contract manufacturing in Asia, Mexico, and Eastern Europe, where NatSteel had a presence.

Less spectacular but no less important was the massive reorganization of relationships between contract manufacturers and their major brand-name customers in the wake of the crisis. Cooperation and control of outsourced production had developed in relatively decentralized ways during the 1990s (mostly between certain business units or regional organizations of brand-name firms and contract manufacturing plants). But production relations were massively centralized after 2001. Cisco provides a typical example. The company ran up a huge excess inventory of chips, printed circuit boards, and components, amounting to US$2.5 billion in the first quarter of 2001 alone (SJMN, April 27, 2001). Under the pressure of massive write-offs, Cisco completely reorganized its global production networks by reducing the number of its contract manufacturers from nine to four and its worldwide EMS manufacturing facilities from thirty to sixteen. At the same, production was shifted to lower-cost contract manufacturers from Taiwan such as Foxconn, with rapidly growing factories in mainland China (2003 interview data).

The centralization of production was accompanied by a new and unprecedented wave of outsourcing of manufacturing by brand-name companies. The most prominent example was Lucent, formerly part of the US telephone monopoly AT&T. At the beginning of the twentieth century (under the name Western Electric), it was the biggest manufacturer of telecommunications equipment in the world. This manufacturing tradition of more than a hundred years was abruptly ended with the transfer of twenty-nine manufacturing facilities to contract manufacturers Celestica, Solectron, Sanmina-SCI, and Jabil. These companies took over about 95 percent of Lucent's production capacity between 1999 and 2003. Along with the sale of subsidiaries in chip making and telecommunications equipment servicing, Lucent's revenues shrank from US$38.5 billion to $8.5 billion while its workforce was downsized from 157,000 to 32,500. The radical shift in production came with massive centralization of manufacturing and logistics chains, exerting pressure on contract manufacturers to reduce capacity in their newly acquired plants (Takahashi 2004).

Hewlett-Packard's takeover of Compaq reveals the dimensions of this industry-wide restructuring. In the wake of the merger, explicitly designed to take large chunks of overcapacity out of global PC markets, the purchasing, manufacturing, and logistics systems of both companies were integrated. As table 2.5 shows in detail, the number of manufacturing facilities of both companies worldwide was reduced from 63 to 32, of distribution centers from 142 to 88, and of direct suppliers from about 1,500 to 700. Part of this restructuring was a company-wide reorganization of IT systems, drastically reducing the number of IT programs, data servers, and computing centers. According to official figures from HP, this reorganization saved about US$3 billion during the first two years after the merger.

Massive centralization of relationships with contract manufacturers was also part of this restructuring. Compaq had relied on contract manufacturers to only a relatively small extent (see Lüthje, Schumm, and Sproll 2002, 58–59). But HP had become one of the biggest customers of the EMS industry during the 1990s (Lüthje 2001). The relationships between HP and its contract manufacturers had evolved through numerous business units and departments, operating with little coordination among the units. This mirrored the almost unintelligible corporate structure of HP and the different business models within the company. In 2001, still before the takeover of Compaq, HP began a large-scale reorganization of contract manufacturing to cope with the inefficiency of its existing structure. Three EMS companies were designed as preferred providers, and contracts with these companies were centrally administered at HP's corporate level (2002 interview data). This reorganization sought to counter the growing bargaining power of contract manufacturers over prices for manufacturing services and component purchasing. Eighty percent of HP's annual purchasing volume (about

Table 2.5. Global Consolidation of Manufacturing and Logistics HP/Compaq, 2002, 2004

	Pre-merger Compaq/HP	*HP 2004*
Manufacturing locations	63	32
Distribution centers	142	88
Suppliers	1,500	ca. 700
Logistics partners	385	119
IT application	7,000	ca. 4,000
Data servers22,000	22,000	19,000
Data centers	ca. 300	88

Source: HP company information.
Note: US$3 billion cost savings in the first two years.

US$40 billion) was concentrated among thirty-five first-tier suppliers (ESM, October 1, 2004). For key electronics components, such as chips, motherboards, and hard disk drives, HP reassumed exclusive responsibility. Direct purchasing of components by contract manufacturers was limited to lower-end and nonelectronic components, such as metal parts or cable assemblies. HP introduced a new policy called *price masking*, designed to keep prices of components purchased by HP secret from contract manufacturers and eliminate contractors' hidden profits from cost calculation for components (2004 interview data).

In the wake of the recession, price masking became a widespread policy among big brand-name firms, including Motorola, Siemens, and Sony-Ericsson (EN, April 1, 2004). According to iSuppli, about 40 percent of the top-tier companies in the electronics industry operated price-masking schemes of various kinds (EMSNow, October 19, 2004). This development had a deep impact on the role of contract manufacturers. On the one hand, it limited their ability to extract profits from the purchasing and resale of electronics parts and components. On the other hand, key elements of supply chain management were relocated to brand-name firms, essentially limiting the profile of contract manufacturing as a highly integrated service (Sullivan 2003).

EMS companies reacted with massive centralization of their own supply chains. Solectron, for instance, relocated responsibilities for component purchases from individual factories or customer teams to a newly created company-wide materials management organization—a strategy imitated by most other contract manufacturers. This policy sought to substantially reduce the number of component suppliers. Solectron selected 250 of its 550 first-tier suppliers, who accounted for 80 percent of its annual purchasing volume of US$14 billion. The corporate purchasing department developed company-wide models of supplier evaluation, bidding procedures, and purchasing agreements. Standardization also allowed expanded use of Internet-based tools for supply chain management. The proportion of web-based purchasing was to be raised from 35 percent to 75 percent of the entire purchasing volume (Carbone 2002).

RESTRUCTURING OF BRAND-NAME GLOBAL PRODUCTION NETWORKS

The consolidation of production and logistics chains in the IT industry resembled restructuring strategies in older industries dominated by Fordist-Taylorist mass producers. Centralization of control over global production and supply networks normalized relationships between brand-name firms and contract manufacturers in the IT industry, comparable to the reduction of suppliers in the auto industry as a result of *lean production* during the 1990s (see Jürgens and Sablowski 2004). The centralization of supply chains by major IT brand-name companies also revealed that the leading EMS companies lacked key organizational capabilities (contrary to what was advertised as a "full-service" model of manufacturing) and were overwhelmed by their enormous expansion during the late 1990s.

Some aspects of restructuring indicate a revival of vertically integrated forms of innovation and production. However, the trend to outsource production continued unabated in most areas. In particular, product development was increasingly outsourced in the wake of the 2001–2002 recession. Various industry segments used distinct strategies for restructuring. Three segments that were at the center of the Wintelist transformation of markets and production networks illustrate these changes. All three examples demonstrate the fundamental instability of norms of production across the IT sector, which became particularly visible after the 2001–2002 recession.

Computers: The Global Retreat from Manufacturing and Product Development

During the 1990s, the computer industry made an almost complete transition to fabless manufacturing. US-based world-market leaders Hewlett-Packard/ Compaq, IBM, Dell, and Apple transferred most of their production to contract manufacturers. This model was also imitated by the most important new brand-name company, Acer, from Taiwan. During the 2001–2002 recession, leading brand-name firms concentrated and centralized their production systems and shifted product development to contract manufacturers operating under the *original design manufacturing* (ODM) model.

After the takeover of Compaq by Hewlett-Packard, IBM's retreat from PC manufacturing was the second fundamental change among brand-name firms. This began in 2001, when IBM gave up manufacturing of consumer PCs and limited its presence in the PC segment to business computers and notebooks, often sold as part of larger IT-outsourcing and IT-servicing arrangements with corporate customers. In 2002 IBM sold production of business PCs and notebooks to Sanmina-SCI, at the time the world's third-largest EMS contract manufacturer, including three major factories in North Carolina, Mexico, and Scotland. The facilities in Mexico and Scotland were closed after a short time, and production for IBM was relocated to three factories in Malaysia, China, and Hungary (see chapters 3 and 4). In addition, IBM located manufacturing of desktop and notebook PCs for the rapidly growing Chinese market in a joint venture facility with Chinese computer maker Great Wall in Shenzhen, South China. However, this cooperation was rather short-lived. IBM, the pioneer of mass-produced PCs in the 1980s and 1990s, finally sold its entire PC business to another major newcomer from China,

Lenovo, which subsequently became one of the largest players in the post-IBM PC industry (*DigiTimes*, December 6, 2004).

Less visible but equally important was the shift of PC production to ODM contract manufacturers from Taiwan, mainly driven by HP, Dell, and Apple. Dell, with its unique model of direct sales through the Internet, relied on contract manufacturers from the beginning of its phenomenal growth in the 1990s. In Dell's manufacturing model, EMS companies such as Sanmina-SCI or Solectron operate as large-scale producers of motherboards or preassembled kits, which are configured to individual customer orders in Dell's own assembly plants in the United States, Asia, and Europe. This organization is intrinsically linked to Dell's web-based sales model, which combines customer-specific configuration with large-scale mass production. Dell's assembly plants perform only the very final stages of product assembly and packaging, as a part of delivery logistics rather than manufacturing (see Lüthje, Schumm, and Sproll 2002, 57–58). In 2007, due to shrinking market share, Dell was forced to depart from its total focus on Internet distribution and establish channel distribution to keep up with competition from HP. There are no clear signs of change in Dell's production organization in its worldwide production facilities. Notebook computers and smaller mobile devices, as well as television sets, are manufactured under ODM arrangements. The ODM supplier also provides the product design. This production model was not changed during the crisis of 2001–2002. However, Dell increasingly employed low-cost EMS and ODM contract manufacturers from Taiwan, in particular Foxconn.

At Hewlett-Packard, PC manufacturing during the 1990s became largely based on the EMS model. However, in the wake of the takeover of Compaq, PC manufacturing for consumers, and partly for business customers, rapidly changed to an ODM model. Two companies from Taiwan (Tatung and FIC), and one from Korea (Trigem), became its main manufacturing partners. HP sold its manufacturing facility near Lyons, France, to Sanmina-SCI and sold another factory in Scotland, acquired from Compaq, to Jabil. In the wake of this development, between 2002 and 2004 HP's entire PC manufacturing and product development of consumer PCs was transferred to contract manufacturers. Thousands of relatively well-paid jobs at HP were eliminated. Following Dell, the development of PC hardware was no longer seen as a core competency. Only the design of the case, logos, and software interfaces (i.e., the outer appearance of the products) was seen as a strategic resource. The largest PC maker in the world, once famous for its engineering culture, became purely a marketing and distributing company with no in-house resources for manufacturing and product development (2004, 2005 interview data).

The Limits of Wintelism: Restructuring of Mobile Phone Manufacturing

In the manufacturing of mobile phones, the Wintel model rapidly gained importance during the second half of the 1990s. However, this change was less clear-cut than in the PC industry and differed markedly from company to company. The US- and Europe-based world-market leaders of the 1990s (Nokia, Motorola, Sony-Ericsson, and Siemens) used contract manufacturing as part of a broader scenario of restructuring. Cell phone manufacturing was released from vertically integrated corporate organizations that had historically dominated the telecommunications industry (Esser, Lüthje, and Noppe 1997). The key development was the spin-off of telecommunications handset manufacturing into separate corporate units, subsidiaries, or joint ventures. New companies appeared, such as Sony-Ericsson and Siemens-BenQ. In the course of this process, short-term profit imperatives dominated the traditional long-term perspective governing technology development and production in telecommunications (see Voskamp and Wittke 2008b).

By the end of the 1990s, leading mobile phone companies had shifted major production capacity to contract manufacturers. Ericsson from Sweden took the lead and announced in 2001 that it would give up in-house manufacturing of mobile phones entirely. Flextronics became the biggest manufacturer of Ericsson phones. Siemens also started a large-scale shift into contract manufacturing, accompanied by sales of smaller manufacturing facilities in Europe to contract manufacturers. Nokia was more conservative and maintained a relatively integrated manufacturing structure. EMS companies mainly provided components and preassembled cell phone kits while Nokia performed the final assembly. This model resembled Dell's manufacturing organization for PCs. Here, contract manufacturers such as Foxconn from Taiwan and Elcoteq from Finland became long-term manufacturing partners and the preferred EMS providers (Bengtsson and Berggren 2002).

During the 2001–2002 recession, a certain swing back to in-house manufacturing took place. Motorola and Siemens Mobile limited outsourced production to 30–40 percent of manufacturing revenues. Siemens also reacted to demands from trade unions and works councils to maintain its only remaining cell phone manufacturing plant in Germany, in the town of Kamp-Lintfort. Ericsson suddenly regained substantial manufacturing resources through its merger with Sony in 2002, which included Sony's factories in Japan and other locations in Asia (2004 interview data). However, Sony-Ericsson's proportion of outsourced manufacturing remained high during the postmerger period (at about 60 percent), using Flextronics and Taiwanese ODM company Arima as its major contract manufacturers.

The massive relocation of cell phone manufacturing to East Asia, and particularly China, actually slowed outsourcing of manufacturing. In order to gain access to the Chinese domestic market, major manufacturers had to set up factories in China in joint ventures with national and local state-owned enterprises. Siemens built a new factory in Shanghai with Shanghai Audio and Video (SAV), which soon became Siemens's largest cell phone production site worldwide. Ericsson has a joint venture with the Putian group (later renamed Potevio), a major state-owned corporation in China. The joint factory serves as a production base for the rapidly growing Chinese market (*Digi-Times*, September 23, 2004). Motorola and the emerging top players from Korea, Samsung and LG, built their own large-scale manufacturing facilities on the mainland, mostly in the city of Tianjin. These factories were part of the Asian manufacturing networks of these companies, which are based on broad vertical integration of the development and manufacturing of chips, imaging technology, and handset systems. Along with the world-market leaders came major multinational component suppliers from Europe who had been long-term partners in vertically integrated manufacturing networks, such as Philips Audio Systems, a world-leading provider of tiny speakers and microphones for mobile communications devices (2004, 2005 interview data).

A distinctively new development in cell phone manufacturing (and the flip side of the partial vertical reintegration of production in brand-name firms) was the rapid expansion of ODM contract manufacturing. The conditions for this development were set by the "commodification" of key product know-how caused by the standardization of transmission technology in mobile phone handsets (called the RF component of the phone). Chip manufacturers, such as Texas Instruments and Infineon, made RF technology increasingly available in modules (i.e., sets of chips and software in a standardized package linking the phone to the network). As a result, non-brand-name firms, including ODM contract manufacturers, were able to develop their own handset designs. Integrated producers of telecommunications network equipment and handsets thereby lost their traditional competitive edge in phone design. The shift toward ODM production was initially supported by Motorola and mobile phone network operators such as Deutsche Telekom or Vodafone trying to market handsets under their own brand. Around 2004, Motorola had a well-established network of ODM providers based on four companies from Taiwan (BenQ, Chi Mei, Compal, and HTC). Siemens, Ericsson, and Nokia followed suit in 2003 and 2004. Nokia quickly established an ODM relationship with BenQ for manufacturing clamshell phones after analysts criticized Nokia for the absence of such phones from its product portfolio (Taipei Times, August 24, 2004).

The growing significance of ODM models in cell phone manufacturing marked another break with the traditions of the telecommunications industry. Companies previously cultivated the integration of in-house manufacturing know-how and proprietary technology standards (see Esser, Lüthje, and

Noppe 1997). In the new world of ODM, leading producers of mobile communications imitated the PC industry. They rapidly limited their technological core competencies to the exterior design of handsets, user interfaces, and the related software. Handset manufacturing and hardware development were no longer considered strategic know-how. ODM contract manufacturers offered both elements as an integrated service under one roof, promising smooth and speedy transition of newly designed products into volume production (2004, 2005 interview data).

These strategies were not without risk, dramatically illustrated by Siemens. The rapid decline of Siemens Mobile during the years 2004 and 2005 (a hotly debated issue in German industrial and labor politics) was directly related to its retreat from strategic development of technology. This was driven by the short-term profit imperatives of *shareholder-value* capitalism. As financial investors (popularly called "locusts" in Germany) increasingly took control over Siemens, the corporation increased outsourcing relationships with ODM makers from Taiwan. After some disastrous failures in new product introductions (NPIs), Siemens finally sold its cell phone manufacturing arm to ODM company BenQ from Taiwan. This created the unprecedented takeover of a global brand-name business in the telecommunications industry by a contract manufacturer from an emerging economy, nurtured by the transfer of manufacturing and design know-how from traditional hightech regions. BenQ's venture into branded cell phone manufacturing, however, was unsuccessful. Siemens burdened its "partner" from Taiwan with massive liabilities, hidden in the mobile phone unit's balance sheets. This financial scandal, together with massive protests by trade unions and politicians in Germany, caused BenQ to retreat from the venture (see Müller 2009).

This disaster, widely reported in Asia, did not cause major damage to ODM as a manufacturing model, however. The massive drop in sales of 2008–2009 caused some of the major players in the mobile phone industry to pull back major orders from contract manufacturers, once again shifting the risks of global overcapacity onto EMS and ODM companies. The withdrawal of another global brand from the mobile phone handset market, Motorola, also left contract manufacturers such as Foxconn with massive losses and overcapacity. The crisis shifted the center of gravity in the global mobile communications industry further to the China Circle, since China's giant phone operators have become leading forces in the development of new telecommunications infrastructures and services. With massive backing from the Chinese government and its economic rescue packages, China Mobile and China Telecom have begun to invest in 3G telecommunications networks, supporting the growth of an industrial base of cell phone manufacturers, chip makers, and software companies mostly located in China and Taiwan. Big brand names in China and Taiwan, such as Huawei and Acer, are entering the market for mobile phones and smartphones to develop brand-name recognition but without building extensive in-house manufacturing capacity. Most of these rapidly growing industry players are using ODM contract manufacturers (*DigiTimes*, April 23, 2009).

This transformation circle ("virtuous" for Asia and China but "vicious" for industrialized countries) was turned one round further with the emergence of smartphones as a lead product in the mobile phone market since about 2007. Apple's famous iPhone defined and created this market. This increasingly important subsegment of the industry became dominated by three major players, Apple, Samsung, and HTC from Taiwan, all of them distinctively post-Fordist technology companies (Lüthje 2008). None of the traditional makers of telecommunications equipment, including Nokia, Motorola, and Ericsson, were able to gain a leading position in this field. The dominant players in smartphones integrate their know-how from the production of mobile phones and mobile computers and from the production of Internet-based software and media content, the famous "applets" in particular. Apple controls its own operating system, which gives it a certain advantage over its competitors. Samsung and HTC use Google's Android operating system as a technological backbone for their products and specialize in the broad customization of Android's graphical interface and its integration with their distinct hardware. Manufacturing and the overwhelming part of component supply are based in East Asia around the China Circle. Production of Apple's iPhone and related products (iPad and iPod in particular) is based on an EMS model with Foxconn as the major manufacturer. Samsung and HTC operate their own factories in China but under a high-performance, low-cost model similar to contract manufacturing factories (2010, 2011 field research).

Video Game Consoles: Wintelism versus "Japan Inc."

Similar to the situation in mobile phone manufacturing, the restructuring of large areas of the consumer electronics industry did not proceed according to Wintelist textbook projections. New growth sectors in digital consumer devices, especially leading-edge audio and video systems and the associated LCD displays, saw confrontation between production networks based on the Wintelist model and highly integrated electronic conglomerates, mainly from Japan and South Korea. Video game consoles offer a particular example in case (Pawlicki 2005, 2008).

The economics of the game console industry differs in some important respects from common consumer electronics, such as television or audio sets. The average product life cycle for standard consumer electronics is estimated as eighteen months, whereas game consoles have life cycles of more than five years. Game console systems also feature leading-edge technology. The main processor of the PlayStation 3, the Cell chip, is being used for three-dimensional medical imaging applications, in blade servers (stripped-down computer servers with modular design), and in supercomputers, such as the IBM Roadrunner supercomputer for the Los Alamos National Laboratory. The development of such leading-edge technologies results in very high up-front costs, which cannot be fully passed onto consumers. Game console companies therefore use a form of the "razor blade" business model, tying subsidized game consoles to the revenues and license earnings from software sales for the respective systems.

In 2001 Microsoft entered this market with its newly developed Xbox game console, intending to break the dominance of the vertically integrated companies from Japan—Sony and Nintendo. As a software company, Microsoft did not possess the technological know-how nor the necessary manufacturing facilities. The company therefore relied on contract manufacturers from the beginning, using an EMS model to ensure rapid manufacturing ramp-up with high production volume. The production network was developed in partnership with Flextronics, with initial manufacturing locations in Guadalajara, Mexico, and Sarvar, Hungary, both close to the main end-user markets in North America and Europe. This production network was based on a complex supply chain. Intel and Samsung supplied microprocessors and memory chips, respectively, fabless chip design house Nvidia developed the graphic processor, chip foundry Taiwan Semiconductor Manufacturing Company (TSMC) manufactured it, and Western Digital designed and manufactured the hard disk drive. Flextronics designed important nonelectronic parts, especially the injection-molded plastic case, and coordinated the complex supply chain of hundreds of components. The production volume of one hundred thousand devices per week was achieved within one month (Carbone 2002).

This genuinely fabless production model was confronted with massive competition from the Japanese market leaders Sony and Nintendo, who both rely on vertically integrated production systems. Although Sony owns huge system production capacity, it also uses contract manufacturers for cost reduction—Asustek and Foxconn from Taiwan—granting only minor competences in design and logistics to the contract manufacturer. This is very similar to classical OEM subcontracting. The Japanese electronics conglomerate outsources production of only mature products, and only when its own production capacity falls short. Sony retains full control over product design for hardware, both for the whole system and for major components such as the microprocessor. To use the long product life cycle to push the production cost of the system below retail price, game consoles, especially their main processor and their graphics processor, are constantly redesigned (Pawlicki 2008; Takahashi 2006). The high level of control, based on the ownership of design and necessary technological capability, gives vertically integrated companies the ability to efficiently align the engineering schedules for their game console components.

In 2002, a year after product introduction, a price drop by Sony on its PlayStation 2 forced Microsoft to lower the retail price of its Xbox. As the initial retail price was already US$150 below production cost, Microsoft's loss on each unit increased even more. Lacking tight control over the main components and the engineering schedules, Microsoft could not align the price drop with a redesigned version of the system. This situation was exacerbated by massive production problems at Flextronics. Increased pressure from Microsoft forced Flextronics to restructure its global production network. The cornerstone of the restructuring program was the closure of the recently ramped-up production locations in Mexico and Hungary, leading to massive layoffs. Worldwide production was concentrated in the Flextronics industrial park in Zhuhai in South China. At the same time, Microsoft assigned a second contract manufacturer to system assembly, the Taiwanese company Wistron, which also operated dedicated production lines in South China. Solectron won the contract for global after-sales repair services (2003, 2004 interview data). Problems in its production system was only one aspect of Microsoft's mixed record in the game console market. Its aim to break the dominance of Japanese competitors, especially market leader Sony, was never achieved. By the beginning of 2005, just before the launch of its next-generation game console Xbox 360, Microsoft had sold twenty-one million Xbox systems (Shilov 2005). It ceased Xbox production in 2007. In 2008, after nine years on the market, Sony's PlayStation 2 was still in production and shipped over 140 million units (Nuttall 2008).

For the Xbox 360, Microsoft partly retreated from its initial model of production and development and comprehensively restructured its supply chain. The software company realized it needed tighter control over the design of the central components and therefore built up internal hardware and chip design capabilities (Takahashi 2006). Because it now owned the intellectual property (IP) on the chip, Microsoft hoped not only to schedule the redesigns more effectively but to choose the manufacturer for its chips—the foundry—and organize these relations under its control. This newly established relationship moved Microsoft toward managing manufacturing-related issues. The changed strategy toward IP ownership met with problems at Intel and Nvidia, who were very reluctant to hand over chip designs and lose substantial profits in this area. With IBM and ATI, Microsoft found suppliers that were open to discussing the ownership of IP, as they were already used to working with game console system companies. They started joint development projects for the main and graphics-processing units, resulting in heavily customized processors. These semicustom processors constituted another major difference in the initial Xbox system design. That original design was based on standard parts, with only marginal customization from Intel and Nvidia (Takahashi 2006, 151). Along with its deeper involvement in hardware and system development, Microsoft took also control over relations to other silicon suppliers. For system assembly of the Xbox 360, Microsoft relied on its previous manufacturing partners Flextronics and Wistron. Celestica was assigned as a third EMS company for system assembly. All three companies manufacture the Xbox 360 in their facilities in the Pearl River Delta, continuing assembly's focus in China.

ODM AND THE CHANGING INTERFACE OF INNOVATION

The examples from PC and the mobile communications industries show that the definition of technological and organizational core competencies has become increasingly blurred. Most core technologies for today's consumer electronics are being commodified. Only a dwindling part of the end-user system consists of the intellectual property of the system vendor. Less and less room is left for brand-name companies to differentiate themselves from their competitors through innovations in product technology or architecture. Thus, innovation outsourcing can lead to the hollowing out of core technological capabilities by brand-name companies. It facilitates market entry of new competitors from the rank of ODM contract manufacturers or brand-name companies. They come from emerging economies, such as the large number of vendors of cell phones, consumer electronics, and sophisticated networking equipment in China.

This trend indicates fundamental changes and new contradictions in the economics of the high-tech industry and in the social regulation of technology development beyond the Wintel model. The economic virtues of Wintelism are contested, both as a competitive strategy for firms and because of its effects on industrial competitiveness for industries and regions. The traditional model of innovation, bound to the vertically integrated corporation since the 1990s, has broken up. That model produced a massive commodification of technological know-how. The logic of Wintelist firm strategies, however, aimed at the creation of short- or mid-term monopoly control over certain technology and market segments. At the same time, profitable product marketing concepts are increasingly created through the bundling of new hardware devices with certain IT-related services, such as Apple's iPod, with its related download services for music, video, pictures, and so on. These unintended consequences of Wintelism show that the socialization of technology is changing, setting the stage for further global competition. The newly emerging economies of Asia are becoming core locations and have autonomous capabilities for developing new models and trajectories of innovation (for reflections and more detailed empirical analysis, see chapter 5 and Ernst 2005a; Lüthje 2007a, 2008; Pawlicki 2005).

The theoretical and analytical implications go beyond the scope of this book. However, our analysis would be incomplete without pointing to the changing interface of manufacturing, organizational, and technology development in the IT industry. This change is driven by falling profit margins, growing R&D costs, the need to supply a constant stream of new consumer electronic products on tight time schedules, and strong pressures from financial markets. The key feature is that restructuring in the IT industry has become more and more "triangular," with simultaneous modularization of global system firms, contract manufacturers, and providers of chips and complex restructuring of the division of labor.

Modularization is apparent in not only the assembly and manufacturing of electronic systems but at the "component level," that is, the development and manufacturing of the microelectronics core components, which provide the building blocks for mass-produced industrial and consumer goods. This is particularly true for the most complex segment of technology development and manufacturing, the chip industry. The constant reduction of transistor size—popularly labeled as "Moore's law"—allows most system functions to move from printed circuit boards onto chips. System development then focuses increasingly on the adaptation of the related chip designs. The process is pushed by technological possibilities and the drive by systems companies to outsource more and more product development activities. Chip companies have built up considerable system development knowledge and capabilities in order to provide complete solutions in the form of SoC chipsets and reference design kits (Cravotta 2007).

This commercialization of IP coupled with the trend toward complete design solutions facilitated the push of ODMs into the market for mobile phones, described above. ODM contract manufacturers such as Arima, Quanta, Compal, and Flextronics are able to design mobile phones in easy and cost-effective ways by adapting reference designs from major chip makers, which require only minor final configuration. To integrate these components into a functioning system, ODMs do not need thorough expertise in chip design (2007 interview data). Their main development task is the development of drivers, application software, and industrial design. This model of innovation pushes more and more system knowledge to the technology suppliers, the chip companies, who are increasingly inclined to supply complete solutions as the demand from ODMs rises. The resulting power relations within these innovation networks are quite obvious. System companies and major chip solution suppliers control the major decisions on core technologies for the mobile phone design process.

Historically, semiconductors were the first segment of the electronics industry in which vertical specialization took shape, as specialized merchant producers—independent semiconductor companies such as Fairchild, National Semiconductor, and Texas Instruments—were established in the United States in the beginning of the 1960s (Angel 1994; Ernst 1983; Lüthje 2001, 85ff.). These integrated device manufacturers, or IDMs, specialized in the development, design, and manufacturing of integrated circuits, selling them to system companies on the market. The success of the IDM model in the 1970s cemented the relative division between component and system development, pushing vertical specialization deeper into the electronics industry. As manufacturing costs and related investment in factories grew higher, a new generation of fabless chip design companies emerged at the beginning of the 1980s. Fabless chip makers specialize only in the development and marketing of integrated circuits (ICs). The actual manufacturing of their semiconductor devices is outsourced. This development spurred the creation and phenomenal growth of a new generation of chip contract manufacturers called "foundries," located mostly in Taiwan and Singapore. With heavy assistance from the Taiwanese government, which wanted to establish an independent local electronics industry, so-called pure-play foundries were established in the late 1980s. TSMC and United Microelectronics Corp. (UMC) became industry leaders. Vertical specialization has developed further since then, with the emergence of specialized design services firms that focus on only a few specific "blocks" of intellectual property integrated in IC designs.

Technological innovation allowed the semiconductor industry to constantly push miniaturization. However, the related technological advances in chip manufacturing developed much faster than the ability of engineering organizations to create manufacturable chip designs. This produced an entirely new set of contradictions, commonly called the "design productivity gap." It is increasingly hard to make use of the ever-growing number of transistors in chip designs in a cost-effective and timely manner. Different concepts of modular chip design, focusing mainly on possibilities of IP modules and their reuse, were developed to cope with this problem. Design factories in low-cost locations created hope that standardized IP modules could be developed that were fast and cost effective, needing only to be stitched together in SoCs by integration engineers in developed countries (Chang et al. 1999; Rowen 2004).

As the growing complexity and financial requirements of chip design foster vertical specialization, the miniaturization of transistor technology creates increasing problems because of the deintegration of manufacturing and chip design. The costs of process technology R&D and ownership of IC manufacturing operations are becoming prohibitive. Even large IDM companies must outsource major parts of their wafer manufacturing to foundries and look to consortia with other chip manufacturers for innovations in process technology. The need for knowledge integration between design and manufacturing should imply integration at the organization level, but vertical integration is not apparent. These contradictory dynamics are leading to triangular restructuring (Lüthje 2006), superseding the simple division between

IDMs and fabless design houses dating from the 1990s and creating new complex structures of industry organization.

The move of EMS and ODM electronics contract manufacturers into chip design is one important aspect of these new industry structures, which go beyond the Wintelist model of specialization. The push of the ODM model into the mobile phone market is causing changes in the innovation interface and pushing chip companies into becoming system developers. This has distinct geographical consequences. ODM companies have their main manufacturing as well as design locations in Taiwan and China. The success of the mobile phone market is therefore causing a geographic relocation of system development to these regions. Chip companies need to partner with brand-name companies, but they also have to establish close links to ODMs, which offer technical help and service. Increasingly, design activities of chip companies in mobile communications are being relocated closer to their ODM customers. This leads to the increased offshoring of innovation, driven by "cluster economics" to locate around large factories of ODM contract manufacturers, chip foundries, and chip design firms in Taiwan and mainland China.

This relocation produces complex changes in the international division of labor in global design networks, supplanting the classical world order of technology development in industrialized countries with mass production in peripheral countries. The example of Flextronics's global network of ODM design in mobile phones (developed in response to the Taiwanese challenge in this field) provides a striking example. As shown in table 2.6, test and software development and other routine work is almost completely located in low-cost regions, while architectural decisions are still concentrated in developed countries. At first glance, this is a rather classical division of labor in engineering. But significant upgrading dynamics can be expected in low-cost locations, as happened in manufacturing, driven by increasing technological capabilities and their cross-linkages and favorable labor cost. The criteria used for locating architectural functions will remain proximity to final customers (2005 interview data). However, as the mobile phone mass markets in developing countries increasingly define new applications and services, especially in the low-cost field, architectural functions of handset development are increasingly migrating to such regions. These complex dynamics are further explained in the following chapter.

Table 2.6.   Flextronics Worldwide Design Operations 2007

	Number of Employees (approximate)	*Design Functions Performed*
China	300	Testing, basic platform development, routine work
Eastern Europe	150	Routine work
India	4,000	Software, testing, routine work
Korea	150	Integrated system development, including architectural work for CDMA-based mobile phones
Singapore	200	n/a
Western Europe	400	Architectural work

Source: Interviews, 2007.

Chapter Three

Reshaping the International Division of Labor

Global Production Networks in Electronics Contract Manufacturing

In this chapter we analyze the concept of production as a globally uniform "service." We examine the way it affects the relocation of electronics contract manufacturing and determines the strategies developed by the leading companies in the industry. This includes a closer analysis of the differences in strategy between US-based contract manufacturers, following the electronics manufacturing services (EMS) model, and their competitors from Taiwan, most of them linked to the original design manufacturing (ODM) production model. We also look at the specific economic, social, and legal conditions in the major locations involved in this global restructuring process.

Do today's global production networks locate complex functions of the production process in developed industrialized countries and standardized mass production in low-cost locations, following the model of the "new international division of labor" analyzed by Folker Fröbel, Jürgen Heinrichs, and Otto Kreye in the 1970s? Do they produce a relatively stable complementary specialization between "lead factories," with top-end technologies and organization in traditional industrial centers, and simple volume production in developing locations? Will this be superseded by vertical reintegration, resulting in a new pattern of integrated high-tech production in various locations of the former "Third" or "Second" World?

For an adequate answer to these questions, it is important to determine the differences between the locational strategies of contract manufacturers in the three major regions of the capitalist world market: North America, Europe, and East Asia. In chapter 1 we explained the widely accepted assumption that global production networks are embedded in national and regional systems and that these include industrial and labor policies and the distinctive dynamics of national and regional economies. In the face of the global character of electronics contract manufacturing, we cannot expect one-dimensional local "path dependencies" as a result of certain strategies of industrial development. We have to consider the specific position of the major facilities and clusters of electronics contract manufacturing developed during the past ten years, during a period of disruptive social, political, and economic transformation.

In chapter 4, we describe the transnational production systems of major IT contract manufacturers. We then investigate the production and supplier networks of contract manufacturers in North America, East and Southeast Asia, and Europe. We look at the regional lead economies in the United States, Western Europe, and Japan and the emerging regional hubs in East and Southeast Asia, including Singapore, Hong Kong, and Taiwan. We present extensive data on the production systems in the most important low-cost regions: Mexico, Malaysia, China, and Eastern Europe.

"ONE-STOP SHOPPING": IT CONTRACT MANUFACTURING ACROSS THE TRIAD

The transnational production networks in IT contract manufacturing are essentially shaped by the concept of manufacturing as a global service. These networks produce a highly sophisticated and flexible system, which allocates different functions among the three major regions of the triad of the capitalist world market (North America, Europe, and East Asia) and their respective low-cost locations. The development of these networks resembles the internationalization process of the pioneering brand-name firms of the newer segments of the IT industry since the 1970s. It is characterized by highly disaggregated and specialized models of corporate organization and by a strong geographical orientation to the economies of the Pacific Rim (Ernst 1983; Lüthje 2001, 94ff.). Low-cost contract manufacturing facilities initially emerged in the preferred offshore locations of the first and second generation of chip and computer manufacturers of Silicon Valley: Singapore, Malaysia, and Taiwan. After the mid-1990s, Mexico and Eastern Europe were rapidly developed as low-cost locations, followed by China at the end of the 1990s.

Silicon Valley, the "Detroit of the information age" (see Lüthje 2001), became the major launching pad for the internationalization of large-scale contract manufacturing. It was the most important location of contract manufacturers' headquarters and their central development and production facilities. The production networks of Taiwanese contract manufacturers were also primarily anchored in Silicon Valley. They developed from the large sector of small and medium-sized component and contract manufacturers run by Taiwanese immigrant entrepreneurs (see Saxenian 1994). However, the structures of North American EMS and Taiwanese ODM contract manufacturers differed significantly from the beginning.

Historically, the emergence of electronics contract manufacturing followed the example of the massive relocation of production from traditional US industrial regions to the South, a seminal trend of industrial restructuring since the 1950s and accelerated by the crisis of postwar capitalism since the 1970s. In the electronics industry, this development was driven by the sell-off of major manufacturing facilities by large brand-name companies, which had previously shifted important production facilities to the non-union South. Contract manufacturing initially emerged in relatively remote locations such as Huntsville, Alabama, home of SCI, the largest EMS firm of the mid-1990s (see Lüthje, Schumm, and Sproll 2002, 69ff.).

Figure 3.1 presents the example of Solectron in 1996, at the time the fastest growing EMS company. With revenues of roughly US$3 billion, the firm had more than ten production facilities worldwide, the largest ones at its headquarters in Milpitas, California, and in Penang, Malaysia. Although the internationalization of contract manufacturing was then in its infancy, the contours were already visible of a global provider of manufacturing services with production facilities in every major region of the triad. The most important volume production factories were in Silicon Valley, Austin, Texas, and Charlotte, North Carolina. Employment in the latter two facilities grew to five thousand each in the year 2000, placing them among the largest electronics factories in the United States. Penang, Malaysia, functioned as the central location for low-cost manufacturing within this global organization, rapidly growing to over nine thousand employees, also in the year 2000. The factories in Texas, North Carolina, and Malaysia were acquired from Texas Instruments and IBM, and the other factories outside Silicon Valley from Hewlett-Packard (ibid.).

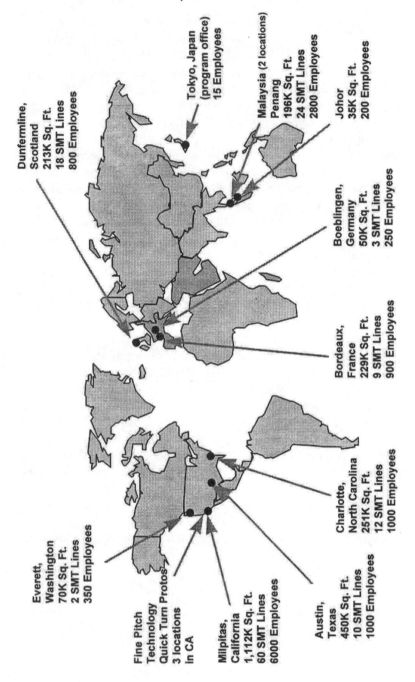

Dunfermline, Scotland
213K Sq. Ft.
18 SMT Lines
800 Employees

Tokyo, Japan
(program office)
15 Employees

Malaysia (2 locations)
Penang
196K Sq. Ft.
24 SMT Lines
2800 Employees

Johor
35K Sq. Ft.
200 Employees

Boeblingen, Germany
50K Sq. Ft.
3 SMT Lines
250 Employees

Bordeaux, France
229K Sq. Ft.
9 SMT Lines
900 Employees

Everett, Washington
70K Sq. Ft.
2 SMT Lines
350 Employees

Fine Pitch Technology
Quick Turn Protos
3 locations in CA

Milpitas, California
1,112K Sq. Ft.
60 SMT Lines
6000 Employees

Austin, Texas
450K Sq. Ft.
10 SMT Lines
1000 Employees

Charlotte, North Carolina
251K Sq. Ft.
12 SMT Lines
1000 Employees

Figure 3.1.   Solectron's Manufacturing Operations 1996 Lüthje, *Silicon Valley*, 258.

The numerous acquisitions of factories led to the emergence of global production systems within less than half a decade. The number of factories owned by Solectron grew fivefold between 1996 and 2000 to over fifty, accompanied by rapid vertical integration. In 2000 Flextronics commanded a global production system of similar scope, driven by massive acquisitions in Europe. The company's global strategy clearly aimed at establishing an international division of labor between high- and low-cost locations, with relatively strong integration in the major regions of the triad. Low-cost factories or industrial parks were usually established in geographical proximity to developed industrial regions, particularly in Europe. This included a massive buildup of manufacturing facilities in locations near the eastern side of the former "iron curtain."

At that time, a separation of labor seemed to develop between lead factories in industrial countries, which undertook product development, new product introduction, and low-volume production, and mass production with low variations in products and processes, which was assigned to low-cost locations. This concept was extensively advertised in industry magazines and business media. Contract manufacturers tried to establish themselves as expert contractors, exploring new low-cost locations seen as socially and politically risky. Flextronics in particular became a pioneer, establishing large-scale industrial parks using a uniform model and integrating a wide range of production, supply, and logistics functions. A number of supply and logistics firms selected as partners, with facilities in various industrial parks, were established almost simultaneously between 1997 and 2000 in Mexico, Hungary, and Southern China. Plans were made for further projects in Poland and China.

In the course of this development, however, a more complex international division of labor quickly emerged. The rapid expansion of contract manufacturing, combined with the full-scale sell-off of factories by brand-name firms, led to vertical integration of manufacturing functions in low-cost sites. Complex production structures developed, with distinct specialization among various regions of the world market. More sophisticated and complex manufacturing processes were shifted to low-cost locations, including new product introductions. In 2006, the global map of contract manufacturing displayed a complex picture of manufacturing capabilities, specialization profiles, and geographical focus for different groups of EMS and ODM firms (see table 3.1).

- The "big five" contract manufacturers from North America (Flextronics, Solectron, Sanmina-SCI, Celestica, and Jabil) command production networks with relatively comprehensive specializations in each region of the triad. Each region has a different geographical focus and production structure. Flextronics has a distinguished presence in Europe and Asia, while

Table 3.1. Global Locations of Top Ten EMS Providers 2006

Company	Headquarters	Americas	Asia-Pacific	Europe
Foxconn	Taipei, Taiwan (including global R&D center)	11 PIC	15 Manuf (including 14 DesDev)	7 Manuf/Logistics
		2 Manuf		
Flextronics	Singapore	6 Manuf	15 Manuf	14 Manuf
	San Jose, CA	5 DesDev	7 DesDev	12 DesDev
		2 PCB	1 PCB	3 Encl
		1 Plastics	3 Plastics	1 PCB
		1 Encl	3 Encl	5 Logistics
		1 Logistics		
Sanmina-SCI	San Jose, CA	19 Manuf	6 Manuf	15 Manuf
		5 Des	1 Design	1 PCB
		3 PCB	1 PCB	2 Encl
		5 Encl	2 Encl	
Solectron	Milpitas, CA	21 Manuf	13 Manuf	9 Manuf
		3 RepServ	2 Des	2 RepServ
		1 Logistics	1 Encl	
			4 RepServ	
Celestica	Toronto, Canada	12 Manuf	12 Manuf	5 Manuf
		1 Des	1 PIC	1 PIC/Logistics
		1 PIC	1 RepServ	1 RepServ
		2 RepServ	1 Logistics	
Jabil Circuit	Tampa, FL	14 Manuf	11 Manuf	12 Manuf
		3 Logistics/RepServ	2 DesDev	5 Logistics/RepServ
			1 RepServ	
Elcoteq	Espoo, Finland	3 Manuf	4 Manuf	5 Manuf/PIC
		1 NPI	3 RepServ	2 PIC
				2 DesDev
				2 RepServ
Benchmark	Angleton, TX	11 Manuf	4 Manuf	1 Manuf (Fulfillment)

Company	Headquarters	Americas	Asia-Pacific	Europe
			1 Des/ Logistics	
Venture	Singapore	2 Manuf	7 Manuf	2 Manuf
		4 DesDev	2 DesDev	
Universal Scientific	Taipei, Taiwan	5 Manuf	2 Manuf	5 Logistics/Rep
		7 Logistics/Rep	8 Logistics/ Rep	

Source: Company information (websites).
Des = Design
DesDev = Design and development of components, end products, and software
Encl = Metal enclosures and frames
Manuf = Assembly of printed circuit boards, end products, backplanes, cables
NPI = New product introduction
PCB = Design and manufacturing of raw printed circuit boards
PIC = Production and inventory control
Plastics = Plastic enclosures and parts, injection molding
Rep = Repair
RepServ = Repair and product services
Various functions may be integrated in specific locations. Classifications reflect predominant type of operation in respective locations. Listing does not include sales and administrative offices.

other companies are more concentrated in North America. Sanmina-SCI has the fewest factories in Asia. Flextronics and Sanmina-SCI have a large number of in-house supplier factories making printed circuit boards and plastic and metal enclosures. With the exception of Celestica, the companies do not operate specialized factories for product introduction. Those capabilities are integrated into major manufacturing sites. In the area of product design, Flextronics stands out with a high number of specialized design centers located in Europe.
• Industry giant Foxconn and Universal Scientific (USI), the two major EMS companies from Taiwan, show an entirely different profile. These companies also have a worldwide presence, but their key production facilities are all located in Asia, especially in the People's Republic of China. Their manufacturing facilities in Europe and North America are mostly final assembly shops, with adjacent logistics and service centers. Foxconn maintains a number of sales and prototyping facilities in the United States as a contact base for major customers. Research, development, and the key elements of product introduction are concentrated around the corporate headquarters in Taiwan. However, Foxconn has shifted substantial functions of product engineering to its manufacturing centers on the Chinese

mainland, taking advantage of the low-cost engineering workforce there (2003, 2004 interview data).

- The three smaller non-Taiwan-based global EMS companies, Elcoteq (Finland), Benchmark (United States), and Venture (Singapore), are concentrating manufacturing facilities in their respective home regions, with extended production networks in high- and low-cost locations. Elcoteq was the first among these companies to establish a major presence in China, with three manufacturing facilities, a decision strongly driven by its two major customers, Nokia and Ericsson (2004, 2005 interview data).

This diverse picture indicates that a clear-cut international division of labor between industrialized and developing countries along quality- versus cost-based criteria does not exist in today's electronics contract manufacturing industry. The majority of the low-cost facilities also undertake product development and introduction as well as specialized production processes with lower volumes. In addition, individual companies and production sites also exhibit relatively complex vertical specialization. Finally, a transnational division of labor can also be seen in a hierarchy among low-cost locations, particularly in Asia and Eastern Europe.

The big ODM contract manufacturers from Taiwan have created a transnational division of labor that differs markedly from North American and non-Taiwan EMS firms. Their production facilities are almost entirely concentrated in the China Circle, as are the Taiwanese EMS companies mentioned above. The five leading ODM companies (see table 3.2) locate headquarters together with product development and introduction and global logistics in Taiwan. Large factories or industrial parks are located in mainland China, mostly in Shanghai and its neighboring cities Suzhou and Kunshan. Most non-Asian locations are confined to final assembly, logistics, repair, and customer relations. Product introduction does not exist in these areas.

Table 3.2. Global Locations Top Five ODM Companies, 2006

Company	Headquarters	Asia-Pacific	Americas	Europe
Quanta	Taoyuan, Taiwan: R&D, PIC	1 industrial park: Shanghai, China 8 factories assembly and components, 1 Manuf: Kunshan, China 1 Manuf displays: Suzhou, China	1 Manuf/Logistics/S 2 Manuf displays Joint venture with Sanyo Sales/Serv	2 Manuf/Logistics/S 1 Manuf displays Joint venture with Sanyo Sales/Serv
Asustek	Taipei, Taiwan: R&D, PIC	2 industrial parks Manuf notebooks, LCD, TV, PDA: Shanghai, China Manuf motherboards, PC: Suzhou, China		
Compal	Taipei, Taiwan: R&D, PIC	1 Manuf notebook PC/mobile phones: Taiwan 1 Manuf displays: Kunshan, China 1 Manuf notebook: Kunshan, China	1 Logistics/Serv: Milpitas, CA	1 Logistics/Serv: Manchester, England
Inventec	Taipei, Taiwan: R&D	2 Manuf notebook, server: Taiwan 1 industrial park 5 Manuf, R&D, Logistics, 2 supplier factories: Shanghai, China 1 Manuf displays: Shanghai, China	2 Manuf/Logistics, 2 R&D: Dallas, Houston, TX	2 Manuf/Logistics: Scotland, Czech Republic

Company	Headquarters	Asia-Pacific	Americas	Europe
		5 R&D/Software: Beijing, Tianjin, Shanghai, Nanjing, Xian, China		1 RepServ: Den Bosch, Netherlands
		1 Logistics: Tianjin, China		
		1 Manuf: Malaysia		
Wistron	Taipei, Taiwan: R&D	1 PIC/Logistics: Hsinchu, Taiwan	1 Manuf (final assembly): Ciudad Juárez, Mexico	
		2 Manuf: Zhongshan, Kunshan, China	2 RepServ: Dallas, El Paso, TX	
		1 Manuf, RepServ: Subic Bay, Philippines		
		1 R&D: Shanghai, China		
		1 RepServ: Tokyo, Japan		

Sources: Company websites, *DigiTimes*, EMSNow, *Taipei Times*, interview data ranking according to EB Top 300—*Electronics Business Magazine*, August 1, 2006.

LCD = liquid crystal display

Manuf = Assembly of printed circuit boards, end products, backplanes, cables

PDA = Personal digital assistant

PIC = Production and inventory control

RepServ = Repair and product services

S = Sales

Serv = Product services

In contrast to the acquisition-led globalization process of US contract manufacturers, the internationalization of Taiwanese ODM and EMS manufacturers was more production oriented. This reflected their development from original equipment manufacturing (i.e., classical supply manufacturing without capabilities in development and logistics) to original design manufacturing or electronics manufacturing services with their related vertical integration. Thus, Taiwanese contract manufacturers have developed complex firm structures, which are overwhelmingly concentrated on Taiwan and the Chinese mainland. They exclude most other relevant low-cost locations, especially those in Southeast Asia, such as Malaysia. As a result, a distinctive, China-centered path of internationalization has been established. It brings together the technological and innovative capabilities of globally oriented overseas Chinese firms with the distinctive advantages of production locations on the Chinese mainland. This historically new pattern of globalization follows a complex set of divergent dynamics within the three major regions of the capitalist world market. We analyze this in the following sections.

NORTH AMERICA: NETWORK-BASED MASS PRODUCTION IN THE AGE OF NAFTA

In the motherland of electronics contract manufacturing, the United States, the first mass-production facilities employing a workforce of low-paid immigrants from Latin America and Asia emerged during the 1990s in Georgia, the Carolinas, Florida, Texas, and California (see Lüthje, Schumm, and Sproll 2002, 80–94, 123–85). The rapid growth of these locations was primarily driven by relocating manufacturing from brand-name firms to contract manufacturers. At the same time, an even faster buildup of new mass-production facilities and industrial parks occurred in Mexico. The centers of this development were Guadalajara, in the state of Jalisco, which became a location of IT manufacturing for US multinationals during the 1980s, and Monterrey, in the state of Nuevo León, which is located not far south of the US border region. In the emerging global division of labor in the contract manufacturing industry, Mexico became an important base for export to the United States. The *North American Free Trade Agreement*, NAFTA, in effect since 1994, completed a policy shift in Mexico from a protectionist strategy of import substitution toward an export-oriented model. This affected industrial policy in the electronics sector.

However, the crisis of the IT industry after the Internet bubble burst in 2001 caused deep changes in regional production networks, increasing competition between the various locations involved. The transfer of mass production from North America to China brought about massive cuts in production and employment in factories in Mexico and the United States. Mexican contract manufacturing facilities consolidated after a period of crisis and expanded further. More complex and higher-priced products were relocated to Mexican factories, resulting in some upgrading of their facilities.

Brazil developed as a second important location for electronics contract manufacturing in Latin America. Beginning in 1997, and at an accelerated pace after 2000, all major US and Canadian contract manufacturers set up shop in the country. In part they acquired advanced factories of brand-name firms, such as Ericsson, IBM, and Compaq. These facilities are mostly located in the São Paulo region, producing small and medium volumes of higher-end products as well as small quantities of cell phones. A second major regional center developed in the free trade zone of Manaus in the Amazonas region. Here manufacturing mostly focused on mass consumer electronics products and mobile phones. However, in spite of protracted efforts, contract manufacturers in Brazil were not able to export a substantial amount of their production to markets outside of Latin America. Production is mostly confined to Brazil and the surrounding South American market, especially the Mercado Común del Sur (Mercosur). In 2005, the Brazilian electronics industry, with 133,000 employees, achieved annual revenues of 92.8 billion Brazilian real (app. US$42.2 billion in 2006). According to the national electronics industry confederation, about US$7.7 billion were exports (Abinee 2006). The eight largest factories alone employ more than twelve thousand people.

Brazil's role in the international division of labor cannot compare with Mexico, however, which owes its importance to its special position as a manufacturing base for the US domestic market. Employment at major contract manufacturers here is around fifty thousand (see table 3.3). In the following paragraphs we therefore concentrate on the United States and Mexico.[1]

Table 3.3. Locations of Contract Manufacturing in Mexico

Company	City	State	Production	Year	Employees
Sanmina-SCI	Guadalajara (3 plants)	Jalisco	PCBA, SA, backplanes	1997	12,000
	Guadalajara	Jalisco	Box build		
	Apodaca	Nuevo León	PC assembly		
	Monterrey	Nuevo León	Assembly cable/electromechanic components		
Jabil Circuit	Guadalajara	Jalisco	PCBA	1997	over 10,000
	Chihuahua	Chihuahua	PCBA—automotive	2002	
	Reynosa	Tamaulipas	Jabil Global Services–Repair		
Flextronics	Guadalajara	Jalisco	Industrial park	1997	6,200
	Aguascalientes	Aguascalientes	Assembly	2001	
	Cd. Juárez (opened November 2006)	Chihuahua	Box build, logistics, repair	2006	1,700
Solectron	Guadalajara	Jalisco	PCBA, SA, new: box build, technology/development	1997	6,000
	Chihuahua	Chihuahua	PCBA PCs, server	2005	600

Company	City	State	Production	Year	Employees
Celestica	Monterrey (Apodaca)	Nuevo León	PCBA, SA, test, repair	1998	5,500
	Querétaro	Querétaro	Plastics		
	Reynosa	Tamaulipas	2 assembly plants		
Foxconn	Ciudad Juárez	Chihuahua	Electronics/plastics	2003	4,500
	Guadalajara	Jalisco	PC assembly for Hewlett-Packard	2003	
Elcoteq	Monterrey	Nuevo Leon	PCBA	1999	1,400
	Ciudad Juárez	Chihuahua	Set-top boxes communication, network, test development	2006	1,600
Benchmark	Guadalajara	Jalisco	assembly	1999	1,900

Sources: Original research, company information, press releases, May 2006.
PCBA = Printed circuit board assembly
SA = System assembly

United States: The Short-Lived Revival of Mass Production in the New High-Tech Centers

The emergence of electronics contract manufacturing in the US West and South was part of the massive relocation of production to the "sunbelt," which became a key element of restructuring of the US manufacturing system after the late 1970s (see Davis 1986). Contract manufacturing created a new relationship between the vertically specialized IT industry in Silicon Valley and other high-tech centers in the West and the Southern strategies of older sectors of industrial capital. Silicon Valley firms took advantage of the non-union environment, large-scale supply of low-wage labor from mostly nonindustrial milieus or recent immigrants and the existing labor market segmentation along racial lines (see Lüthje and Scherrer 1997). But while most older industries in the South developed considerable long-term expansion, IT contract manufacturing was characterized by short and rapid growth followed by a steep decline within a period of less than ten years.

The expansion of IT contract manufacturing followed the strategy of leading Silicon Valley chip and computer manufacturers, which relocated mass-production facilities to regions with previously limited industrial development in Texas, Arizona, Oregon, and New Mexico after the mid-1980s. In the case of contract manufacturing, this geographic expansion was organized through the acquisition of manufacturing facilities from established electronics manufacturers. Large-scale contract manufacturing facilities were created between 1995 and 2000 in Austin, Texas, Charlotte and Raleigh, North Carolina, Atlanta, Georgia, Tampa, Florida, and Denver, Colorado. The two largest locations were Huntsville, Alabama, home to the early industry leader SCI (initially a manufacturer of printed circuit boards for the IBM PC) and Silicon Valley, California (Lüthje, Schumm, and Sproll 2002). Silicon Valley, better known as a location for highly sophisticated research and technology firms, is also a low-wage location for manufacturing. Contract manufacturers followed major chip and computer firms in recruiting a workforce from mostly female immigrants from Mexico, Central America, and East Asia, adding new forms of flexible and insecure employment during the 1990s, particularly temporary labor (Lüthje 2001).

The expansion of this new American model of manufacturing (see Sturgeon 1997) remained largely confined to the computer and the data network equipment industry. Production of most consumer electronics vanished from the United States after the 1980s. Contract manufacturing took hold in some remaining segments of the US electronics industry with mostly localized production, such as defense, aerospace, and automobile electronics. The growth of electronics contract manufacturing had the potential for "reindustrializing" the US economy, based on low-wage manufacturing work, an often forgotten element of the so-called New Economy of the 1990s (see

Brenner 2002). However, this development was short-lived, since contract manufacturers simultaneously erected large-scale manufacturing facilities and industrial parks in Southeast Asia, Mexico, and finally Eastern Europe. Companies showed little interest in US facilities as lead factories for developing new mass-production sites in Mexico, a marked difference from the strategy employed in Europe at that time (see chapter 3). Expansion in Mexico was mostly under direct control from corporate headquarters in the United States.

The crisis of 2001 caused factory closures in every major location in the United States; Silicon Valley was hit hardest. In this region, almost eighty thousand layoffs were recorded for the electronics industry in 2001, leading to a record unemployment rate of 8 percent (*SJMN*, November 21, 2001). The exact figure of layoffs in electronics contract manufacturing is difficult to determine, since a large segment of workers was employed through temporary labor agencies (Lüthje 2001, 308ff.). The California Employment Department registered a massive drop among temporary employees, many of whom were undoubtedly workers from contract manufacturers (*SJMN*, October 13, 2001).

A survey prepared during our field research at the end of 2003 found that half the manufacturing facilities of contract manufacturers in Silicon Valley were closed or up for sale. Solectron, then the largest local employer in the industry with about seven thousand workers, closed four major manufacturing buildings and sold the facilities of its subsidiaries Zhone and Smart Modular. At Flextronics, almost all production facilities in Silicon Valley (with three thousand employees) were closed down, including a model factory working for Cisco. Only a small prototyping operation remained at the corporate headquarters in San Jose. Sanmina-SCI transformed a former SCI factory of 1,500 workers into a design center and closed a major printed circuit board manufacturing plant in Santa Clara (2003, 2004 interview data).

Other locations saw similar drastic job cuts. In Austin, Texas, Solectron's workforce was reduced from approximately 4,500 in 2001 to 1,800. Flextronics closed a highly sophisticated PCB manufacturing facility of its subsidiary Multek, with roughly 1,200 employees, and Sanmina-SCI closed another PCB manufacturing plant with about 180 workers (*AAS*, August 1, 2001). In Atlanta, Georgia, a Solectron facility with 1,800 workers, previously acquired from NCR, was closed (*CO*, January 10, 2002). In Huntsville, Alabama, several thousand jobs were lost, mostly due to the restructuring of former industry leader SCI in the wake of its acquisition by Sanmina (*Huntsville Times*, April 20, 2004). EMS companies also acted as agents for the closure of newly acquired facilities from major brand-name firms. One Lucent factory (formerly Western Electric) in North Andover, Massachusetts, was acquired and closed by Solectron, while another major Lucent production site for telecommunications switching equipment in Oklahoma was taken over and closed by Celestica (2002 interview data).

This massive downturn had deep consequences for the structure of electronics contract manufacturing in the United States. The production systems of North American contract manufacturers, with the exception of Flextronics, remain largely centered on the United States. Today, however, most US facilities are specialized operations for prototyping, development, customer service, or logistics. Mass production has vanished almost completely. Mexico now is the most important location for volume production in North America (see table 3.3). The growing number of facilities of Taiwanese contract manufacturers in the United States has not changed this picture substantially, since these relatively small operations are mostly confined to the acquisition of new customers (see table 3.3). In some areas of the United States such as Silicon Valley, a small number of highly specialized contract manufacturers emerged after 2002, focusing on technology-intensive niche products. This development does not alter the fact that large-scale manufacturing of IT systems in the United States has disappeared almost entirely.

Mexico: Upgraded Production at Low Costs

Well before the enactment of NAFTA, Mexico had a reputation for offering favorable conditions to multinational companies for direct investment in the "backyard" of the United States. Those conditions included cheap and relatively skilled labor and lax enforcement of labor rights and environmental protections. These conditions, the product of industrial policies on sectoral, national, and international levels, set the stage for relocating electronics contract manufacturing to Mexico.

Economic integration with the United States and the relocation of production to Mexico was already at the heart of the *Border Industrialization Program* (BIP) of the Mexican government in the 1960s. It marked the first significant step away from the policies of industrialization through import substitution, pursued from the 1930s. That policy sought to protect the national market and support the development of a national industrial base in key economic sectors. Under the BIP, foreign companies benefitted from tax incentives and tariff-free trade with the United States for manufacturing operations along the border. In these areas, the *maquiladora* industries emerged, which assembled semifinished products under special conditions for the US market. Since the late 1980s, the *maquiladora* concept, which had been geographically limited to the border areas, has been expanded to the whole country (Bacon 2008).

During the following decades, Mexico experienced low economic growth, mass unemployment, declining real wages, and a vast increase in poverty (see Boris 1996; Schirm 2001). The abrupt decline of oil prices and the debt crisis of 1982 led to a drastic devaluation of the Mexican peso. As its market was opened beginning in the mid 1980s, Mexico experienced disruptive changes. Import tariffs and restrictions were eliminated, a large number of state-owned enterprises and banks were privatized, and foreign direct investment was encouraged (see Boris 2001; Dedrick, Kraemer, and Palacios 2001). Mexico's adherence to the General Agreement on Tariffs and Trade (GATT) in 1986 led to new growth in the *maquiladora* industry, which employed more than four hundred thousand workers in roughly a thousand factories in 1990. For 2005, the Mexican Statistics Office counted more than three thousand *maquiladoras* with more than 1.1 million employees (INEGI 2006).

NAFTA, which went into effect January 1, 1994, led to a new wave of foreign direct investment in export production facilities. The agreement was the culmination of successive waves of trade liberalization. Tariffs were abolished or suspended in order to encourage foreign investment. Liberalized trade, promised by Mexican president Carlos Salinas de Gortari, would create jobs and income growth in Mexico. Opened markets, deregulation, privatization, and promotion of export industries would bring Mexico closer to the "First World," he claimed. Liberalized trade, however, confronted Mexico with a new level of world competition.

In the fifteen years after NAFTA's enactment, foreign direct investment and exports rose to unprecedented levels. The proportion of exports in Mexico's GDP went from 16 percent in 1994 to 35 percent in 2003 and lifted the country into being the second-largest manufacturing exporter in the world, after China (Moreno-Brid, Valdivia, and Santamaría 2005). Almost 90 percent of Mexican exports are bound for the United States. NAFTA consolidated Mexico's position as a low-cost production base for industrial and agricultural goods. However, the promise of rising living standards was unfulfilled (see Boris 2001, 140ff; Zapata 2002; Schiemenz 2006). According to the OECD, more than half of Mexico's population live in poverty, and 56 percent of the younger workforce between fifteen and twenty-five years of age is unemployed and without professional education (OECD 2002; Hainzl and Wimmer 2006). The number of (mostly undocumented) immigrants to the United States increased (Moreno-Brid, Valdivia, and Santamaría 2005, 26).

The strong export machinery did not create sustainable growth for the Mexican economy as a whole. The export model itself, through tax-free imports of manufacturing supplies, detaches export production from national supply industries (ibid.; Dussel Peters 2004; Contreras and Carillo 2003). Skilled suppliers of electronics parts, for example, could not develop when industrial production was focused on assembly industries. The wide-ranging exemption of exporting industries, not only from tariffs but also from taxes, also caused enormous problems (Dussel Peters 2001). Privately produced profits did not flow into social consumption. The status of Mexico as a peripheral economy was not substantially changed by a trade agreement that for the first time allowed the relatively free flow of capital and goods across the border between "North" and "South."

Industrial Policy in the Mexican Electronics Industry

The electronics industry is among the key sectors of the Mexican economy contributing to the dynamic growth of exports during the post-NAFTA period. The industry provides about three hundred thousand jobs. Exports almost doubled between 1996 and 2004, reaching US$43 billion at the end of that period and surpassing exports of other industrial goods such as auto parts or garments. In computers and telecommunications equipment, along with TV, audio, and video equipment, the proportion of exports reaches almost 53 percent (Ruiz Chávez 2005).

The computer industry in Mexico dates back to the 1960s, when the first subsidiaries of multinational companies settled in Guadalajara. After Germany's Siemens set up a manufacturing facility in 1962, Motorola de México and Industrias Mexicanas Burroughs opened factories. Mexico's second-largest city, one thousand miles south of the US border, became the center of the Mexican IT industry during the 1980s. Major companies such as IBM, Kodak, Hewlett-Packard, Texas Instruments, Intel, NatSteel, and AT&T/Lucent followed with a number of joint ventures and smaller start-ups. Other centers of electronics manufacturing emerged in the major *maquiladora* cities along the US border, including Tijuana, Mexicali, Ciudad Juárez, and Reynosa. In addition, household appliances are produced in the region around Mexico City and in the northeast. Asian manufacturers of audio and video equipment, including Sony, Sanyo, Samsung, Hitachi, Matsushita, Toshiba, and JVC have facilities in Tijuana. Production is focused on TV sets and household appliances. Components for PCs and mobile phones were also manufactured until recently (Barajas and Curry 2003). Ciudad Juárez has become a major center for automotive electronics. Figure 3.2 shows the various centers of contract manufacturing throughout Mexico.

Mexico provides an interesting example of the importance of industrial policy in the development of export-oriented industry. Under its old policy of import substitution, the Mexican government tried to develop national production capabilities and technology control in the IT industry during the 1970s and 1980s. A number of regulations and laws were put into effect to control foreign investment in the computer industry. The National Council of Science and Technology, CONACYT, was formed, and government control was centralized under the Secretariat of Trade and Industry Development (SECOFI). In 1981, a government program for the computer industry was set up in order to balance export production and local technology development. Foreign direct investment would be allowed only through joint ventures with

Figure 3.2. Locations of Contract Manufacturing in Mexico

Mexican firms in order to promote local development. However, this policy soon came into conflict with trade liberalization under NAFTA.

The emerging debt and currency crisis and seminal changes in the global computer industry kept this program from having much effect. It was finally derailed by persistent pressure on the Mexican government by IBM, which opposed a joint venture because it wanted to produce PCs in Guadalajara under its own control. IBM finally obtained a license, and others were subsequently awarded to other companies as well. Foreign companies had to accept certain concessions to ensure technology transfer and the development of local suppliers. This decision was a turnaround in national industrial policy in the computer industry, since protection of national producers was no longer prioritized over exports. In 1990, the Mexican government opened the borders to foreign companies, allowing the import of computer parts at preferential tax rates. Import tariffs were limited to a maximum of 20 percent and were finally abolished in 1998 (see Dedrick, Kraemer, and Palacios 2001; Barber 2005).

The Mexican "Silicon Valley": Guadalajara as a New Center of Contract Manufacturing

With the inauguration of NAFTA, foreign direct investment in the electronics industry in the Guadalajara region started to grow rapidly. New industry segments emerged, particularly in the field of computers and telecommunications. Traditional industries, such as mining, food, textile and garment, wood, metal, and leather manufacturing rapidly lost significance. Traditional industry structures, dominated by small and medium enterprises mostly producing for the national market, shifted toward the large electronics multinationals focused on exports (see De la O Martínez 2001; Woo 2001). This trend was supported by various initiatives of the state government of Jalisco, which encouraged foreign direct investment in local industries. Electronics emerged as the main industrial and export sector for the entire state, and Guadalajara became known as "Mexico's Silicon Valley."

After 1997, contract manufacturers were among the most important new companies to locate in Guadalajara, benefitting from a relatively developed local industrial economy and infrastructure. Within the matter of a few months, contract manufacturers erected new production facilities, rapidly growing in size and creating many jobs. As in Eastern Europe, some contract manufacturers used smaller local companies as a launching pad. SCI, for example, acquired a factory from ADTEC (Adelantos in Tecnología), an electronics supplier which had emerged in the wake of IBM's big investment in Guadalajara in 1993. However, contract manufacturers did not take over facilities from major brand-name firms. Instead, they built their own large-scale factories in the new industrial parks on the outskirts of Guadalajara and in the neighboring municipalities of Tlaquepaque, Zapopan, Tonalá, El Salto, and Tlajomulco. This investment boom initially centered on the mass production of simple consumer goods for the North American market from a geographically close, low-cost location. A strong demand for labor was driven by the high production volumes of this business. New factories expanded rapidly. In the year 2000, Flextronics employed about fourteen thousand workers in its new industrial park, Solectron had ten thousand, Sanmina-SCI six thousand, and Jabil four thousand employees. The labor market could not provide the necessary number of workers, so recruitment was soon expanded into the surrounding rural areas. Rapidly changing orders and production volumes led to a regime of highly flexible employment. This included temporary labor as well as consigning overflow work to small local manufacturers.

Monterrey, capital of the state of Nuevo León and near the Texas border, also emerged as a center for electronics contract manufacturing after 1997. Development here, however, was severely affected by the global industry recession in 2001. A Solectron facility was closed in 2001 and production was relocated to Guadalajara. Sanmina made a similar decision but maintained a fulfillment center for PCs and a manufacturing facility for cable assemblies and power adaptors. Two other contract manufacturers, Celestica and Elcoteq, maintained their operations and made Monterrey their main location in Mexico. In 1998, Celestica took over a factory from Lucent and further expanded in the border region, with two new factories in Reynosa. Flextronics opened a new location in Aguascalientes, the state neighboring Jalisco, taking over a facility from Xerox in 2001. In addition, Jabil acquired a facility from Philips in the city of Chihuahua in 2002. In recent years contract manufacturers have increasingly set up logistics, fulfillment, and repair centers near the US border.

Guadalajara, however, remains the center of the Mexican IT and telecommunications industry. Its protracted efforts to develop a local industry structure as well as its pleasant cultural and climatic conditions make the city attractive to expatriate managers, a considerable advantage over the border regions. The location offers ample support services for new factories as well as financial subsidies from the state government and a growing infrastructure of skilled suppliers (see Partida Rocha 2004; Palacios 2001; Woo 2001). The region boasts 13 brand-name companies, 16 contract manufacturers, 26 design centers, and 360 specialized suppliers, justifying its classification as an electronics cluster. This development is supported by concerted efforts of several local institutions, such as the Office for Economic Development (SE-PROE), the industry association CANIETI, and Cadelec, an organization supporting industrial development in the electronics industry established in 1997 by electronics companies with support from the United Nations Development Program (UNDP). Cadelec works systematically to develop a supplier base serving multinational electronics companies. Research and academic institutions and technical colleges such as CINVESTAV extended their programs and curricula to provide skilled engineering personnel. In addition, many companies support professional education and knowledge transfer through in-house training programs and donations of industrial equipment for educational purposes (Woo 2001).

The local labor market, therefore, provides a skilled workforce of manufacturing workers and engineers, taking advantage of the long-term presence of international brand-name firms. This is an important advantage over the border regions in the north, where skilled technicians and engineers are scarce. In addition, turnover rates and wages in Guadalajara are lower, and the overall stability of the labor market is higher. Last but not least, workers in Guadalajara do not have a reputation of being militant (Flores 2002), and local trade unions do not oppose poorly paid jobs and employment conditions that violate existing law (see chapter 4).

Guadalajara has had undeniable success in developing local industrial capabilities, including design and development. But regional integration of industrial structures in the electronics sector remains limited. Major brand-name firms almost completely ceased their manufacturing operations in Guadalajara in the wake of the global crisis in the IT industry after 2001. Complex electronics components are not usually manufactured locally but are imported from Asia or the United States. The main industrial activities remain confined to assembly, particularly at contract manufacturers.

Mexico in the Context of the Global Crisis: The New Competition with China

The impressive boom of electronics contract manufacturing in Mexico was suddenly interrupted by the crisis of the global IT industry beginning in early 2001. China emerged as a major threat to the Mexican economy. Multinationals in many industries shifted significant proportions of their production from Mexico to China. In fact, the crisis had tremendous impact. Between 2001 and 2004, more than eight hundred factories in the Mexican *maquiladora* industry were closed and more than two hundred thousand jobs eliminated. Although the shift of production to Mexico was massive, much of the public debate in Mexico did not focus on the underlying cost of global production and export-dependent strategies for industrial development. Instead, blame was placed on the wages of Mexican factory workers. As in Hungary (see the discussion later in this chapter), companies and business associations complained about the high wages, not mentioning the fact that the relative disadvantages in comparison to China were at least in part caused by the appreciation of the Mexican currency under the NAFTA regime.

In the state of Jalisco 21,217 jobs were lost among electronics manufacturers and 23,880 among suppliers and related businesses (Dussel Peters 2005, 111). Exports for PC and telecommunications equipment dropped to US$7.8 billion in 2003, well below the double-digit figures of 2001 and before. These figures showed a massive downturn in contract manufacturing. Major projects and customers were lost, and employment declined rapidly. The headcount at Flextronics and Solectron, the two largest contract manufacturers, fell from fourteen thousand in 2001 to three to four thousand in 2003. A massive shift of EMS production to China occurred. Mass manufacturing of key high-volume IT products such as PCs, printers, and cell phones became almost entirely relocated to East Asia. Manufacturing of the Xbox game console for Microsoft by Flextronics was transferred from Guadalajara to Zhuhai in China. In April 2003 another large-scale project for the assembly of printers for Hewlett-Packard was withdrawn at the last minute, after the project had received praise in local media (2004 interview data). Such examples illustrate the massive competition between the locations of contract manufacturers on a global scale.

The crisis started a new round of restructuring in the global electronics industry and a further shift of production from brand-name companies to contract manufacturers. Guadalajara saw a massive exodus of manufacturing among IT brand-name companies. Many of them did not leave the region entirely but retained such activities as software development and sales. IBM retreated from PC manufacturing, handing server manufacturing to Sanmina-SCI and later selling its entire PC division to Lenovo, as described in chapter 2. In Mexico, IBM handed its big production facility in Guadalajara to Sanmina-SCI. In a similar move, HP transferred its business PC and server assembly operation to Foxconn, helping the Taiwanese giant to gain a presence in Guadalajara after an earlier takeover of a cell phone assembly plant from Motorola in Ciudad Juárez.

In the wake of the crisis of 2001, Mexico also reaped some "gains" from the massive closure of contract manufacturing facilities in the United States. This contributed to the consolidation of the Mexican contract manufacturing base beginning in 2004, after massive workforce reductions. As production in Mexico expanded, three older Celestica factories in Mount Pleasant and Raleigh, North Carolina, Salem, New Hampshire, and Fort Collins, Colorado, were closed. A company spokesperson explained that closing the Colorado facility had nothing to do with its economic situation but rather with the geographic preferences of its customers for the most cost-efficient manufacturing solutions (Martínez 2005).

Consolidation after the Crisis: Successful Industrial Upgrading among Contract Manufacturers in Mexico?

The consolidation of contract manufacturing was part of the larger recovery of the Mexican economy after 2004. Production resumed previous levels, and the proportion of exports in the national GDP was back to 26 percent in 2006. In electronics, major contract manufacturers stabilized, and some expanded their Mexican operations, indicating that Mexico was surviving as a significant low-cost location. In 2005, Sanmina-SCI even received an award from the state of Jalisco as its leading exporter (EMSNow, December 6, 2005). Substantial changes were made in the specialization and skill portfolios of Mexican contract manufacturing facilities. The major effects of this industrial "upgrading" can be summarized as follows:

(1) Mexican factories won a significant role as centers for product configuration close to major end markets. In the PC industry, Mexico retained full-scale manufacturing for business PCs. For consumer PCs, however, essentially a high-volume product, Mexican facilities perform only final assembly and configuration. In related fields like printer manufacturing for Hewlett-Packard, the complete relocation of production to Asia was in part reversed. HP also adopted an international division of labor, in which final configuration was performed in Mexican EMS factories. This relocation occurred in spite of the fact that shipping costs for simple printers across the Pacific are relatively low, compared with heavier products such as PCs. Final configuration in proximity to the end market substantially reduces the time span for product delivery, configuration changes, and after-sales services, which are located in repair and service centers close to the US border.

EMS contract manufacturers and Taiwanese ODM companies opened facilities in the border region near Ciudad Juárez, previously a center for automotive electronics. In 2005, Solectron opened a new configuration and repair center for PCs and servers. Flextronics followed suit with a new logistics center in 2006. European contract manufacturer Elcoteq opened a second Mexican facility, while Jabil had a repair center in the city of Reynosa. In other areas, such as cell phone manufacturing, production that had been relocated to China partially returned, driven by a boom of demand for such products in the Mexican domestic market. The move of Taiwanese ODM companies to Mexico makes it possible for Mexico to consolidate its role as a location for final assembly and product configuration. This trend also indicates an international division of labor, however, in which the manufacturing of more complex components is increasingly concentrated in East Asia.

(2) The product portfolio of Mexican factories changed significantly. The efforts of local management to attract products of higher complexity and value proved at least partially successful. In particular, the diversity of products increased. Computer and telecommunications devices still play a significant role, including products of higher added value such as servers, network equipment, and routers in small and medium volumes. Auto electronics has become an important segment of production in which contract manufacturers tried to get a foothold while facing the protracted resistance of large automotive suppliers. Some companies with a strong presence in northern Mexico, such as Delphi (Contreras and Carillo 2003), began to reorient their own attitudes toward contract manufacturing, a potential gain for EMS companies in this region. Jabil, for instance, focused its facility in Chihuahua on automotive electronics. This industry also played an increasing role in Guadalajara, along with an expansion of medical products, industrial electronics, and household appliances, such as electronic control systems for washing machines. For these products, which usually are smaller in volume than PCs or cell phones, the manufacturers cite proximity to the US market as a distinctive advantage. In addition, cooperation among engineers is facilitated by the proximity of time zones and lower language barriers.

(3) Contract manufacturing factories in Mexico are mostly vertically integrated facilities, combining electronics manufacturing with local production of enclosures (i.e., injection molding for plastic parts, metal manufacturing, and assembly of racks and cable harnesses). As in other low-cost regions, different strategies for integration can be observed at the firm level. Flextronics, for instance, locates these capabilities within a large industrial park, which includes a number of previously independent supply firms. Foxconn also integrates manufacturing of plastics parts and electronics assembly in one factory. Solectron had its own center for enclosures manufacturing in Guadalajara. Sanmina-SCI and Celestica have special business units for enclosures throughout the company, also with a strong presence in Mexico. Although its factories were not located at the sites of its electronics manufac-

turing units, Sanmina-SCI opened a new facility for enclosures in Guadalajara in 2006, emphasizing the importance of local integration.

The electronics manufacturing cluster in Guadalajara is well developed, with a considerable number of suppliers, but local integration of manufacturing in Mexico remains limited. Most electronics components are not manufactured locally but are imported from the United States or China by global procurement organizations. Mexico's export regime favors such arrangements since the import of parts is subsidized by the lack of tariffs and taxes if the final products are exported. This encourages massive centralization of the supply chains of contract manufacturers. Often, major brand-name firms have direct contracts with major suppliers, further limiting the contract manufacturer's abilities to localize procurement.

(4) Production of higher value-added and diversified products in smaller volumes has changed the profile of contract manufacturing facilities. This resulted in a changing ratio of production workers to technical personnel, dropping from a 67 to 33 percent ratio in earlier years to a 60 to 40 percent ratio in 2005 (2005 interview data). The companies seek to enhance their ability to introduce new products, which increases the need for manufacturing-related engineering work. Frequent product changes have a similar effect. Sanmina-SCI, for example, reported in a press release that 3,500 different products would be produced in its manufacturing facilities in Guadalajara (Evertiq, June 21, 2006). Quality-control requirements have also been increased with the changing product portfolio, since quality standards are significantly higher in telecommunications and automotive electronics than in mass consumer goods. The increased number of ISO certifications, which define worldwide quality standards, obtained by EMS facilities in Guadalajara are a good indicator of this development.

In spite of the significant development of Mexican factories, product development and design were not relocated to Mexico. In this area, the traditional division of labor between the United States and Mexico seems to persist. According to our interview informants, Mexican engineers were sent to the United States to learn the technical specifications for mature products. For products under development, the allocation of engineering work depends on the prospective end-user market. Usually, R&D is done at US locations (2003, 2005 Guadalajara interview data). Some smaller projects were more localized, so in this area Guadalajara made some progress. The local government and Cadelec waged major efforts to relocate product design and development by brand-name firms in Guadalajara but achieved only limited success. HP developed a laser printer in Guadalajara in 2005 and expanded software development, especially systems solutions for business customers. After giving up local manufacturing, IBM invested in a new center for software development, employing one thousand engineers. To a limited extent, contract manufacturers are also upgrading local production. The technology centers of Flextronics and Solectron not only perform materials analysis but also develop basic knowledge for new products and testing procedures.

Generally, Mexico retained its importance as a regional production center for the North American market—at the expense of locations in the US South. In contrast to the situation in Eastern Europe, mass production was consolidated after the crisis, and Mexico maintained its ability to compete with locations in East Asia by including higher-value segments in its manufacturing portfolio. The rise of employment to fifty-one thousand after 2004 in the Mexican contract manufacturing industry (see table 3.3) is a result of this development along with expansion into new regions of the country. The enormous rise of China does not mean that electronics manufacturing will remain concentrated in only one region of the world. Former Flextronics CEO Michael Marks told an industry newsletter, "Electronics production may shift closer to consumer countries as manufacturing costs rise in Asia. If the China Yuan and Malaysia Ringgit appreciate, manufacturing costs there will increase in dollar terms, potentially deterring companies who are rushing to build factories there. I think China is overdone" (Custer 2005).

Economic and political factors favor the development of regional industrial centers for export production, and electronics contract manufacturing found beneficial conditions in Mexico. Low labor costs, favoring labor-intensive industries and processes, are only one factor. The productive base of contract manufacturing was upgraded through logistics and repair centers and further vertical integration near markets. Mexican locations are integrated in a complex international division of labor within the corporate organizations of contract manufacturers. This clearly goes beyond the role of an "extended assembly line." However, there are few endogenous opportunities for innovation for local factories, and the local supplier base remains limited—a development comparable with that of other major manufacturing industries in Mexico (see, for instance, Contreras and Carillo 2003; Barajas 2000).

This trend continued during and after the global financial and economic crisis of 2008 and 2009. Contract manufacturing in Mexico has not only been consolidated in the wake of the crisis, but the industry has grown considerably. The product range has not changed significantly, as mobile phones and BlackBerry devices account for the major part. Facilities in border regions such as Chihuahua and Reynosa have expanded, but Guadalajara remains the most important center of the Mexican IT industry, with the highest concentration of contract manufacturing facilities. Flextronics alone employed eighteen thousand people in its two facilities in Guadalajara in October 2009. Since its merger with Solectron in 2007, Flextronics now owns a second huge plant in its industrial park. Jabil built a second factory in Guadalajara and employs nine thousand people overall there. Sanmina-SCI has twelve thousand employees (2009 interviews). This employment has grown well above the data for 2006 compiled in table 3.3. It is all the more remarkable since contract manufacturers have not been spared the effects of the current international financial crisis.

Following this crisis, seven hundred thousand jobs in Mexico were slashed between October 2008 and October 2009 (CEREAL 2009). Contract manufacturers downsized their workforces considerably in the first half of 2009 but avoided shutting down operations. Sanmina alone reduced its Mexican headcount from sixteen thousand to twelve thousand. Salary levels at contract manufacturers were affected. After a period of growth, they slipped back to levels lower than those of 2005—an average wage of about US$7 per day in 2009 (Cereal 2009, 7). After mid-2009, contract manufacturers in Mexico began recovering and showing growth, which was not the case for overall development in Mexico. A noticeable improvement in the manufacturing sector was linked in part to an increased interest by multinational companies in direct investment. This development was driven by the massive devaluation of the Mexican peso in the wake of the international financial crisis. The attractiveness of Mexico as a manufacturing location has increased. Costs for wages, production, and transportation, as well as tax levels, are favorable even in comparison with China (Spiegel 2009). But the Mexican manufacturing sector still exhibited an overall negative growth rate of –7.3 percent in August 2009 (CANACINTRA/UNAM 2009). Nevertheless, employment in contract manufacturing has shown robust growth, with a potential for new projects.

EAST AND SOUTHEAST ASIA: GLOBAL PRODUCTION AND INTRAREGIONAL DIVISION OF LABOR

In the global production networks of IT contract manufacturing, East and Southeast Asia play a central role, with low-cost locations in China, Malaysia, Thailand, the Philippines, and Indonesia. This macroregion is home to the most comprehensive infrastructure of transnational contract manufacturing and the largest factories. Malaysia, Thailand, and the Philippines were among the first generation of low-cost locations in the electronics industry. China's phenomenal rise as the sector's "workshop of the world" is a recent phenomenon, which took place mainly after the industry's global recession in 2001. The international division of labor in East and Southeast Asia differs markedly from that in North America and Europe since there were no developed industrial countries in the region until the 1980s except Japan. The regional headquarters of electronics contract manufacturing are located in the emerging industrial countries of Singapore, Hong Kong, and Taiwan, three of the four Asian tigers. Taiwan plays a special role as home of both the world's leading ODM companies and the largest EMS contract manufacturer (see chapter 2).

The production networks of contract manufacturing in the region have a distinctive Chinese face. The most important locations, lead and mass-production facilities alike, are in China or the China Circle—which includes Taiwan, Singapore, Hong Kong, and Penang in Malaysia. All have a large Chinese population. At the same time, the large proportion of ethnic Chinese among management and skilled workers gives contract manufacturing the appearance of a "Chinese business network," different from the small and medium enterprises usually associated with this concept (see Hsing 1998; Yeung and Olds 2000).

Unlike in North America and Europe, contract manufacturing in Asia did not develop through a network of lead facilities in industrialized countries. Instead, Japan played a special role in the global electronics industry. The EMS model of contract manufacturing shaped by US companies took hold in Japan to only a very small extent. Most contract manufacturers maintain only sales and service facilities in the country. The situation in South Korea is similar (see table 3.4 and figure 3.3). After the 1980s, Japanese and also Korean electronics companies expanded production massively in low cost locations in Southeast Asia and, more recently, China. Their facilities and subsidiaries, however, are fully owned by the respective companies, and are not contract manufacturers. Compared to American and European brand name firms, the production networks of Japanese and Korean companies appear relatively "closed," with only minor relationships to external suppliers and contract manufacturers (Ernst 1994, 2005b). Only in recent times has cooperation with mostly Taiwanese contract manufacturers increased. The predominant vertical integration of Japanese and Korean electronics multinationals has not changed substantially (see chapter 2).

Table 3.4. Locations of Top Six Contract Manufacturing Companies in Asia, 2006

Company	Malaysia, Singapore	China/Hong Kong/ Taiwan	Other	Function, Basic Capabilities	Number of Employees
Foxconn		Taipei, Taiwan		HQ, R&D, Log, Manuf	> 3,000
		Shenzhen		Industrial park	> 130,000
		Kunshan		PCBA, SA	> 10,000
		Beijing		PCBA, SA	> 10,000
		Zhongshan		PCBA, SA	< 3,000
		Several smaller sites in China		n/a	n/a
Flextronics	Singapore			Global and regional HQ, Precision manuf, Plastics	n/a
		Tampoi		PCBA, SA, Plastics	> 3,000
		Senai		PCBA, SA, Plastics	> 3,000
		Melaka		PCBA	> 3,000
		Shah Alam		PCBA/SA	> 2,000
		Penang		SA	< 500
		Beijing		Software	n/a
		Hong Kong		Regional office	n/a
		Doumen		Industrial park: PCBA, SA, PCB Manuf, Plastics	> 10,000

Company	Country	City	Capabilities	Employees
		Shenzhen Gongming	Plastics	> 1,000
		Shenzhen Xixiang	PCBA, SA, Plastics	> 2,000
		Shenzhen Shajing	PCBA, SA	> 2,000
		Shenzhen	Des	n/a
		Dongguan	Plastics	< 3,000
		Guangzhou	Des	n/a
		Shanghai Pudong	PCBA, SA, Plastics	> 3,000
		Shanghai Malu	PCBA, SA	> 4,000
		Changzhou	Sheet metal encl	< 1,000
		Nanjing		< 500
		Qingdao	Encl	> 1,000
		Taipei, Taiwan	Regional office, PIC	n/a
	India		PCBA	< 1,000
	Thailand		Encl	> 1,000
	Japan		Des, SA	< 1,000
Sanmina-SCI		Singapore	PCBA	> 1,000
		Penang	PCBA, SA	< 1,000
		Kunshan	PCBA, Encl, Des	> 3,000
		Shenzhen	PCBA, Encl, Des	> 3,000
	Thailand		PCBA	n/a
	Indonesia		PCBA	n/a

Company	Malaysia, Singapore	China/Hong Kong/ Taiwan	Other	Function, Basic Capabilities	Number of Employees
Solectron	Singapore			Regional HQ, Encl, Des	9,000
	Penang			PCBA, SA, PIC, Des, Rep	>6,000
		Suzhou		PCBA, SA, Rep	n/a
		Shenzhen		PCBA, SA	n/a
		Shanghai		Des, Rep, PCBA, Encl	
			Indonesia	PCBA, SA	2,000
			Japan	Sales, NPI, rep	n/a
		Taipei, Taiwan		Sales, NPI	n/a
Celestica	Singapore			PIC, precision manuf, ink cartridges	
	Kulim			PCBA	1,500
	Johor Baru			PCBA, SA, rep	n/a
		Hong Kong		Admin, Log	<500
		Dongguan (2)		PCBA, SA	>5,000
		Shanghai		PCBA	n/a
		Suzhou		PCBA	1,800
			Thailand	PCBA	>2,000

			Activities	Employees
Jabil				
	Singapore	Japan (3)	Sales, Log, Rep, PCBA	n/a
		India	PCBA, SA	> 2,000
	Penang	Philippines (2)	PCBA, SA	
			PCBA, Rep	
	Shanghai		PCBA, SA	> 3,000
	Suzhou		PCBA, Des	< 1,000
	Wuxi		PCBA	< 500
	Guangzhou		PCBA	> 2,000
			PCBA	5,000
		Japan (2)	Sales, SA	n/a
		India (4)	Sales (1), PCBA (4)	n/a

Source: Company information.
Admin = Administration and office work
Des = Design
Encl = Metal enclosures and frames
HQ = Headquarters
Log = Logistics
Manuf = Assembly of printed circuit boards, end products, backplanes, cables
PCBA = Printed circuit board assembly
PIC = Production and inventory control
Rep = Repair
SA = Systems assembly

Because top-tier Asian brand-name firms have only rarely been customers of the EMS industry, the development of electronics contract manufacturing in Asia can be described as the expansion of an "American model of manufacturing" (Sturgeon 1997). This process developed directly through the expansion of low-cost manufacturing locations in Southeast Asia and their regional hubs, Singapore in particular. It was driven by the emerging production networks of vertically disintegrated US companies in the PC and hard disk drive industries (see Borrus, Ernst, and Haggard 2000). Brand-name firms from Silicon Valley usually followed the earlier internationalization of chipmakers, who built assembly factories in the Philippines, Thailand, and Indonesia in the 1970s (see Ernst 1983; Henderson 1989; McKendrick, Doner, and Haggard 2000).

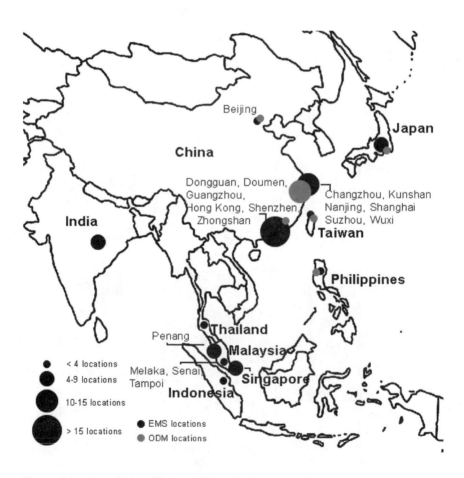

Figure 3.3.   Locations of Contract Manufacturing in Asia

The Asian production systems of contract manufacturers are extensively interlinked, distributing tasks within the region. Flextronics shows the complexity of this production infrastructure. Its headquarters in Singapore coordinates twenty-five facilities with around fifty thousand employees—more than half of the company's global workforce of ninety-five thousand (2003 figures). A design center is located in Singapore, with two hundred employees, and a high-end plastic and metal manufacturing facility brings its employee total to seventeen hundred. Flextronics has two main production bases, in Southern Malaysia near Singapore, and in the Pearl River Delta in South China. Large-scale metal and plastics factories making parts and enclosures are a key element of this production system. Extensive vertical integration goes along with the specialization of facilities and locations. For example, southern Malaysia is the global hub for production of ink-jet printers, whereas South China focuses on cell phones and consumer electronics.

The Regional Hubs: Singapore, Hong Kong, and Taiwan

In the Asian production networks there is no distinctive hierarchy between lead and mass-production facilities divided between traditional industrial countries and low-cost locations, as advertised by the major EMS companies since the late 1990s. Rather, regional headquarters are concentrated in those newly industrializing countries that during the 1990s became the major bases for multinational capital in East and Southeast Asia: Singapore, Hong Kong, and Taiwan. The intraregional division of labor resembles a *hub-and-spoke* system. Different locations show varying dynamics of development, which are shaped by their geopolitical positions and the industrial policies of particular countries.

Singapore

Singapore is the historic base for the development of the production systems of US contract manufacturers in Asia. Their most important headquarters are located there. In Singapore, contract manufacturing emerged with the growth of a broad-based electronics components industry heavily focused on manufacturing hard disk drives (Dedrick and Kramer 1998, 174ff.; McKendrick, Doner, and Haggard 2000). Multinational corporations drove the growth of a number of local manufacturing services companies. They grew as the production networks of their major customers expanded during the 1990s. Among those were JIC, a major supplier to Compaq. Venture today is among the ten largest EMS companies in the world. Foreign companies also grew, such as Flextronics, at the time a mostly unknown component supplier from Newark, California (Beane, Shukla, and Pecht 1997, 57–58). The most important company of this kind became a subsidiary of Singapore's state-owned National Steel, and by the end of the 1990s it was number six in the global EMS industry.

The diversified infrastructure of IT contract manufacturing was decisively supported by the industrial policy of Singapore's government. It was lauded for its sophisticated development strategy, systematically improving local production conditions for multinational firms (see Wong 2000). After the second half of the 1990s, industrial policies shifted from their initial focus on the chip and hard disk drive industry to the development of a skilled manufacturing base in specialized electronics components (Chew and Yeung 2001). Those policies concentrated on printed circuit boards, metal and plastics precision parts, and related machinery (Beane, Shukla, and Pecht 1997, 48–49). Extended technical training programs for workers, technicians, and engineers in these fields were an essential component, along with support and active involvement by the electronics industry trade union. In Singapore, the electronics industry is extensively unionized, including major contract manufacturers (2004 interview data).

The computer industry and its subsegments, including contract manufacturers, were heavily affected by the crisis of 2001. In hard disk drives, the key sector of the local manufacturing base, massive layoffs occurred. In contract manufacturing, major Singapore firms were taken over by global EMS companies. JIC was bought by Flextronics, and Omni by Celestica (FT, June 16, 2001). The 2001 acquisition by Solectron of Singapore's leading EMS firm, NatSteel, became a widely publicized event. It signalled the rapid demise of electronics mass production in Singapore and the end of the aspirations of local companies to become global players in contract manufacturing. Solectron's acquisition of NatSteel went hand in hand with the subsequent downsizing of the company's major facilities in Singapore, Malaysia, and Mexico. These were caused by overcapacity and the need to consolidate the company's global production system. Singapore also lost major contract manufacturing capacities to nearby Malaysia and other low-cost locations in the area, especially the free trade zone of Batam, Indonesia. In spite of the loss of most volume manufacturing during that period, however, Singapore maintained its central position in regional contract manufacturing networks. Major US contract manufacturers expanded design, engineering, and logistics for their Asian subsidiaries, using Singapore as an "engineering transfer station" (Wong 1999) especially for the buildup of large-scale facilities in China.

Hong Kong

Hong Kong provides a marked contrast to Singapore's continuously growing role in the global production networks of the IT industry. Historically, Hong Kong was the first offshore location in the electronics industry in Asia, dating back to the mid 1960s, with early investments from companies such as Philips and Fairchild Electronics (see Henderson 1989, 50ff.). Hong Kong's position in contract manufacturing grew rapidly during the 1990s but declined at an even faster pace after the year 2000. After the 1970s, a considerable infrastructure emerged of medium-sized producers of electronics parts and assembly shops. This provided an important base during the 1990s for the rapidly expanding activities of firms from Taiwan in the neighboring Pearl River Delta, with the special economic zones around the cities of Shenzhen, Zhuhai, and Shantou. Hong Kong's role as a hub for the Chinese market is often associated with its political transition from a British colony to a special administrative region of the People's Republic of China in 1997. However, Deng Xiaoping's famous formula, "one country, two systems," had become reality in South China even before the handover.

Investments from Taiwan were mostly channelled through proxies in the British crown colony. The doors for these investments were opened after the political crisis in China in 1989 and the subsequent economic boycotts from many Western states. They rapidly gained significance with Deng Xiaoping's historic "southern tour" to Shenzhen and other cities in Guangdong Province, which ushered in the period of accelerated market reforms in China (Naughton 1997). Taiwanese entrepreneurs took particular advantage of long-standing cultural and family ties to this region of the Chinese mainland, a factor especially important for the growth of small and medium-sized companies (Hsing 1998). At the same time, many electronics companies from Hong Kong started to shift their operations to the mainland to take advantage of the extremely low wages in and around the special economic zones (Lee 1998).

This development caused a rapid erosion of Hong Kong's manufacturing base in electronics. Employment in electronics assembly in Hong Kong declined from roughly twenty-five thousand in 1985 to nine thousand in 1994 (Dedrick and Kramer 1998, 203). At the same time, the strong influence of family-based capital, often organized under opaque arrangements between entrepreneurs and local authorities on the Chinese mainland, produced a massive concentration of small and medium-sized factories, most of them sweatshops with extremely low wages and poor working conditions (Lee 1998).

To a great extent, electronics contract manufacturing in South China developed in this milieu. Beginning in the late 1990s, transnational EMS firms built a presence in the region, often through acquisition of small and medium-sized factories acquired from Hong Kong companies. These were subsequently integrated into global production systems. Management and technical personnel for the new contract manufacturing facilities were often hired from Hong Kong and Taiwanese electronics firms. These transnational EMS companies were not interested in using Hong Kong as a manufacturing base.

Instead, they wanted a hub for logistics and management and a point of dispatch for expatriates to the Pearl River Delta, with its difficult living conditions for foreigners. Some contract manufacturers, including Flextronics, Celestica, Sanmina-SCI, Jabil, and Elcoteq gave their Hong Kong subsidiaries regional headquarters status. This development was short-lived, however. Management and engineering was rapidly transferred to the major facilities on the mainland, often to other regions and cities such as Shanghai and Beijing. Hong Kong lost its role as regional hub for Asian production networks almost completely to Singapore (2003, 2004, 2005 interview data).

Taiwan

Taiwan, the third major hub of contract manufacturing in Asia, is the central location of ODM companies and the world's leading EMS contract manufacturer. It is also a highly developed base of skilled providers and contract manufacturers of electronic components, including microchips. After humble beginnings in the 1970s and 1980s, Taiwan's electronics industry took off with the rapid growth of vertically specialized mass production under the Wintelist industry model during the 1990s (Borrus 2000). Well into the 1990s, the industry structure was shaped by small and medium-sized firms who competed fiercely against each other but at the same time developed forms for local cooperation, often reminiscent of industrial regions in Europe using models of "flexible specialization." Relationships with international clients often developed through networks of emigrant engineers and entrepreneurs in high-tech centers in the US West, especially Silicon Valley (Saxenian 2002, 2004). Taiwan's government also played a pivotal role in the development of a first-class manufacturing base for the global IT industry. Not only did it give massive support to technology development in areas such as chips, printed circuit boards, and optoelectronics, but it also became involved as a direct owner or tacit shareholder in some of the country's leading industrial groups (Pohlmann 2002, 265ff.; Amsden and Chu 2003; Berger and Lester 2005).

With the consolidation of vertical specialization in the IT industry, Taiwanese company networks rapidly lost their small and medium-sized character. Large-scale contract manufacturers for microchips (called *foundries*), today among the technologically most sophisticated semiconductor companies in the world, became flagship companies of the Taiwanese high-tech industry during the 1990s (see chapter 2). In components manufacturing and systems assembly, rapidly growing contract manufacturers initially focused on producing desktop and notebook PCs. They changed their operations from classical system assembly to original design manufacturing (ODM). Contract manufacturers such as Quanta, Compal, Tatung, and Lite-On developed considerable logistics know-how and became providers of integrated manufacturing services, competing with North American EMS firms (Chen 2002). At the same time, a number of large producers emerged, producing sophisticated electronics components such as motherboards, storage devices, and computer screens. According to Ernst (2000, 111), 60 percent of all desktop PCs worldwide were either manufactured in Taiwan or had a motherboard from a Taiwanese manufacturer.

Taiwan benefitted particularly from the massive restructuring of multinational brand-name firms in the wake of the 2001 crisis. Foxconn rose to become the industry's number one electronics contract manufacturer, but other ODM manufacturers also became multinational corporations with a global presence. The attractiveness of Taiwanese contract manufacturers as partners in production triggered the movement of multinational technology development companies to Taiwan. Its capital, Taipei, can rightfully be called "the world's ODM capital" (Chen 2004). In 2003 and 2004, brand-name companies, including Hewlett-Packard, IBM, Motorola, Apple, and Siemens, opened new technology sourcing centers in the city or expanded existing ones, each handling several billion US dollars per year (see table 3.5).

Rapid upgrading along the technology chain came at a price, however. Taiwanese manufacturers shifted ever larger volumes of production to the mainland. This trend began during the 1990s as computer and motherboard manufacturers built factories in South China. By 1995, 50 percent of manufacturing capacity in the main product categories was located on the mainland (Dedrick and Kraemer 1998, 152). As shown in table 3.2, after 2005, the overwhelming proportion of facilities belonging to major Taiwanese contract manufacturers were located on the mainland. Taiwan has rapidly become a headquarters economy, concentrating on management, development, and global logistics. "*Made in China by Taiwan*" aptly characterizes this division of labor across the Taiwan Strait, transforming the island's electronics firms into "hybrid companies with dual citizenship" (Leng 2005). These firms are especially sensitive to any instability in the political relationships between

Table 3.5. Procurement Volume of Leading PC Companies in Taiwan

Company	2005 (US$ billions)	2006 (US$ billions)
HP	19	More than 20
Dell	10	12.5
NEC	5.2	6.6–7.2
Sony	5.2	6.0
Lenovo	5.0	n/a

Source: DigiTimes, May 2006.

Taiwan and the People's Republic. In recent times, political changes in Taiwan are of utmost significance; the pro-independence government of former prime minister Chen Shui Bian tried to slow down the relocation of advanced technology to the mainland (most visibly in chip manufacturing). But the Kuomintang government in power since 2007 is actively promoting further integration of Taiwanese electronics companies as an important part of its policy of strengthening economic and cultural ties with the mainland.

New production and innovation networks are rapidly developing across the Taiwan Strait. The main players in the mobile phone ODM market, ODM companies from Taiwan, have located large manufacturing and design facilities in China, mostly around Shanghai and Suzhou. Most architectural tasks are still performed at company headquarters in Taiwan, but routine engineering and manufacturing-related design takes place on the mainland. Not only are new markets for mobile phones becoming the main drivers of dynamic sales growth in developing countries such as China and India, but also local brand-name companies and "white-box" handset vendors are entering the market. These local companies do not have enough knowledge for full-scale mobile handset development, but they are eagerly using complete or semi-complete handset models or components offered by ODM companies or chip design houses.

Mediatek, a Taiwanese chip company specializing in the design of complete wireless chip solutions, was able to establish itself as the major chip company in the Chinese mobile handset market, with around 40 percent of market share in 2006 (Cravotta 2007). Mediatek not only provides chipsets that are cheaper than those from multinational chip vendors but also offers reference designs and complete software packages for handsets. With Mediatek's mobile handsets, design teams need only design the user interface and the plastic shell. The increasing importance of the Chinese market and its specific characteristics have had a profound influence on innovation—at least for the mobile handset industry—advancing the geographic relocation of architectural activities to countries where they didn't exist previously.

As innovation is offshored to countries like China—to enable geographical proximity to manufacturing and cost reduction—intense contradictions develop in local labor markets. The design labs of multinational companies, as well as of local upcoming brand names and design houses, are competing for talent in local labor markets. This causes a permanent shortage of skilled engineers. China's shortage is similar to the "golden years" in Silicon Valley, when engineers job-hopped for better salaries or career possibilities. Engineering salaries in countries such as China have been rising fast, at annual rates of up to 15 percent (Lüthje 2007a). This threatens internationalization strategies that aim at reduced labor costs. But Chinese engineers are not only asking for salary increases. They also seek interesting design projects that allow them to develop their personal skills and enhance their future employability.

Malaysia: Testing Ground for New Forms of Mass Production in Asia

Malaysia was one of the first low-cost locations for electronics contract manufacturing. Beginning with Solectron's acquisition of a manufacturing facility from Texas Instruments in 1992, Malaysia saw a rapid expansion of this industry. It benefitted from geographical proximity to Singapore, an investment climate favorable to multinational companies, and the availability of an English-speaking workforce. The five biggest US contract manufacturers each developed an extensive presence in Malaysia, accompanied by the emergence of a number of local contract manufacturers and a rapidly expanding infrastructure of local suppliers of nonelectronic components. After the late 1970s, Malaysia became a low-wage location on the global assembly line (Fröbel, Heinrichs, and Kreye 1977; McGee 1986). A massive influx of foreign direct investment during the second half of the 1990s, however, rapidly transformed the industrial base and made Malaysia a model of export-driven industrialization (Ernst 2003c).

The electronics industry was the backbone of Malaysia's transformation from a postcolonial producer of raw materials, such as rubber, palm oil, and tin, to an important exporter of industrial goods. This change took place in less than two decades (Rasiah 1995). Electronics manufacturing began around 1970 with investment from multinational corporations such as Ericsson in telecommunications, audio products, and video products, initially directed at the national market (Hobday 1999, 78). The main drivers of export production were US chip makers such as Intel, National Semiconductor, Fairchild, and AMD. They established large factories for microchip assembly in the newly created free trade zone in Penang in northern Malaysia, beginning in the mid 1970s. These factories employed sixty thousand workers in 1985 (O'Connor 1993, 213). However, the chip industry remained limited to a very narrow spectrum of activities in the final assembly of semiconductors. Ironically, its position at the back end of global production systems made Malaysia seem like the world's biggest exporter of semiconductors during the 1980s and 1990s. In reality, the country hardly possessed any local resources to manufacture the core components of microchips, the chip wafers (Beane, Shukla, and Pecht 1997, 42). During the 1990s, a remarkable diversification of the industrial base in electronics took place, driven by another boom in foreign investment. Malaysia emerged as one of the most important recipients of foreign direct investment worldwide. Between 1990 and 2000, foreign direct investment stock quintupled and reached over US$52 billion (UNCTAD 2004, 379).

The main drivers of this development were PC and hard disk drive manufacturing (Dedrick and Kramer 1998, 204ff.) as well as audio and video electronics. The production of computers, networking equipment, and disk drives (led by Hewlett-Packard, Compaq, Dell, NEC, and Seagate) grew at an annual average rate of 35 percent between 1990 and 1995. Audio and video equipment, which was manufactured in more traditional industrial environments dominated by vertically integrated multinational corporations (including Sony, Hitachi, Sharp, Bosch, and Grundig) expanded by 15 percent per year (Beane, Shukla, and Pecht 1997, 65). The export of electronics products grew at an average annual rate of 25 percent between 1990 and 1995 (Ernst 2003c). A push toward more complex products and local cluster economics occurred in the hard disk drive industry. Two highly specialized producers of disk drive heads and storage media from Silicon Valley, Read-Rite and Komag, established important facilities in Malaysia (McKendrick, Doner, and Haggard 2000, 98ff.; Ariffin and Bell 1999, 163).

Industrial Policy and Regional Structure of Electronics Production

The development of the Malaysian electronics industry was backed by ambitious industrial policies, often obscured by the free market image presented by the Malaysian government. The country opened for foreign investment after 1970, in reaction to a political crisis with roots in the struggle for national independence from British colonial rule. Malaysian politics is based on a difficult balance among the three main ethnic groups: the Malays, most of them Muslims, the Chinese, and the Indians. Malayan riots against the commercially more successful Chinese population in 1969 started a process of economic modernization aiming at economic promotion of ethnic Malays and accelerated growth driven by multinational investment in labor-intensive industries (Rasiah 1995). The creation of free trade zones in certain regions was the most important element of these policies. They established designated spaces for foreign capital, governed by liberal market policies. This regime had major implications for the ethnic and gender structure of the workforce and labor policies in the electronics industry.

This constellation has shaped industrial policy in the Malaysian electronics sector until today. It is characterized by the continuing coexistence of import substitution and export orientation (Rasiah 1995, 74ff.). Leading representatives of the state speak against the global rule of neoliberal capitalism, as they did in the wake of the so-called Asian financial crisis in 1997 (Mahathir 2000). In the electronics industry, numerous programs assist the development of local enterprises (with Malayan background), their technological capabilities, and workforce education. In the 1990s Malaysia also set up ambitious programs for quantum leaps into the "information age," for example, the *Second Industrial Master Plan (IMP2)* of 1996, the much heralded but ill-fated project of the *Multimedia Super Corridor* near the capital, Kuala Lumpur, or massive government investment in a national chip foundry called Silterra (Ernst 2003c). On the other hand, austerity in the assembly industries was dictated by global competition, with a negative impact on living standards and skill levels of the workforce (Felker and Jomo 1999; see chapter 4).

Although Malaysia is relatively small in geography and population (about twenty-three million), the electronics industry is highly regionalized. It is concentrated in the three major industrial centers, each representing certain stages of the development of the industry:

- The oldest location surrounds the capital, Kuala Lumpur, and the cities Petaling Jaya and Shah Alam. The first generation of electronics manufacturing was concentrated here and included production facilities of vertically integrated multinational companies such as Motorola, Matsushita, and NEC. Most were established around 1970. These older plants were complemented by some chip and hard disk drive assembly factories during the 1980s (Beane, Shukla, and Pecht 1997). The only contract manufacturer in this location is Flextronics, with two factories acquired from Ericsson and Casio in 2000. One of them was closed in 2009. Most electronics factories in this area have between five thousand and ten thousand employees, and the total number of electronics workers was roughly seventy thousand in 2003–2004.
- The most important location of the electronics industry and of contract manufacturing in Malaysia is Penang, with four large industrial parks. These emerged from the free trade zone established in the 1970s. The leading companies are US, Japanese, and German brand manufacturers of semiconductors, hard disk drives, PCs, audio-video equipment, and automobile and medical electronics. Solectron, Jabil, Flextronics, Sanmina-SCI, and BenQ from Taiwan (the only ODM company) are the major contract manufacturers. Penang's large manufacturing base is complemented by another industrial park in nearby Kulim, hosting multinational chip makers such as Intel and Infineon, Malaysia's Silterra chip foundry, and some contract manufacturers including BCM, the leading Malaysian EMS company. In Penang there were around eighty thousand employees in electronics manufacturing in 2000; in Kulim, roughly fifteen thousand (Toh 2002).
- The youngest location is the southern province of Johor near the border of Singapore, which grew rapidly with the relocation of electronics manufacturing from Singapore in the second half of the 1990s. In this region, there are almost no brand-name companies but relatively large facilities of contract manufacturers and suppliers. The leading company here is Flex-

tronics, with two large factories in Tampoi and Senai, each with three to four thousand employees.

This regionalization also reflects different local industrial policies in the three areas. The development of vertically integrated production sites in the Kuala Lumpur area benefitted historically from the capital's role as economic center of the country and the proximity of relevant government bureaucracies. The facilities of world-known brand-name companies are icons of the Malaysian government's export-oriented modernization strategy. Regional industrial policy directed at improving local production conditions hardly exists in the area, which can also be said for the southern region of Johor. The policies of the local government mainly aim at attracting production from Singapore in a variety of industries, based on the development of traffic and communications infrastructure and the construction of industrial parks. Dedicated support of the skill base of specific industries exists only in rudimentary ways (Rasiah 1999a).

In contrast, Penang is a relatively successful example of regional industrial policy (Rasiah 1999b, 192–93), closely interlinked with local Chinese communities as the largest and politically dominant ethnic group in the area. Beginning in the mid 1980s, the local government created a number of organizations to support the region's technological and human resources. It assisted the development of sectoral industrial clusters and a skilled base of local suppliers. It sought to overcome the relatively narrow concentration of the local economy on microchip assembly and to develop a more diversified industry structure (Toh 2002). The *Penang Development Corporation* (PDC) serves as a link between multinational companies and local suppliers. The PDC is connected to a number of organizations in research and education, such as the *Penang Skill Development Center* (PSDC), a technical college for local workers and engineers, and the *Socio-Economic and Environmental Research Institute* (SERI), a think tank that researches the social and ecological consequences of local industrial development. Another important field is the development of localized IT data networking infrastructures and skills for small and medium-sized suppliers. This includes RosettaNet, a global Internet-based network for electronic data interchange (EDI) for electronics suppliers, begun in the late 1990s (ibid.).

The Production Base in Contract Manufacturing

The expansion of contract manufacturing formed a key element of the Malaysian electronics industry's rapid development during the 1990s. As depicted in table 3.4, a total of ten facilities emerged among the big five EMS companies from the United States, mostly in the range of two thousand to four thousand employees. Malaysia became the most important location for contract manufacturing in Southeast Asia. The second wave of expansion of contract manufacturing after 2000 in Asia, however, was centered in China and mostly bypassed Malaysia. Contract manufacturers from Taiwan have almost no presence in Malaysia. The major areas of production in the Malaysian contract manufacturing industry, which almost exclusively uses the EMS model, reflect the specialization of IT manufacturing in Malaysia. PCs, servers, networking equipment and computer peripherals, and printers and hard disk drives became the focus of manufacturing beginning in the 1990s. Flextronics near Kuala Lumpur produces significant volumes of cell phones. Dell, Cisco, HP, IBM, Motorola, and Ericsson are among the largest customers of the EMS industry in Malaysia.

Contract manufacturing facilities in Malaysia all feature state-of-the-art manufacturing technology and organization. In this respect, the EMS plants differ fundamentally from the first-generation electronics assembly factories of the 1970s and 1980s. As in Mexico and Eastern Europe, the rapid growth in the 1990s was mainly based on the expansion of volume manufacturing of computer motherboards and printed circuit boards for disk drives and networking equipment. After the year 2000, a gradual shift took place toward products with lower volumes and higher customer-specific configuration requirements. Relatively few product introduction centers exist in Malaysian facilities; however, this function is still mostly performed in Singapore. Solectron has a large-scale facility performing this function in Penang, which became part of Flextronics in 2008. Jabil and Flextronics factories in Penang also have product introduction capabilities. Production of plastic parts and metal enclosures is relatively insignificant in Malaysia. With the exception of Flextronics's high-volume factory assembling computer printers in Senai and Tampoi, EMS factories in Malaysia do not have manufacturing capacities in this area (see table 3.4).

Production in Malaysian factories features a high degree of vertical integration in printed circuit board and systems assembly. Solectron's industrial parklike production site in Penang implements *integration at the facility level*. With 7,700 employees in recent years, it is the company's biggest facility in Asia. In 2005, it consisted of five factories located at various sites of Penang Prai IV Industrial Park. In *Plants 1 and 1a* (which also housed administration and management), computer products were manufactured on a 500,000-square-foot floor. *Plant 2* makes networking equipment (340,000 square feet), while *Plant 3* makes computer peripherals, including hard disk drives (approximately 150,000 square feet). *Plant 4* was a final assembly facility for various IT products (280,000 square feet), and *Plant 5* is a product introduction facility and repair center serving all of Asia. In 2002, the whole factory had sixty automated assembly lines for printed circuit boards (known as surface mount devices, or SMD) and sixteen lines for final product assembly (2005 company information). This broad portfolio of products and services was created by the rapid development of the facility during the 1990s. The factory started with only six hundred employees in 1993, but by 2000 it employed more than ten times as many (2003 interview data).

Flextronics's production in southern Malaysia was an example of *vertical integration between facilities at a regional level*. The factories in Senai and Tampoi in the Johor Province specialize in manufacturing ink-jet and laser printers. In 2005, the main client was world market leader Hewlett-Packard, whose world headquarters for the printer division is in nearby Singapore. Flextronics maintained a lead factory for southern Malaysian operations at its technology and logistics center near Singapore's Changi Airport, which also serves as the company's world headquarters. Apart from engineering functions, this facility housed a manufacturing facility for highly complex commercial printers for HP, using skilled manual labor. A second Flextronics facility in Singapore served as a lead factory manufacturing plastics parts for printer enclosures. Tool development and maintenance for injection molding machines were also located here. The injection molding operation, with several hundred employees, was located on the Malaysian side at the Senai factory, which also housed assembly operations for a diversified group of products. The assembly of the printers was housed in the Tampoi factory, with about 4,500 employees. A product introduction facility for standard consumer printers and a class 100 clean room for the production of printing media was also located there. Printed circuit boards were supplied from another Flextronics factory, about two hundred kilometers away in Melaka, with thirty-two SMT assembly lines and three thousand employees, producing for the Tampoi factory. Tampoi served as the introduction center for new HP consumer printers worldwide. It was also the lead factory for Flextronics's printer assembly operations in Sárvár, Hungary, and Zhuhai and Shanghai in China (2003, 2005 company information).

Vertical integration and industrial network formation in Malaysia occur mostly within or between multinational actors in the IT sector. They cluster in the area of PC and peripheral production. In some cases, EMS companies and the local operations of multinational brand firms become vertically integrated. Contract manufacturers act as integrated suppliers, becoming a virtual factory for brand-name companies, as is the case of motherboard manufacturing by Solectron, Sanmina-SCI, and Jabil for Dell. Dell has its largest assembly plant for notebook computers outside the United States in Penang. As is the case in every Dell factory, it is merely a final assembly center, customizing individual orders from Dell's Internet-based sales system. The technologically more sophisticated, capital-intensive elements of production, particularly the manufacturing and assembly of printed circuit boards, is performed by contract manufacturers.

Local contract manufacturers and suppliers enjoy only limited success in the production networks of multinationals. Local purchasing by large contract manufacturers is limited to nonelectronic components. The bulk of the huge supply volume is imported from outside Malaysia. Big contract manufacturers view the quality of local suppliers as rather low, although lip service is paid to efforts by local government agencies to improve quality and to develop comprehensive certification (2003 interview data). Although a relatively broad spectrum of local suppliers has developed for technologically sophisticated parts with support from government industrial policies (Rasiah 1999a), long-term linkages between contract manufacturers and suppliers exist in only a few niche markets, such as precision enclosures for commercial printers, plotters, and scanners. The absence of broader spillover effects is related to the fact that specialized low-volume manufacturing has remained relatively limited in the product portfolio of multinational contract manufacturers in Malaysia (2005 interview data).

The situation of government-supported Malaysian contract manufacturers is similar (Rasiah 1999a). BCM is a company run by local management with Indian and Malayan background in Kulim, near Penang. It gained a reputation as a manufacturer of handheld VHF radios for Motorola and works for a number of smaller electronics companies from Europe and the United States. The production model of this and similar companies can mostly be characterized as *original equipment manufacturing* (OEM; see chapter 2) since these companies cannot provide extensive services in design, logistics, and supply-chain management. Integration into the global production networks of brand-name companies usually does not occur without the "visible hand" of the Malaysian government. In the case of BCM, Motorola provided orders to the Malaysian contract manufacturer in return for government subsidies to help expand its facilities in Kuala Lumpur (2005 interview data).

Restructuring during Crisis

The structural problems of vertically integrated mass production, focused on printed circuit boards and system assembly with a relatively low degree of diversification, became visible during the global crisis of the IT industry in 2001. That crisis hit Malaysia particularly hard (Toh 2002, 16). Production and employment slumped nationwide, resulting in factory closures and lay-offs (see chapter 4). In Penang alone, twelve thousand jobs in electronics manufacturing (about 15 percent of total employment) were eliminated (BW, October 22, 2001). During the crisis, Malaysian industry felt massive competition from China, the new big location for contract manufacturing in Asia. Malaysia's competitive advantages resulted from the dense interlinkages between multinational corporations, the well-developed infrastructure in transport and communications, and its political stability. But these factors lost clout by comparison with China's lower wages and land costs. More important, economies of scale emerged in China due to the size and the rapidly developing vertical integration of contract manufacturing facilities. Manufacturing PC motherboards, until then a backbone of IT production in Malaysia, was almost completely lost to China. This especially affected the Penang facilities of Solectron, Sanmina-SCI, and Jabil. At the same time, Malaysia suffered from the speculative overexpansion of major contract manufacturers at the end of the 1990s. Singapore's leading contract manufacturer was taken over by Solectron, leading to the closure of the NatSteel factory in Penang (2002, 2003 interview data).

In spite of its dramatic impact, the recession did not signal the end of Malaysia as a location for production. Production and employment in contract manufacturing stabilized quickly after the downturn of 2001–2002 and recovered at slower but relatively steady rates in the following years. Malaysia benefitted from the relocation of higher-end manufacturing from Singapore, which in some cases led to upgrading Malaysian facilities. Some major sites also acquired lead functions for the ramp-up of manufacturing operations in China, including the dispatch of skilled Chinese-speaking engineers and technicians from Malaysia (2005 interview data). The biggest benefit for Malaysia, however, came from the policies of multinational brand-name firms, which wanted to maintain a second major location for low-cost mass production in Asia. This strategy, known as "China plus one," was designed to minimize the social and political risks of China as a manufacturing location.

In some areas of contract manufacturing, this restructuring process upgraded facilities in Malaysia. As mass production of low- to mid-end systems was shifted to China, major US vendors shifted the manufacturing of their latest and most sophisticated network routers to Malaysia. The main reason cited for this strategy was the danger of unwanted transfer of intellectual property to competitors in China (2005 interview data). The relocation of relatively complex products to Malaysia produced a trend toward flexibilized high-volume production—a type of production that gained importance in contract manufacturing after 2001. Under this model, relatively large manufacturing volumes are combined with frequently changing product configurations and sophisticated supply-chain concepts and logistics.

Production of ink-jet printers by Flextronics for Hewlett-Packard in southern Malaysia is a good example of high-volume, high-mix manufacturing, but there are numerous other cases. At Solectron's Penang facility, production was refocused on server and networking products after 2003, following the almost complete loss of printed circuit board assembly for PCs and hard disk drives during the crisis. These new products have high requirements for customer-specific configuration. The previously dominant assembly-line production was complemented by cell-based manufacturing structures, particularly in systems integration. Inventory logistics is now based on *vendor-managed inventory*, in which the parts supplier manages most inventories and assumes financial responsibility for them. Systems integration and testing were improved significantly (2005 interview data).

The industry tended toward production of relatively complex products in lower volumes. Sanmina-SCI's facility in Penang was historically a high-volume assembly facility for printed circuit boards. The factory was transformed for the assembly of specialized products with a relatively high number of mechanical components, such as security printers for credit and identification cards. Smaller facilities of multinational contract manufacturers also cooperate extensively with local suppliers in the area of mechanical components (2005 interview data).

However, in spite of the relatively comprehensive respecialization in manufacturing, product development was shifted to Malaysia to only a small extent. The general character of contract manufacturing is primarily a production-related service, separated from the development of the products by brand-name customers. Malaysia could not reap benefits from the massive relocation of product design from developed industrial countries, which became a characteristic trend in the IT industry after 2001 (see chapter 2). It has a relatively weak position as a destination for "innovation offshoring" (Ernst 2006a) because only a small number of ODM contract manufacturers exist there that might make use of the available low-cost engineering workforce. The number of second-tier design companies, developing specialized chips, chip modules, or other IC-related components, has traditionally been low (Hobday 1999, 98).

Malaysia's trajectory took it from a low-end assembly site, under the once "new" internationalization of labor of the 1970s and 1980s, to a diversified base of advanced components and systems assembly. The development of the country's IT industry remains highly dependent on "manufacturing-related learning" (Best 1999). Malaysia is one of the most important locations for electronics manufacturing in the world, but a pathway of upgrading from OEM over ODM to brand-name manufacturing had not developed, unlike in the most successful emerging economies in Asia, South Korea and Taiwan (see O'Connor 1993, 229; Wong 1999, 56ff.). Malaysia's important position within the "China plus one" scenarios of global flagship companies does not guarantee further upgrading of electronics production in the long term.

As a consequence, in the area of components and systems assembly, Malaysia may be relegated to a "global shipping dock," as it was previously in the chip industry. Its largest single exporter of electronics products, Dell, announced in 2006 that it would concentrate worldwide assembly of notebook computers in its Penang facilities, involving significant relocations from North America, Europe, and China. Production in this field, however, involves only final assembly and product configuration. The production of electronic components and most of the product design is provided by ODM companies from Taiwan and their facilities in China. Dell accounted for almost 30 percent of Malaysia's electronics exports and 10 percent of its total exports of industrial goods in 2005. A gradual hollowing out of much of the country's IT manufacturing base seems to be imminent unless a major paradigm shift in industrial development can be initiated (figures according to *DigiTimes*, January 26, 2006).

China: New Center of Globalized Mass Production in the IT Sector

The most important location of electronics contract manufacturing today is the People's Republic of China. About 30 percent of IT contract production worldwide took place there in 2005, according to Technology Forecasters, a market research firm. Beginning in the late 1990s, large-scale factories and manufacturing infrastructures were built up in the major areas of export production along the Chinese east coast. This process gained strength in the wake of the 2001 recession. The rise of China in IT manufacturing is the most dramatic consequence of the crisis of the Wintelist industry model and the changed conditions of global competition following the demise of the so-called New Economy. This development was driven by the relocation of contract manufacturing from North America, Europe, and Asia, particularly from the "older" low-cost locations of the EMS industry in Mexico, Malaysia, and Eastern Europe. The expansion of the Chinese contract manufacturing industry reflects the rise of the ODM model, the special role of Taiwan as the "global factory" (Ernst 2006c), and China's aspirations for a global leadership position in the electronics industry (see Berger and Lester 2005).

This macroeconomic context differs fundamentally from the other low-cost countries under investigation here. *First*, China developed a rapidly growing mass market for electronics products of all kinds—including the most advanced and technologically sophisticated products. *Second*, productive resources grew rapidly throughout the IT industry, including high-end segments such as chip manufacturing and a wide variety of product development and specialized design services (Lüthje 2006, 2007a). *Third*, China is rapidly developing its own multinationals in the electronics industry, with leadership aspirations in global production and design networks. They are supported by massive government spending and strategic industrial policies in key technology sectors, such as mobile communication, digital television and broadcasting, and chip design (Ernst 2006b).

The term "low-wage production" alone does not describe this global relocation to China of advanced production in the electronics industry. Rather, the picture is dominated by the rapid growth of modern, vertically integrated mass production. The enormous size and scope of the new factories might suggest that we are facing a revival of a Fordist-Taylorist model of production and work (see Lüthje 2004b). But the rapid growth of contract manufacturing, with state-of-the-art technology and organization, is just one element in this scenario. There is a great variety among the underlying models of industrial organization and their flexible combination (Liu, Lüthje, and Pawlicki 2007). The political and social context is shaped by almost three decades of policies of gradual market transformation. These policies did not use the neoliberal "shock therapies" favored by financial institutions. This was clearly different from the experience of Eastern Europe, as we will see in the next section of this chapter. The Chinese state plays a strong role in formulating industrial policy at various levels, although competing interests and policies often produce fragmentary and contradictory political regulation. As a result, significant differences exist in the conditions of production within the country and, as we will describe in chapter 4, in working conditions and labor standards. This is a characteristic feature of the emerging model of "capitalism with Chinese characteristics" (Lüthje 2006).

Political Context and Regional Structure

IT contract manufacturing in China developed from the relocation of simple assembly operations of electronics manufacturers from North America, Taiwan, and Asian low-cost locations to the South Chinese Pearl River Delta (PRD). Taiwanese manufacturers of PCs and PC components operating in Hong Kong spearheaded this development (Hsing 1998; Lee 1998), which finally led to a huge concentration of companies in the area. They were followed by American contract manufacturers that acquired existing facilities and opened new ones in the PRD beginning in 1998.

The Pearl River Delta was already the site of increasingly diversified export production in light industries such as garment, shoes, and consumer goods of all kinds, as well as chemicals and plastics. After the mid-1990s, the PRD became the fastest-growing industrial region in China. With roughly twenty-five million factory workers since the late 1990s, the region is the largest industrial area in the world (Guangdong Sheng Tongji Nianshu 2006). The major locations of industrial production are in Shenzhen, with more than 9 million inhabitants and 3 million industrial workers in 2006, Dongguan, with more than 5 million industrial workers, and Guangzhou (better known in the West as Canton), with about 3.5 million industrial employees. The region is located at the center of global communication and transport networks, which historically had been centered in Hong Kong but then expanded rapidly on the mainland.

In the manufacturing base of South China's "Red capitalism" (Lin 1997), electronics contract manufacturing represents one of the technologically most advanced industries. Its emergence at the end of the 1990s marks a major step in the industrial development of the region. The early industrial development of the 1980s and early 1990s took off in the special economic zones of Shenzhen and Zhuhai and was shaped by smaller companies from

Hong Kong and Taiwan. More capital-intensive forms of production developed after 1995. After 2004, a third phase of industrial development took place, characterized by rapid growth of more knowledge-intensive enterprises, not only in electronics but also in other industries such as steel or petrochemicals (T. Chan 2005, 81). The emerging Chinese electronics multinationals based in the region have been key drivers of this latest stage of development—Huawei, ZTE, and Konka in Shenzhen and TCL in Huizhou.

The development in Guangdong Province was shaped by the special economic zones. It was different from the older industrial regions along the coast, such as the Beijing-Tianjin corridor in the north and the greater Shanghai region. Here, substantial investments from foreign multinationals began in the 1980s, usually as joint ventures with European, Japanese, and sometimes US multinationals, particularly in consumer electronics and telecommunications (Harwit 2008). These regions developed as locations for contract manufacturing only with the massive expansion of the industry in China after the year 2000. Small and medium-sized assembly firms operating under sweatshop conditions were relatively insignificant in the greater Shanghai and Beijing areas. At the same time, industrial development took place in a more planned and regulated fashion, particularly in relation to the environment. Contract manufacturing facilities are often located in large and modern industrial parks, with infrastructure meeting high international standards. Labor standards are also controlled more strictly (see chapter 4). Shanghai and Beijing became preferred locations for headquarters of multinational brand-name companies with research and development facilities as well as important production complexes, such as Nokia in Beijing, Motorola and Samsung in Tianjin, and Siemens and numerous Japanese multinationals in Shanghai.

Important differences exist among the "second generation" of contract manufacturing locations. Areas shaped by companies from Taiwan feature distinctively modest urban environments compared to the "five-star" industrial parks in Beijing, Tianjin, and Shanghai. Such differences are particularly visible around Shanghai. Here, the Suzhou Singapore Industrial Park (SIP), run by the city of Suzhou in cooperation with investors from Singapore, has become one of the most attractive locations for multinational enterprises in China. The seventy-square-kilometer area, with world-class infrastructure, is one of the most ambitious urban developments in China. It includes tens of thousands of apartments and single-family homes and research institutions and universities for eighty thousand students. It accommodates factories of major electronics multinationals, such as Nokia, Bosch, Infineon, AMD, National Semiconductor, Philips, and Samsung, and of EMS companies Flextronics (Solectron before 2008) and Celestica. In contrast, the nearby town of Kunshan is the most important location on the Chinese mainland of Taiwanese ODM companies, which manufacture about 70 percent of the world production of notebook computers in this area. In Kunshan, which grew from a rural township of 50,000 to an industrial city with 2.3 million inhabitants within a decade, multinational brand-name companies have almost no presence. The urban environment caters to the needs of Taiwanese managers, technicians, engineers, and their families, forming a community of tens of thousands. The biggest contrast, however, is in the situation of production workers. In contract manufacturing facilities in Suzhou SIP, rural workers make up around 10 percent of the workforce. Kunshan's workforce consists almost exclusively of migrant workers, whose living conditions are much worse. Divisions exist even within cities: some of the older industrial areas of Suzhou, with a large concentration of Taiwanese ODM manufacturers, have conditions similar to those of Kunshan (2004, 2005, 2006, 2009 interview data and field visits; see chapter 4).

Such differences show the decentralization of industrial policies in China—one of the most important but least understood characteristics of the capitalist transformation of the country since 1978 (see Hsing 1998; Nee and Su 1996; Lüthje 2006). Informal coalitions between local governments and party organizations and the respective investors in their communities have driven this process, creating massive competition between cities and regions. Local urban "growth machines" (Hsing 2006) offer massive incentives and tax rebates for investment. Local industrial policies usually include nonenforcement of existing labor laws and occupational health and safety regulations. Such policies give the major industrial cities in the Pearl River Delta, such as Shenzhen or Dongguan, a reputation as "lawless cities." In the newer locations in northern China and the Yangtze River delta, solid infrastructure and sustainable environmental policies have become standard. Nevertheless, many locations offer similar financial incentives and tax breaks to investors, often undermining national regulations. This is particularly true in locations dominated by Taiwanese firms, where the local branches of the Chinese government's Taiwan Affairs Office and the related associations of Taiwanese businesses influence local policies (Dongguan 2004, Kunshan 2005 interview data).

The Production Base in Contract Manufacturing

In all of these locations, electronics contract manufacturing is characterized by large-scale operations. As shown in table 3.4, the five major North American contract manufacturers in 2006 had over thirty facilities in China, with roughly sixty thousand employees. The majority were located in the Pearl River Delta and in the greater Shanghai area. Elcoteq, the only major contract manufacturer from Europe, had three factories in Beijing, Dongguan, and Shenzhen. Foxconn from Taiwan, the world's biggest contract manufacturer, had between 200,000 and 300,000 employees in China in

2006, 130,000 in its industrial park called "Foxconn City" in Shenzhen's Longhua district, the largest electronics factory in the world.

Foxconn's enormous expansion resulted in an explosive growth of its factories and workforce. Before the beginning of the recession in 2008, its overall headcount in China was seven hundred thousand, with three hundred thousand workers in "Foxconn City" and another one hundred thousand in surrounding facilities in Shenzhen. This development led to concerns about overexpansion and social instability, causing a major overhaul in Foxconn's locational layout in China. According to plans published in Chinese business media in early 2008, the company was planning a massive downsizing of its Longhua complex from 300,000 to 120,000 workers. This was to be accompanied by a massive buildup in new locations with previously little or no electronics manufacturing, such as the port city of Yantai in Shandong Province, Wuhan, Taiyuan, a number of places in the industrial "rustbelt" provinces of the northeast, and rural provinces such as Guanxi or Inner Mongolia (see table 3.6). Certainly, such gigantic plans will not be completely realized, and many of these figures are designed to lure local governments into the competition to offer tax incentives and investment subsidies. Foxconn's expansion was affected by the 2008–2009 recession, as we explain in further detail later, but the company highlights the enormous concentration of electronics manufacturing resources China has seen in recent years.[2]

ODM contract manufacturing is concentrated in the Shanghai region. The five leading companies are Quanta, Asustek, Compal, Inventec, and Wistron, which all have major factories or industrial parks (see table 3.2). In addition, BenQ (renamed Qisda after the disaster with Siemens Mobile) has ODM and own-brand manufacturing in a big factory in Suzhou and in the facility in Shanghai taken over from Siemens in 2005. Shanghai and Suzhou are also important locations for US-based EMS companies. After the takeover of Solectron in 2007, Flextronics had five major facilities in the greater Shanghai area, with the former Solectron factory in Suzhou SIP as regional lead factory. A major ODM facility was taken over from Arima, located on its seven-factory campus in the older industrial area of Suzhou. In northern China, there are only two EMS assembly factories. Besides Elcoteq, a Foxconn facility in Beijing serves as a product introduction center for major multinationals headquartered in the capital, such as Nokia and HP. A metal and plastics enclosure facility belonging to Flextronics in Qingdao supplies major Chinese home appliances manufacturers concentrated in this city, such as Haier.

Table 3.6. Existing and Future Industrial Parks of Foxconn in China, June 2008

No.	City (Province)	Products/Function	Workforce	Projected Investment (US$ billions)
1	Shenzhen Longhua (Guangdong)	IT products and parts of all kinds	300,000	
		China headquarters	120,000 proj.	
2	Shenzhen (Guangdong)	Cell phones, consumer electronics	70,000	
3	Kunshan (Jiangsu)	Connectors, computer, power supply	100,000	
4	Taiyuan (Shanxi)	Magnesium and aluminum products	50,000	1
		Cell phones	65,000 proj.	
5	Yantai (Shandong)	Computer	50,000	1.2
		Consumer electronics	100,000 proj.	
6	Zhunan (Jiangsu)	Connectors, computer	120,000 proj.	n/a
7	Wuhan (Hubei)	Digital cameras, computer	150,000 proj.	1.2
8	Langfang (Hebei)	Cell phones and spare parts	60,000 proj.	1
9	Qinhuangdao (Hebei)	Printed circuit boards	35,000 proj.	1
10	Yingkou (Liaoning)	Printed circuit boards, motherboards, power supply	30,000	1
11	Shenyang (Liaoning)	Numerical control precision tools	n/a	1
		Automotive electronics		
12	Nanjing (Jiangsu)	Software	30,000	1
13	Hohot (Inner Mongolia)	Computer products	n/a	1
14	Nanning (Guanxi)	Various	n/a	3

Source: China Entrepreneur (Zhongguo Qiyejia), December 2008.

Volume production of PCs, digital consumer electronics, and mobile communications devices are concentrated in South China, including production of cell phones, game consoles, and small devices such as PDAs, MP3 players, and Apple's well-known iPods and iPhones. Production volumes are considerable. In the city of Shenzhen, more than one hundred million cell phones, with a market value of US$25 billion, were manufactured in 2005, fifteen million of them by Foxconn alone for Motorola and Nokia, according to the Shenzhen Wireless Communication Association (Xinhua, August 7, 2006). In the Shanghai area and North China, EMS contract manufacturers mainly focus on telecommunications infrastructure products, particularly base stations for mobile communications. ODM production in the region focuses on notebook computers as well as cell phones and higher-end mobile communication devices. Most ODM manufacturers also have subsidiaries for manufacturing LCD displays for mobile phones, notebooks, and digital TV sets. These are also mostly located in the Shanghai region. Independent providers of PC motherboards and other computer components are another important element of this manufacturing infrastructure. Their large factories are located mainly in South China.

Vertical integration is particularly strong in China. Vertical integration *within* facilities is characterized by large-scale industrial parks. At least six major parks exist in China, owned by Foxconn and Flextronics in the PRD and ODM companies Quanta, Asustek, Inventec, and Arima in the Shanghai region (see table 3.2). In 2003, Flextronics built an industrial park in Zhuhai consisting of two large facilities for PCB assembly, a factory for the production of raw printed circuit boards with top-of-the-line process technology, facilities for injection molding and manufacturing of metal enclosures, final assembly and product configuration, and logistics terminals. The workforce increased from twelve thousand workers in 2003 to almost fifty thousand in 2008 but dropped to about thirty thousand in the wake of the global financial crisis of 2008–2009. Production is focused on mobile phones, game consoles, and ink-jet printers, the latter in cooperation with Flextronics's factories in southern Malaysia (company information and 2003, 2004, 2009 interview data).

"Foxconn City" in Shenzhen is the ultimate model of vertically integrated mass production. This complex features fifteen major factory buildings, each housing production for one major brand-name customer, and large-scale facilities for metal stamping and manufacturing, plastics injection molding (probably the largest of its kind in the electronics industry worldwide), cable assembly, and other auxiliary functions. The manufacturing concept is dedicated to in-house mass production of nonelectronic components (metal, plastics, cable), which carry higher profit margins than automated assembly of printed circuit boards. In 2004, four thousand engineers were working in the Shenzhen facility. Foxconn City forms a preferential customs area with on-site customs inspection, the only private factory in China to which such a status has been awarded (2004, 2009 interview data).

Along with vertical integration at the facility level, various forms of vertical integration *between factories* are also seen at regional levels. Flextronics's production network in South China provides a good example. The company's smaller factories in the region form a production cluster of considerable size, with one regional manufacturing center for medium-volume production of consumer products (2,300 employees), two injection molding facilities with about 1,500 employees, a smaller factory for metal enclosures, and a design center in Guangzhou (2003 interview data). In 2003, two injection molding facilities in Dongguan were added; these formerly belonged to Singapore's NatSteel. In 2007 a major design center was opened in Shenzhen, concentrating on mobile communications and multimedia products (2008 field data). Elcoteq, with two complementary production facilities in Dongguan and Shenzhen, and Sanmina-SCI, with several smaller assembly and enclosure manufacturing facilities in Shenzhen, are further examples of vertical integration at the regional level. The company has a similar regional production cluster in the Shanghai region, with facilities in Kunshan and Wuxi and a logistics center in Shanghai, together employing about three thousand workers (2005, 2006 interview data).

Forms of vertical quasi integration between brand-name firms and contract manufacturers also exist in China. EMS firms are mostly involved in such arrangements, whereas ODM companies mostly have production models that remain "closed" vis-à-vis customers. Vertical integration between contract manufacturers and brand-name companies is found in mobile phone manufacturing. Nokia is the most prominent case. Two manufacturing clusters were set up in Beijing and Dongguan as part of Nokia's global modular manufacturing system (see chapter 2). A smaller facility was also established for network infrastructure products in Suzhou. Foxconn has a central role as provider for preassembled cell phone shells. Its Beijing facility (located in the neighborhood of Nokia's China headquarters) acts as the interface in this system. Mass manufacturing is provided in "Foxconn City" and another large-scale facility in Shenzhen with about twenty thousand workers (2008 interview data). Elcoteq, Nokia's second contract manufacturer, has a smaller assembly facility in the same location in Beijing and a manufacturing facility acquired from Nokia in Dongguan in the PRD.

Siemens's former cell phone production in Shanghai used a similar but much smaller model of "modular" manufacturing. EMS companies such as Elcoteq and Flextronics manufactured lower- and mid-end volume products. A number of medium-sized contract assemblers from Germany were used for in-house manufacturing of higher-end products in the vicinity of Siemens's Chinese factory. Their assembly plants with several hundred workers performed labor-intensive tasks that could not be done on Siemens's highly automated production lines, such as the wiring of cell phone shells and assembly of cables. Some of these contract assemblers subcontracted simple manufacturing work, such as attaching plugs and connectors to cable assemblies, to smaller companies in the PRD area. After the takeover of Siemens Mobile by BenQ, most of these suppliers lost their contracts and had to close their facilities. BenQ performed most of those labor-intensive segments of the assembly process in-house (2005, 2006 interview data).

The existence of a broad spectrum of small and medium-sized suppliers of nonelectronic components, cables, and simple manufacturing services is another characteristic of the production infrastructure in China. These companies, mostly owned by private entrepreneurs from Hong Kong, Taiwan, or mainland China, are concentrated in South China. According to estimates from Flextronics, around 2,700 such component suppliers exist in the PRD, a major factor encouraging the location of large EMS factories there. These firms specialize in products hazardous to workers and the environment, such as batteries. The quality of these suppliers is often low, but they continue to receive orders—particularly from North American contract manufacturers, which do not make their own cables and passive components. They use selected suppliers that have received some certification and have longer-term relationships with their respective EMS companies (2003, 2004 interview data).

Small suppliers represent the continuing realities of "ultralow-cost" production developed during the early days of the special economic zones in South China. Important cluster effects arise from the massive presence of such companies, especially for mass production of cell phones or PCs. According to the Shenzhen Wireless Association, almost all the roughly two hundred hardware components used in a mobile phone are manufactured in the city and can be ordered by phone within less than half an hour. In addition, there are about one hundred design companies for cell phone components (Xinhua, August 7, 2006). The large production volume of contract manufacturers in the region would hardly be possible without the existence of such an infrastructure. The changing requirements of globalized mass production causes considerable upgrading among some of those suppliers. Many Chinese small enterprises have had to give up their personalized and family-based relationships, often associated with "Chinese business networks," and turn to more formal, market-type relationships. As a senior manager of a US contract manufacturer explained during our field interviews:

> I think there is less and less of the old and informal style. There are just too many components involved and it is too obvious that the quality level doesn't reach and the pricing is reviewed daily by a team of people. So, there is not going to be a competitive advantage to have been somebody's friend unless

you are exactly as somebody else, your pricing is the same, your quality is the same, 100% all the same, then yes, that maybe—but it is much more formal than the old days. That comes from the top down from all these companies, they are publicly listed and there is much more a scrutiny by people nowadays. (2008 interview data)

Large-scale providers of nonelectronics components have emerged in the China Circle, making metal frames (called chassis) for notebook computers and cell phones. As manufacturing of these products became concentrated in large factories on the Chinese mainland, the demand grew rapidly for this kind of component in large volumes at uniform quality, because most Taiwanese ODM contract manufacturers and US EMS providers do not produce them in-house (only Foxconn has this capacity). This opened up growth opportunities for new specialized mass producers with sophisticated knowledge of the related manufacturing processes and led to the development of a new industry subsegment. The three leading companies in this field—Catcher Technology, Ju Teng International, and Foxconn Technology—are all based in Taiwan. The biggest one, Kecheng (or "Catcher Technology" in English), operates a huge vertically integrated factory in Suzhou SIP with modern production equipment. It uses a variety of die-cast and metal manufacturing processes on huge production lines. Before the 2008 recession, this factory had a workforce of thirty thousand (2009 interview data). At the end of 2011, the factory was temporarily closed by the local government of Suzhou, following massive complaints from residents about toxic hazards from the factory and concerns about workplace safety. One of the main products in this factory are the metal frames for Apple's iPod and iPad devices (2011 interview data).

Contract Manufacturing and Industrial Development

The enormous growth of electronics contract manufacturing in China has changed the country's productive base in high tech in less than a decade. The large factories of global contract manufacturers are completely different from the sweatshop-based export manufacturing in China of the 1980s and 1990s. The factories form the backbone of a new base of integrated mass production that has no comparison in any other country. The complexity of production structures is remarkable. Vertical reintegration takes place not only in specific segments of component or system manufacturing but across the entire production system, including nonelectronic components. Other than in Malaysia, sectoral network relationships are not primarily between multinational companies producing for export. There are ample interlinkages between transnational brand-name firms with important interests in China's large domestic market, Chinese brand-name firms, EMS and ODM contract manufacturers, and a huge variety of first-, second-, and third-tier component manufacturers. With their comprehensive integration into the economy of the People's Republic of China, companies from Taiwan today are an integral part of its manufacturing base.

Within a relatively short period, the product portfolio and production capabilities of contract manufacturing in China have been upgraded. Product introduction functions are found in almost every major production site in China. Vertically integrated large factories have a relatively broad spectrum of production and development for sophisticated components, such as raw printed circuit boards, plastics, and metal parts. Most of the maintenance of production equipment, including use of sophisticated tools in metal manufacturing and injection molding, are performed inside Chinese factories. Much of the necessary know-how is still being imported from factories and locations outside China, but localization is progressing rapidly. International vendors and service providers in advanced manufacturing have a major presence in the relevant industrial areas of China and do not operate from outside, as is the case in Singapore and Southeast Asia.

Standardized high-volume manufacturing still prevails in Chinese contract manufacturing facilities, but learning progresses rapidly. This is particularly visible in the manufacturing of telecom network infrastructure products in the Shanghai area. This segment is dominated by high-volume products, such as radio base stations, with a high degree of customer-specific configuration. This type of production is characterized as *flexible-volume production* (*high-volume, high-mix*). This form of production benefits greatly from the enormous investments of Chinese telecom operators in new network infrastructures. That includes products using China's homegrown TD-SCDMA standard for third-generation mobile communications. These cross-sectoral upgrading effects do not exist everywhere, however. Emerging Chinese brand-name multinationals in consumer electronics and telecommunications are customers of major contract manufacturers. They do not promote the upgrading of production and human resources, nor are they pushed by government agencies in that direction. The decoupling of research and design-based innovation and manufacturing is particularly visible in South China. Major Chinese multinationals such as Huawei, ZTE, TCL and Konka have their home bases there, but they do not play any role in upgrading local production capabilities or social standards in manufacturing. Rather, the local governments of cities such as Shenzhen, which in some cases co-own these companies, support company investment in less developed areas of China in order to escape the rapidly rising wages and salaries on the coast (2008 interview data; see chapter 4).

Rapid changes are taking place in competition between the major industrial areas in China. A sophisticated production base, with relatively complex manufacturing processes and growing integration of manufacturing and product development developed in Shanghai, driven by ODM contract manufacturers. South China remains focused on manufacturing standardized high-volume products. The quality of South Chinese manufacturing locations has suffered from massive problems because of an overburdened infrastructure. There were massive outages in the region in summer 2004, a labor shortage during the boom period of 2004–2008, and the plant closures and social unrest in the wake of the recession of 2008–2009. Shanghai has become a headquarters location for brand-name firms and a center for chip manufacturing, the high end of the technology "food chain." In Guangdong Province, a manufacturing-centered development path was based on low-wage production of components and contract manufacturing. There is now massive pressure from major industrial areas in inner China, such as Chongqing, Xian, and Chengdu, the capital of Sichuan Province. These areas want to attract large-scale IT production, a policy given high priority by the Chinese national government.

Competition between locations is developing in China like that between high-tech regions in industrialized countries and emerging economies in low-cost countries. China's status as a key location for manufacturing in the global electronics industry is not in question, but there is new competition between regions in China. Foxconn's large-scale relocation scheme described earlier highlights this development. Whether these relocations will result in further "races to the bottom" in social and environmental standards or will create "competition for upgrading" within China remains speculative. To answer this question, one must look at the working and employment conditions for the new industrial workforce in contract manufacturing and determine whether workers' skills, social status, and migration status are stabilized and upgraded as well (see chapter 4).

EASTERN EUROPE—LOW-COST LOCATION FOR THE EUROPEAN MARKET

The electronics industry in the European states of the Eastern Bloc historically served military defense needs during the arms race with the West. Vertically integrated government-owned companies dominated and often encompassed the entire industry of their respective countries. Companies such as Videoton in Hungary or Mera and Unitra in Poland employed as many as one hundred thousand employees. Electronics became a symbol for the growing technological gap between West and East. During the 1970s, Eastern European countries raised cheap credit on global financial markets to modernize and reconvert their national industries, creating a short-lived Eastern European "economic miracle." However, the "computerization of the country" (Poland) or the "completion of the microelectronics revolution" (German Democratic Republic) did not take place, not least because of the global economic downturn during the 1970s. Cheap credit became massive debt burdens. Cautiously established contacts with Western companies were ended in the early 1980s, following the Soviet Union's invasion of Afghanistan and the coup d'état against the Solidarność movement in Poland. Some large-scale projects to expand national technology and manufacturing bases in the chip and computer industries slowed down or were abandoned—especially in East Germany and Czechoslovakia, the two most developed industrial economies. This further widened the technology gap.

After the political upheaval of 1989, national electronics industries declined rapidly, at different speeds in various countries, but with massive layoffs everywhere. Only fragments were left of the former combinations, or national enterprises, typically in computer manufacturing and defense electronics. Eastern-central Europe became primarily a market for Western multinationals, particularly in consumer electronics, where Western European markets had been stagnant. In Poland, sales by domestic electronics firms dropped by 50 percent between 1990 and 1991 (Radosevic 2002, 2) in areas such as audio and video equipment. Only imported products were available at the time, as a report from the Polish foreign investment agency stated (PAIZ 2001, 10). At the same time, some Western brand-name firms quickly acquired prime quality pieces of Eastern European factories and established their own production facilities in order to secure their market presence in the region. Among the investors of the early 1990s were Philips (in Hungary and Poland) and Samsung (particularly in Hungary). In addition, Western investors often received preferential treatment in contracts for modernizing infrastructure such as telecommunications, which had a further negative impact on the domestic electronics industry in the Eastern countries (Havas 1998). As a result, Western electronics manufacturers rapidly became the dominant players in most countries in Eastern Europe.

This development was caused not only by economic factors, particularly the huge need for capital and the hope for rapid modernization driven by foreign capital. There was also a political purpose—the expansion of the European Union. Eastern European candidate countries had to provide major concessions, eliminating tariffs protecting national industries and opening up for foreign investors. It was made clear that EU membership did not include the harmonization of labor and social policies. On the contrary: a newly created special status was assigned to Eastern European countries, with lower subsidies for economic development from the EU that could be withdrawn in case of "lack of progress" in meeting the conditions for adherence. For labor markets, open borders were denied. Linking economic opening with continuing inequality in labor and social policies became the hallmark of the EU's political strategy, giving full priority to monetary stability and international competitiveness. The EU's traditional principle of achieving equal social and political conditions within its territory was reinterpreted as upholding differences between regions keeping their distinctive "competitive advantages" (Krätke 2005, 88). This orientation primarily served the interests of transnational corporations, widely analyzed in the relevant literature (Ziltener 2003, 19–20). Regions are still encouraged to use differences in social, labor, and fiscal policies to achieve economic restructuring, promoting Eastern European countries as low-wage economies (Bohle 2003, 19–20).

Competition between locations receives massive support from the EU. Many Eastern European countries not only offer low land costs but also favorable tax policies, often in special economic zones designated for foreign investors. The generous tax breaks have raised concerns across Europe, with public criticism of some new member states by the European Commission and a commitment to eliminate long-term tax subsidies. These promises were made shortly before the first group of new member states from Eastern Europe joined the EU in May 2004. Negotiations were conducted behind closed doors on the continuation and even expansion of tax incentives and special economic zones until 2017 (Sepp and Wrobel 2003, 284). In the course of this process, some major contract manufacturers in the electronics industry, such as Flextronics and Sanmina-SCI, had threatened publicly to withdraw from certain Eastern European countries should existing regulations be changed (Poschmann 2004, 6). Although such a position was unpopular in most Eastern European countries (including local management in the respective companies), the tax incentives finally were upheld (2005 interview data).

To what extent can the globally controlled electronics industry in Eastern Europe still be considered a "national" asset of the respective countries? Academic research has emphasized that industrial traditions established before 1989 (sometimes dating back to the 1920s) were an important "pull" factor for investment in the electronics industries of Eastern European countries after the collapse of the iron curtain (Linden 1998, 22ff.). Poland, for instance, had a strong base in the production of traditional TV vacuum tubes, which made the country the number one target for foreign direct investment in TV set manufacturing. Highly developed chip production in Czechoslovakia triggered massive foreign investment during the second half of the 1990s. Hungary had a long history of diversified electronics manufacturing. But after the initial waves of investment from foreign brand-name multinationals, they rapidly reorganized production, using Eastern European manufacturing sites primarily as an "extended assembly line" for labor-intensive products. This caused a massive downsizing of indigenous resources for industrial modernization (Havas 1998). This process was decisively supported by EU policies intended to extend maquiladora-style "passive" manufacturing services in Eastern Europe (Pellegrin 1998).

In critical social sciences, these developments led to an analysis of Eastern Europe as "Europe's new periphery" (Neunhöffer and Schüttelpelz

2002). Our analysis of electronics contract manufacturing, however, does not support concepts like peripheralization. Rather, the short history of contract manufacturing reveals a remarkably rapid development of world-market-oriented industry. The development of different locations and national economies is an integral part of European and global constellations of economic competition.

Expansion during the Boom: The Development of Contract Manufacturing in Central and Eastern Europe after 1997

With its emergence as a model of globalized mass production, electronics contract manufacturing developed rapidly in Europe, although initially almost exclusively in Western Europe. After 1992, North American contract manufacturers began to take over manufacturing facilities of established brand-name firms in Western Europe. IBM's circuit board manufacturing plant in Bordeaux was sold to Solectron in 1992. Solectron also took over manufacturing from Philips in Dunfermline, Scotland, in 1993. Jabil opened its first production site in Europe in this region in the same year.

From the beginning, contract manufacturers set their sights on low-cost locations, particularly in Wales, Scotland, and Ireland. The United Kingdom and Ireland had a reputation for aggressively attracting foreign capital to less developed rural or older industrial areas affected by massive closures of traditional industries such as steel and coal mining. These policies had considerable success, with massive investment from US and Japanese electronics manufacturers during the early 1990s. Ireland primarily used low taxes as an incentive (as the first European country to have abolished corporate income tax). Britain developed extensive support for foreign investors at national and local levels. In addition, both countries had a reputation for strong deregulation of labor markets and employer-friendly labor laws (2004 interview data; Hilpert 2002).

Eastern Europe did not attract great interest from contract manufacturers during the first half of the 1990s. Elcoteq from Finland, the first major European EMS company, opened a manufacturing plant early in 1992 in Tallinn, the capital of Estonia. Before 1997, North American contract manufacturers focused on gradual expansion of their production networks in Western Europe, aiming at acquisition of higher-end production resources. In 1995, for instance, Flextronics acquired the former production plant for raw printed circuit boards from Hewlett-Packard, a technologically sophisticated facility on HP's main European campus near Stuttgart, Germany.

This picture changed significantly after 1997, with the boom of the so-called *New Economy*. Demand for computers, game consoles, and particularly mobile phones grew enormously, creating serious capacity shortages in manufacturing. At the same time, major European brand-name firms started outsourcing complete production processes. Ericsson transferred important parts of its manufacturing organization to Flextronics in 1997, particularly its integrated manufacturing site in Karlskrona (Sweden). That was followed by further handovers of several other smaller operations in Sweden and France to Flextronics and Solectron in the following years. In Germany in 1999, Siemens sold its manufacturing of telephone branch exchanges to Vogt Electronics, a German medium-sized electronics company vying to enter EMS contract manufacturing. In 2000 and 2001, French telecommunications producer Alcatel made headlines, handing several important production facilities in France to contract manufacturers. US corporations such as Motorola transferred production in Europe to contract manufacturers (Celestica and Solectron, in particular) while at the same time Motorola was collecting heavy government subsidies for a new facility in Flensburg, a deindustrialized former port and shipbuilding town in northern Germany. Finally, in 2001, Ericsson decided to hand over all mobile phone manufacturing worldwide to Flextronics, becoming the first fully outsourced company among European telecommunications vendors (see Lüthje, Schumm, and Sproll 2002).

Eastern Europe started to benefit from the outsourcing boom. The locations taken over in Western Europe were mostly older ones, with longstanding manufacturing traditions, that were then operated by relatively unknown contract manufacturers. In Eastern Europe, "greenfield investments" dominated. New production facilities were built in western and southern Hungary, Poland, the Czech Republic, and Estonia, which soon employed tens of thousands of people. Contract manufacturers became important players in national economies. Flextronics became Hungary's biggest private employer with more than ten thousand employees, dwarfing even wellknown auto multinationals such as Volkswagen in this role (ibid.). Figure 3.4 shows the centers of contract manufacturing in Eastern Europe.

Figure 3.4.   Locations of Contract Manufacturing in Eastern Europe

As table 3.7 shows in detail, numerous production sites emerged after 1997. Some locations developed capabilities beyond the assembly of printed circuit boards, the core of electronics contract manufacturing, as well as plastic parts and final assembly of products and systems. Some specialized in industrial electronics and the introduction of new products. Vertically integrated production facilities were built, facilities whose production portfolio went beyond mere assembly operations. Many sites also included tool and die manufacturing and maintenance shops. Different patterns of development emerged among contract manufacturers. Flextronics focused on its worldwide concept of industrial parks and integration between regional production facilities. Elcoteq simultaneously developed several production sites with relatively similar production portfolios in locations such as Romania and the Ukraine, which were less popular at that time.

The new sites in Eastern Europe were explicitly marketed as alternatives to the older Western European locations, including the low-cost sites in Wales or Ireland (2001 interview data). The future for Eastern European sites looked rosy. In Western Europe, new development was not widely perceived as a threat at first to established locations and their jobs, although production was relocated from the very beginning. Flextronics's factory in Sárvár, Hungary, for instance, grew with the transfer of manufacturing from Hewlett-Packard in Spain. Its Polish factory took over production from Sweden (a direct ferry even hauled trucks between the two cities in Sweden and Poland). The workers affected by such relocations were concerned, but the expectations of enormous market growth during that period produced growing orders, and most Western factories still had to hire workers as the transfer of production began (2005 interview data).

Public as well as academic debates on the subject were dominated by the idea of a mutually beneficial division of labor and "complementary specialization," in which less developed products would be manufactured in Eastern Europe and more complex, high-tech items in Western Europe (Kurz and Wittke 1998). Such complementary specialization was predicted in the strategic projections of contract manufacturers. Eastern Europe's role was clearly designed as volume production for the EU market, with low costs and flexible regulations. In its initial phase, this description indeed fit the reality of the new factories and industrial parks in Eastern Europe. They began their production with typical high-volume, low-mix products, particularly PCB and systems assembly. However, Eastern European factories were upgraded after only a few years, and by 2000, most sites were no longer simple mass-assembly locations.

Table 3.7. Locations of Contract Manufacturing in Eastern Europe 2007

Company	Location	Year	Production	Number of Employees
Celestica	Czech Republic (Ráječko, Kladno)	2003	PCBA	2,000
	Romania (Oradea)	2004		
Elcoteq	Estonia (Tallinn)	1992	PCBA, industry electronics, backplanes	3,500
	Russia (St. Petersburg)	2001	PCBA	1,500
	Hungary (Pécs)	1998	PCBA, industry electronics, NPI	5,000
	Romania (Arad)	2006		250
First International Computer (FIC) (ODM)	Czech Republic (Rudná)	2001	PCBA	n/a
Flextronics	Hungary (Zalaegerszeg, Sárvár, Nyíregyháza)	1997–1998	PCBA, industry electronics, SA, NPI	9,000
	Ukraine (Mukacheve)	2004	PCBA	2,000
	Poland (Tczew)	2000	Industry electronics, PCBA, backplanes, NPI	2,500
	Czech Republic (Kladno)	2007	PCBA	1,000

Foxconn	Czech Republic (Pardubice)	2003	PCBA	5,000
	Hungary (Komárom)	2004	PCBA	2,700
Jabil	Ukraine (Uzhhorod)	2007	PCBA	2500
	Poland (Kwidzyn)	2002	PCBA	2,000
	Hungary (Vác, Szombathely, Tiszaújváros)	2004	PCBA, backplanes	3,000
Sanmina-SCI	Hungary (Székesfehérvár, Miskolc, Tatabánya)	2000	PCBA, box build	
Solectron	Hungary (Budapest)	1998	NPI	1,000
	Romania (Timișoara)	2000	PCBA	3,000
	Czech Republic (Plzeň)		n/a	n/a
Videoton	Hungary (Székesfehérvár)		PCBA	1,500
	Romania	2002	PCBA	3,000

PCBA = Printed circuit board assembly
NPI = New product introduction
SA = Systems assembly

In the initial conception, these locations were planned as subunits of Western lead factories. Western sites, many of them close to border regions, provided the bulk of management. They were also in charge of customer relations, purchasing management, and logistics. Product introduction and prototyping were initially located in the West as well. Only mature products and processes ready for "stable" volume manufacturing would be transferred to the Eastern plants. Elcoteq's facilities in Estonia were managed in this way from Finland, Flextronics's Hungarian facilities from Austria, and Solectron's site in Romania from three Western European plants in Germany, Scotland, and France (2002 and 2005 interview data).

All Eastern European sites under investigation in this study developed rapidly from branch plants managed from outside into relatively integrated factories with a broad spectrum of productive functions, including equipment maintenance, tool and die making, procurement, inventory management, and logistics. Within the hierarchical corporate structure of contract manufacturers, production was organized and controlled by local management. Eastern European sites increasingly played a role in the design of electronic and nonelectronic components and in product introduction. Half a decade after the opening of the first facilities in Eastern Europe, management of Eastern European sites felt their capabilities were equal to those of most sites west of the former iron curtain (2003, 2005 interview data).

Global Integration with Minor Regional Effects of Modernization

Upgrading the technology and organization of contract manufacturing sites in Eastern Europe did not engender a related modernization of the respective regions and their national economies. The often-heard notion of "cathedrals in the desert" (initially coined for new factories in Italy's *mezzogiorno* regions) also fits contract manufacturing plants in Eastern Europe. In many locations, roads and other new infrastructure were built to serve the factories, and in some areas cooperation developed between contract manufacturers and technical colleges, or new training centers were created. But the expectation by local political actors of networking between high-tech manufacturing and existing indigenous capabilities mostly remained unfulfilled.

Like any other region, contract manufacturing in Eastern Europe is part of an essentially global structure of production. Flextronics's manufacture of mobile phones for Ericsson is a good example. After the complete takeover of this production segment from Ericsson in 2001, Flextronics managed the complete production and logistics chain for Ericsson's main market, Europe. For this purpose, Flextronics set up a final assembly and delivery plant in Hungary (called a *fulfillment center* in industry lingo), providing final configuration, packaging, and shipping for up to seven million mobile phones per year. This facility received the prefabricated hardware devices without the software (called *dummies*) from the Flextronics industrial park in Zhuhai (South China) and its assembly plant in Shah Alam (Malaysia). Both were taken over from Ericsson. PCB and final product assembly were carried out in Asia, including the production of plastic shells and parts. The highly sophisticated printed circuit boards were also manufactured in Zhuhai. Specialized engineering know-how was provided from Flextronics's PCB manufacturing site in Stuttgart, Germany. The dummy devices were shipped by air cargo to Hungary via the Vienna airport, where the software was added according to the requirements of the final customers, mobile phone operators, or electronics retail chains. After packaging, the devices were shipped by a Dutch trucking firm under contract from Flextronics to fifteen different countries in Europe (Lüthje and Sproll 2003; 2005 interview data).

Similar and equally complex international divisions of labor exist for many other high-volume consumer products. In Flextronics's production of ink-jet printers for Hewlett-Packard, the Hungarian site also has the role of a fulfillment center for the European market. Foxconn has its main focus in Eastern Europe on the Czech Republic, where the Taiwanese company established production facilities in Pardubice in 2000, later expanding to Kutná Hora. Since then, PCs, notebooks, and servers have been assembled for clients in the European market from parts delivered from Foxconn's Asian operations. Its factory in Kutná Hora is one of the biggest PC assembly facilities worldwide. Foxconn also repairs products for companies such as Apple, Acer, and HP at these facilities. Because of its special position, the proportion of exported products from Eastern European contract manufacturing plants is extraordinarily high, in most cases reaching 95 percent. This is significantly higher than for most other multinational companies producing in Eastern Europe (usually between 70 and 90 percent). Even where contract manufacturers produce for brand-name firms providing infrastructure equipment for the respective countries (such as in Poland), the export quota is still around 65 percent (2003 interview data). In the Czech Republic, Foxconn became the second biggest exporter, accounting for about 3.7 percent of the country's exports in 2008, trailing only Volkswagen's Skoda subsidiary. Eastern Europe plays the same role as a transnational delivery center as Malaysia does for many production segments in Asia.

Local suppliers, however, make only a low contribution to contract production of this kind in Eastern Europe, usually not more than 3–5 percent of value added. Local supplies typically include technologically unsophisticated goods, such as office supplies, paper, and packaging materials, as well as auxiliary services such as cafeterias or food supplies. The role of Eastern European providers in delivery logistics is minor. Only in Romania are a number of smaller trucking firms competitive on the basis of very low wages, high flexibility, and low truck-leasing rates (2005 interview data). On the other hand, communication and cooperation within the corporate organizations of contract manufacturers is highly transnational. There is constant contact with the other European and global production sites to ensure smooth production, coordination of production volumes, and transfer of machinery and skilled personnel. Permanent contact is also maintained with transnational brand-name customers. The unequal development of local and global networking relations in day-to-day operations highlights the fact that contract manufacturers are primarily internationalized and do not act "locally" or "nationally."

National and regional governments in Eastern Europe have developed various programs to encourage transnational industrial investments to spill over into the regions. In Hungary a national scheme, known as the Széchenyi Plan, was launched in 1999, aiming at better integration of local industries with transnational production. Such programs usually have little effect, however. In Poland there are no sanctions for international investors that do not keep their commitments to local governments for infrastructure construction, education, or involvement of local suppliers. Local government agencies often are happy that jobs were created at all. Promises by contract manufacturers to support local suppliers did not engender significant increases. A major European EMS company set a target of raising the proportion of local suppliers to 15 percent of local value added between 2002 and 2005. This goal was never reached—local supplies remained at 5 percent at the end of the period. Strategic decisions about the "approved vendor lists" of contract manufacturers were not made in the region but followed the global arrangements between brand-name firms and contract manufacturers in spite of frequent dissatisfaction among local management (2005 interview data).

The governments of special economic zones and national ministries lack power over transnational corporations. Reclaiming ground for local initiative is often not even discussed at the conceptual level. Rather, regional development programs end up nowhere, although "cluster formation" is commonly mentioned as a leitmotif of industrial development. Therefore, the following analysis also can be applied to the case of contract manufacturing:

> According to the definition, clusters are characterized by intensive cooperation, companies in clusters operate in tight networks. As for Hungarian industrial districts, there are no intensive linkages among firms, or among firms and institutions. In the Hungarian growth-poles the co-located branch plants of multinational companies operate isolated from each other. (Szalavetz 2004, 24; for an earlier conceptual critique of cluster formation in Eastern Europe, see Tatur 1998)

From the Crisis of the New Economy to the Crisis of Contract Manufacturing in Europe

The year 2001 marked the end of the IT industry boom called the New Economy and a major turning point in the development of the industry as a whole. Accelerated restructuring and relocation of production were accompanied by significantly lower growth rates, with massive effects on the contract manufacturing sector in both Western and Eastern Europe.

In *Western Europe*, contract manufacturing increased mergers and acquisitions, responding to accelerated outsourcing among brand-name companies. Nokia's network equipment division had been relatively resistant to large-scale outsourcing. But under the pressure of the global downturn in 2001, the company sold two factories for network switching equipment in the United Kingdom and Sweden to contract manufacturer Sanmina-SCI. At the same time, contract manufacturers significantly reduced capacity, causing massive redundancies and closures of facilities, many of them acquired only a short time before. Among the factories closed were Ericsson's former facilities in Östersund, Sweden (acquired by Solectron in 1997 and closed in 2001), and Kumla, Sweden (acquired by Flextronics in 2001 and closed in early 2002). Jabil took over several sites of Britain's Marconi, once an icon of long-distance communications technology, and closed its Liverpool facility after a year. The remaining production was transferred to another factory in Coventry, which also was closed in 2003. In France, Flextronics bought Alcatel's factory in Lunéville in April 2001 and closed it in November of the same year, while acquiring another factory from Alcatel in the city of Laval.

The parallel strategies of acquisition and downsizing were a desperate effort by contract manufacturers to consolidate their market positions under conditions of massive overproduction and industry-wide consolidation. These strategies were only partially successful in Europe. Some contract manufacturers, such as Jabil, survived the crisis relatively well. Others ended up in a downward spiral of permanent restructuring. At Solectron, restructuring and layoffs became a never-ending story after 2001, resulting in the closure of three out of four facilities in France and the continuing transfer of production to Eastern Europe. During 2001 alone, Solectron laid off five thousand people in France. After a series of downsizing agreements with employee representatives, the affected factories were finally closed in 2002 and 2004. In 2004, Solectron's last remaining French facility in Bordeaux faced massive difficulties. A seventh downsizing agreement since 2001 led the French media to ask sarcastically whether this one would be the last (Le Monde, September 1, 2005). Elsewhere in Europe, the once fast-growing, low-cost regions in Western Europe—Scotland, Wales, and Ireland—were also hit. Solectron closed two plants in Ireland in 2001 and 2002. Its facility in Dunfermline, Scotland, was downsized to a workforce of just three hundred (2003, 2005 interview data).

Winner or Loser? Eastern Europe in the Reorganization of the Global Division of Labor

Beyond individual companies, the model of EMS contract manufacturing as a whole experienced massive pressure in the wake of the 2001–2002 recession. This was caused by the new outsourcing strategies in the IT industry, related to the ascent of the ODM model and the simultaneous shift of the epicenter of large-scale contract manufacturing to East Asia. In Europe, this global shift was not very well understood by politicians, trade unions, and researchers. Western European media portrayed the shift of manufacturing to Eastern Europe as the major cause of the large-scale job losses in electronics. Headlines in British newspapers claimed, "Jabil Betrays Coventry as 400 Jobs Go to Hungary," or "We Lose All Our Jobs to Hungary and Romania," referring to the plant closure by Jabil and Sanmina-SCI in early 2003.

At first glance, this picture seemed to be true. In Eastern Europe, another series of factories opened after 2001. Jabil opened one in Poland (in 2001, with expansion in 2002) and another in Hungary (in 2002). Celestica built one in Romania in 2004. In addition, Foxconn invested US$82.55 million in its operations in Pardubice and employed 2,248 people until 2006. Its investment in Eastern Europe after the crisis of 2001 also included Hungary. After Foxconn had invested US$80 million in the production of spare parts for Nokia mobile phones in 2002, the company decided to increase investment by US$120 million in 2005 (Tubilewicz 2007, 69ff.). It seemed that the "new" East was successfully competing against what was called "old Europe," as US neoconservatives claimed during those years. The Eastern European proportion of electronics contract manufacturing rose significantly. At the beginning of the 1990s, less than an eighth of the relevant production volumes were generated in Eastern Europe. That rose to about one third during the boom of the late 1990s and to one half in 2003 (Radosevic 2004).

Such perceptions neglect the global dimensions of industrial reorganization and the related shifts in the international division of labor. Eastern European production sites felt the consequent insecurity constantly in the factories. During 2004 and 2005, only a limited number of facilities in Eastern Europe were running at full capacity. At Elcoteq's big plant in Estonia, relocation of production engendered continual growth of the workforce. Flextronics production sites in eastern Hungary reported high-capacity utilization during that period (with four daily work shifts during peak periods) due to relocating production from England and western Hungary. These locations confirmed the perception of Eastern Europe as a "winner" region (2004, 2005 interview data).

Most locations under investigation in this book, however, suffered from the loss of most large customers in the wake of the 2001 breakdown, and the long-term impact was felt over the following years. Many local managers in the EMS industry saw the existence of their facilities threatened. Orders from significant customers, such as Kodak, HP, Alcatel, Thomson Multimedia, and Motorola were not replaced by contracts at similar volumes. Purchasing systems were reorganized globally by these first-tier brand-name customers (see chapter 2). Manufacturing orders were therefore relocated globally as well, often shifting to Taiwanese EMS or ODM manufacturers. The shift to ODM production models in particular had a massive impact on the production base of contract manufacturing in Eastern Europe since most ODM producers had only relatively small operations in that region. Only one EMS producer from Taiwan, Foxconn, opened major new facilities in Eastern Europe—a large final assembly plant in Pardubice in the Czech Republic, with approximately four thousand workers, and a campus in Komárom, Hungary, mostly working for Nokia, with three thousand employees. These facilities were designed for relatively limited product assembly (final assembly of computers in the case of Pardubice, modules for cell phones in the case of Komárom) with little vertical integration.

Under the impact of those changes, many production facilities in Eastern Europe remained idle, even once the IT industry recovered after 2003. Ample internal restructuring reflected the downsizing of former high-volume production sites. In many facilities, only a limited number of production lines were in operation. Production operations often became more fragmented as high-volume manufacturing on long assembly lines was converted to smaller units doing limited assembly. Massive layoffs resulted from this development, in some locations affecting several thousand employees, as factories felt further pressure to flexibilize employment (2004, 2005 interview data).

In Hungary, the decline of production in major contract manufacturing facilities was one of the driving factors for sudden public debate on the "exit of the multinationals." The debate was highlighted by the relocations of well-known brand-name firms, such as IBM, Philips, and Kenwood, to European countries farther east or to East Asia. Epcos, a spin-off from German multinational Siemens, shifted major production of electronic components for mobile phones from western Hungary to Croatia (Verseck 2003). The most spectacular case of this kind was the closure of IBM's big manufacturing facility for hard disk drives in Székesfehérvár in 2002. This plant was part of IBM's worldwide production organization, with facilities in San Jose (California), Mainz (Germany), Guadalajara (Mexico), and Singapore. With growth spurred by relocations from the German facility, IBM used the former Hungarian electronics combinate Videoton as a contract manufacturer, giving rise to hopes locally that a Hungarian enterprise would become a significant international player in contract manufacturing. But with IBM's exit from manufacturing, Videoton had to lay off the majority of its employees (2004, 2005 interview data).

In Poland, the situation was somewhat different. Flextronics's once high-flying expansion plans for its manufacturing campus in Gdańsk never materialized. Employment growth remained well below initial projections from the late 1990s. Workers were laid off during the recession. The expansion plans had been based on the expectation of rapid growth in production of base stations and other equipment for third-generation mobile phone networks, known in Europe as universal mobile telecommunications systems (UMTSs). As the expectations of major European telecom operators crumbled after the financial bubble behind the boom burst (see chapter 2), Flextronics had to drastically reduce its growth projections for its industrial park in Poland. In spring 2003, only two of the five manufacturing buildings initially planned had been built, and one was half empty. By 2005 the facility finally reached full capacity, employing 2,600 workers (2003, 2005 interview data).

Electronics contract manufacturing as a whole lost capacity and significance in Europe. Production volume and employment were cut back in Western Europe in the wake of downsizing and were relocated to only a limited extent in Eastern Europe. Again, Solectron's sites in Hungary and Romania benefitted from the transfer of production from France, Great Britain, and Sweden in the wake of the recession. Employment in Hungary rose from 1,300 to 3,000 between 2001 and 2002 (2002 interview data). The continuing downsizing in Solectron's Western European facilities, however, did not produce employment growth in the years after that. Rather, massive layoffs occurred in Eastern Europe as well. In Romania, six hundred employees lost their jobs in 2005 (2005 interview data).

Eastern Europe was a "successful" competitor against Western Europe, but it was also affected simultaneously by global competition through the ongoing relocation of production to Asia, especially China. Often relocation went along with a shift of customers to ODM production models and their respective providers from Taiwan. The Flextronics factory in Brno (Czech Republic), with a projected workforce of 3,500, was closed, when all orders were lost to ODM companies from Taiwan (2005 interview data). Eastern European locations lost their recently won function as mass-production bases for the European market to China. In the global reorganization of the production network for the Microsoft Xbox (chapters 2 and earlier in this chapter), production lines in Flextronics's industrial park in Sárvár, Hungary, were removed only a few months after they had been set up with great fanfare in the fall of 2001. According to the local management, the resulting mass layoffs affected 2,100 workers. In the same location, the configuration and delivery center for cell phones from Ericsson was also later closed, and production was shifted to Shah Alam, Malaysia, and China (2005 interview data).

In 2008 the worldwide economic crisis had deep effects on the operations of EMS companies in Eastern Europe. To counteract the severe drop in customer orders, EMS companies slashed employment at the beginning of 2009. Up to 25 percent of the jobs were cut back using the flexibility provided by massive employment of contract workers. The severity of the crisis led to the layoff of regular blue-collar and even white-collar employees. Although these job cuts were fast and radical, EMS companies started to reemploy people as soon as the order situation brightened. Flextronics and Jabil announced a substantial need for additional staff by mid-2009. The overall trend of moving operations to the east was reinforced by the crisis, as most EMS companies, with the exception of Elcoteq, established or expanded successful operations in Romania, Ukraine, and Russia. Flextronics operations in Timişoara, Romania, were inherited from the Solectron takeover. In August 2009, the company officially stated that it regarded these operations as strategic and located and expanded its NPI operations, special business solutions, and even some design capabilities there. Celestica transferred parts of its production from Ráječko, in the Czech Republic, to its facility in Oradea, Romania. This production transfer was allegedly due to a customer request aimed at further cost savings. Both Wistron and Foxconn started to restructure their businesses by diversifying their production from a focus on PCs and notebooks to LCD monitors and TVs. Foxconn also began reworking its regional division of labor in Eastern Europe by moving the assembly of Acer notebooks from the Czech Republic to its newly acquired operations in Székesfehérvár, Hungary, while planning for expansion of its Czech operations.

Management Strategies for Survival in Eastern Europe

Eastern Europe's catch-up was scrambled. The growth benefits from deregulation and liberalization predicted by neoliberal economists did not materialize. Local management in contract manufacturing facilities then made considerable efforts to reposition Eastern European locations as competitors with China and Asia. Eastern European plant managers voiced massive discontent over the centralized corporate decision making. It was often said that the major cost parameters of such decisions were false and that the flexibility and quality of shipments from Asia was substandard: "The quality we get from Asia is simply five times worse than in Europe. This is incredible. We produce telephones with a failure rate of 0.3 to 0.6 percent, from Asia we get them with 5 percent. That means out of one hundred phones five have to be rejected, go away, they are kaputt. . . . And we must ship this with such a bad quality. It is incredible" (2005 interview).

There were two strategies to strengthen Eastern Europe as an alternative to China: on the one hand, local management tried to minimize costs by shifting production to less developed regions and countries to take advantage of lower labor costs in eastern Hungary, Romania, and the Ukraine. On the other hand, specialization on lower volume and niche products was promoted, hoping for competitive advantages by serving the needs of customers in the region. Local management eyed brand-name firms that had already shifted major production to China and wanted to relocate some portions to Europe for higher quality or market proximity (2005 interview data).

In 1998 Flextronics opened a new site in eastern Hungary, citing rapidly rising wages in the western part of the country, where unemployment had been wiped out by the huge demand for labor from foreign multinationals. The new low-wage sites were considered more appropriate for simple products and processes. Production of higher value-added products would remain in western Hungary. In 2005 only the sites in eastern Hungary were running at full capacity, while the plants in western Hungary had difficulties. Production in eastern Hungary benefitted from the use of low-cost suppliers in neighboring Ukraine. That country's "orange revolution" and the related opening to the West led to cross-country industrial parks along the border under unified management. Ukraine appeared particularly attractive as an alternative to Asia, since the country was to join the EU in the near future and wages would remain low (2005 interview data).

The achievements of these relocation strategies made local managers cautiously optimistic. Hewlett-Packard, for instance, had ink-jet printers assembled by Flextronics in Sárvár, western Hungary, for several years but then began to consider relocation to China. Cost reductions due to relocation to the eastern Hungarian-Ukrainian industrial park saved printer assembly in Hungary for a few extra years. Production was finally shifted to China in 2005, however. The low-cost locations in eastern Hungary were far from safe. In February 2006, almost one thousand workers were laid off in Flextronics's Nyíregyháza facility, officially because of seasonal fluctuations in production. In the wake of Hewlett-Packard's exodus, the plant obviously faced difficulties in reemploying those workers (2005, 2006 interview data).

Efforts to convince multinational brand-name firms to locate large-volume contracts in Eastern Europe mostly failed. The local management of contract manufacturers tried to replace big customers with large numbers of small companies. The portfolio of products and processes resulting from this development ranges from specialized repair services to assembly and packaging, and from special shipping logistics all the way to analysis of tariff regulations to determine favorable locations for smaller production batches, choosing between facilities in the EU and China. The key concept underlying such strategies was to move configuration close to final customers and markets, leveraging geographical proximity. Respecialization resulted in substantially lower work volumes, however. One Flextronics facility in western Hungary, formerly specialized in mass production, had seventy-five products for more than thirty customers during the winter of 2005 with relatively high-capacity utilization, according to the local trade union (2006 interview data).

In another facility, a large order from Danish toy maker Lego saved the plastic injection molding operation from closure in 2005. Large redundancies were made just a year later, as the conversion from electronics to plastic building blocks did not turn out to be a growth business (2005 interview data, 2006–2007 company information). In 2008, Lego ended the relationship with Flextronics and relocated production of building blocks and other toy elements (a volume of twenty billion pieces per year) to factories under its own management in eastern Europe, Mexico, and Denmark. Lego still calls intermittent outsourcing a success, but it later admitted that it shifted production to contract manufacturers to learn how to utilize facilities in Eastern European low-cost locations. It was not a long-term manufacturing partnership. A Lego spokesperson explained in a media interview, "Our partner has helped us to shift production to cheap regions such as Hungary or the Czech Republic. This was important. But then it turned out that they could not run the plants more efficiently and better than we can ourselves" (SZ, September 28, 2009).

Precarious Upgrading

Whatever the immediate result of the small-batch strategy in Eastern Europe, massive competition between locations in Eastern Europe and China has paradoxical implications. As facilities are threatened, their capabilities and the skills of their workers seem to move upward. With the growing number of smaller customers, technological, logistical, and organizational complexity of production is growing. Individual sites have to meet a much greater diversity of customer needs. Most products in small-batch production undergo permanent improvement while "on the line." On the other hand, the margin for failure shrinks, since mistakes or delays may result in immediate cancellation of production contracts (2005 interview data).

This situation produced significant modernization of production technology. Considerable investment was made in testing equipment, complementing manual control procedures and visual inspection of printed circuit boards with sophisticated optical equipment. In PCB assembly, multifunctional placement machines were introduced, allowing assembly of six or eight different types of printed circuit boards in one production run. The smaller volume resulted in a more flexible work organization, in order to facilitate frequent product changes and reprogram control software and manufacturing logistics. Production lines were organized along lines of customers or customer groups and structured as cost centers. Almost every site in our investigation had greatly improved quality management programs (2005 field dates; see chapter 4). One of the most unexpected consequences of restructuring was sudden labor shortages, which appeared in spite of general downsizing. The massive deindustrialization of many regions in Eastern Europe, the closure of professional vocational schools and technical colleges, and widespread emigration, especially of skilled workers, produce ongoing bottlenecks in the supply of an appropriate workforce (2005 interview data).

This paradoxical situation, between downsizing on the one hand and accelerated upgrading on the other, marks the end of the Eastern European EMS factories' short journey from dependent mass-production sites, led from outside, to full-fledged manufacturing centers within global production systems. As was the case in Mexico and Malaysia after the end of the New Economy boom, Eastern Europe displays what we have called insecure or precarious upgrading. The situation in Eastern Europe is somewhat unique, since respecialization has been driven by smaller and highly diverse manufacturing volumes. The road to the flexible model of high-volume production (high-volume, high-mix), used in the more successful factories in Malaysia, has been blocked for Eastern Europe. The problem of the region's relatively small manufacturing volumes, as global production is recentralized, is exacerbated by the lack of local cross-linkages with mass production in other segments of the electronics industry and by the absence of government efforts to develop a more integrated manufacturing base. Eastern Europe has been left out of the global restructuring of production that resulted from the rapid development of ODM production.

The international division of labor between Western and Eastern Europe remains highly unstable. As Michael Faust, Ulrich Voskamp, and Volker Wittke (2004, 72–73) aptly state, complementary division of labor existed to some degree in the early stages of relocation during the mid- and late 1990s. Since then, the industrial division of labor has been in flux. Developments in the wake of the 2008 global financial crisis seem to confirm this. The role of Western European operations is increasingly weak due to massive downsizing during the financial crisis. Flextronics alone, with the most intensive presence in both Western and Eastern Europe, shut down four locations in Western Europe, consolidated two locations in Germany (Paderborn and Herrenberg) into one, and reduced employment in two more.

Flextronics emphasizes the strategic character of its operations in Timişoara, Romania, which points to substantial upgrading of this plant as an independent location. If it is integrated in the company's worldwide division of labor, it may be able to move away from being a remotely managed high-volume, low-mix assembly operation. Timişoara has developed into an integrated location, performing high- and low-volume, high-mix production and end-to-end manufacturing that includes prototyping and other engineering activities, such as design for manufacturing (DFM) and PCB layout design, as well as test development and new product introduction (2008 company information).

NOTES

1. For a comprehensive analysis of contract manufacturing in Brazil and Mexico, see Sproll 2010.

2. Foxconn's relocation process was accelerated by the tragic incidents at its factory compound in Shenzhen with the series of suicides among young migrant workers and the related worldwide media attention. After these incidents, the development of new factories was speeded up through the opening of two large plants in Zhengzhou in Henan Province and Chengdu in Sichuan. The latter factory became the major manufacturing site for Apple's iPad tablet computers and gained infamous publicity in the wake of a massive aluminum dust explosion in 2011, which, as widely reported in Chinese and international media, was caused by safety defects in the wake of the extremely rapid construction of the factory. Problems with aluminum dust have been flagged by the NGO SACOM for the Chengdu location prior to this incident. Note, however, that the suicides in Shenzhen were not the main reason for the relocation. Rather, Foxconn had designed this strategy as an answer to the rising labor and land costs in South China, in line with the Chinese government's increased efforts to develop manufacturing in inland locations in the wake of the 2008–2009 global financial crisis.

Chapter Four

Global Taylorism?

Work and Politics of Production in Low-Cost Locations

Electronics contract manufacturing as a system of global mass production includes far-reaching standardization of labor processes. This is a key element of this model of production and distinguishes it from other forms of modular or network-based mass production, for example, production in the automobile or garment industries. In this chapter, we analyze the way contract manufacturers try to achieve a globally uniform labor process by selecting and shaping certain production technologies and forms of work organization. We assess the extent to which these strategies are successful and examine the ways companies try to regulate and control work on the shop floor using specific national and regional labor policies. Our analysis is based on the assumption that global standardization of service portfolios, customer relationships, production processes, and logistics enables comprehensive standardization of labor processes. The social control and regulation of the labor process, however, takes place in the context of very different labor markets, industrial relations, labor migration, and ethnic and gender discrimination (Lüthje, Schumm, and Sproll 2002; see chapter 1).

We contend that the emergence of large IT contract manufacturing complexes has driven a massive expansion of neo-Taylorist forms of work, which are becoming particularly widespread in low-cost locations. Contract manufacturers are using standardized work systems in a similar fashion around the globe, making the parameters of economic and organizational efficiency widely comparable among locations in both developed and developing countries. Technology conditions appear highly uniform between locations since the same manufacturing systems and equipment are used throughout transnational production systems. Globalized neo-Taylorist work, however, needs to

151

be established politically and socially as well. Corporations, therefore, use local and national institutions to recruit the large numbers of workers required for mass production of this kind. The industrial relations of production systems within greenfield locations or free trade zones therefore often differ from normal industrial relations in these countries.

In this chapter, we first trace the organizational aspects of global labor standardization and its key elements within corporate organizations. Following this, extensive case studies examine the way shop-floor relationships are formed through national and regional regulations in various low-cost locations in Mexico, Malaysia, China, and Eastern Europe (focusing on Hungary and Poland). We look at the forms of control in shop-floor-based practices and conflicts of interest between labor and capital. The generic forms of work organization, social control, and labor policies are analyzed as specific production regimes. As explained in chapter 1, we distinguish three basic dimensions of regimes of production: *regimes of work* (work organization and quality management, including occupational safety and health), *regimes of employment* (wages and benefits, working hours, forms of workforce recruitment and training, and the underlying segmentations by gender, ethnicity, and migration status), and *regimes of control* (industrial relations at plant, regional, and industry levels, including relevant governmental policies). We look at company- and plant-based regimes of production in the broader context of the industrial relations systems and industrial and development policies in different countries.

"COMMON PROCESSES": THE GLOBAL STANDARDIZATION OF WORK IN ELECTRONICS CONTRACT MANUFACTURING

Work and employment practices in electronics contract manufacturing facilities around the world have some common characteristics that result from the industry segment's particular role within the IT sector. Although there are often massive differences among individual plants, companies, regions, and national states, the basic characteristics of the labor process are shaped by the typical "service orientation" of production work rarely found in comparable industries. The leading contract manufacturers use state-of-the-art technology in their assembly processes and in IT-based supply-chain management. Work organization in contract manufacturing did not emerge from specific innovations in production technology, however. Rather, the basic methods and processes are generalized throughout the electronics industry. Those in contract manufacturing do not differ significantly from those in more traditional areas and companies.

Electronics contract manufacturing is based on five basic work processes (for a detailed analysis, see Lüthje, Schumm, and Sproll 2002, 44ff.):

Assembly of printed circuit boards: Formerly performed exclusively on manual assembly lines, this "bread-and-butter" activity of electronics manufacturing has become highly automated since the 1980s. The process technology known as *surface mount technology* (SMT) is widely available and used in electronics factories around the world. Small electronics components, such as chips, resistors, and connectors, are mounted on printed circuit boards made of epoxy laminate. This work is performed by programmable precision machines that can place several thousand to ten thousand parts per hour. The placement machines are usually combined on assembly lines with soldering ovens of varying size and configuration, according to the requirements of the product, production volume, and quality management. Today most assembly processes can be automated, but manual assembly remains an integral part of the manufacturing process, particularly in low-cost locations. Manual assembly is used where an excessive amount of software programming would be required. It is used as well for mounting nonelectronic or "hybrid" components such as microphones or coils, or for flexible handling of frequently changing assembly jobs. Manual assembly classically consists of relatively simple, segmented work steps with minor training requirements. However, operators usually need several years of experience to gain multiple skills and to master special soldering, quality inspection, and testing procedures.

Final assembly and system configuration (also known as "box build"): Printed circuit boards are assembled with premanufactured components such as hard disk drives or displays, cables or connectors, and the plastic or metal enclosures into the final product. These production processes are usually not automated since manual labor is still the most flexible method for handling the disparate requirements for inserting preassembled components into enclosures, frames, and racks of different shapes. This kind of work is mostly organized along assembly lines, especially for high-volume products. Group work in the form of "assembly cells" is used for products of higher complexity, such as servers.

Manufacturing of raw printed circuit boards: As opposed to PCB assembly, the production of printed circuit boards themselves is a highly specialized process with many elements and stages of high complexity. They include the design of the circuitry, the production of various layers of the circuit board, metallization, lamination, galvanization, drilling of connection channels, and precision cutting at microscopic levels. Most of these tasks are skilled or semiskilled machine jobs. In up-to-date facilities, most of the chemical processes are performed in closed systems, a precondition for minimizing the considerable health and safety hazards of this work.

Manufacturing of metal parts and enclosures: This work is mostly performed by metal stamping and punching machinery of different sizes. The human component consists of semiskilled machine work at individual workstations with varying degrees of automation. Maintenance and tooling is performed by technicians or engineers. Work at stamping machines often includes physically demanding tasks, such as lifting heavy metal parts and enduring high noise levels, plus other health risks. Health hazards are also involved in spray painting metal parts and enclosures.

Manufacturing of plastic parts and enclosures: Production is performed by injection-molding machinery of varying size, with workplaces for individual operators. Technicians and engineers prepare and maintain the highly complex injection tools. Serious health hazards are caused by fumes, bonding substances, and paint, as well as the physical requirements of lifting heavy parts and tools.

Given the high degree of standardization of the work process, it is not surprising that the technological and organizational level of factories in low-cost locations is not very different from facilities in developed industrial countries. The emergence of large-scale, vertically integrated manufacturing leads to massive expansion of very modern production processes and work organization. Standardized mass production is accompanied by an increasing array of specialized products with small volume and prototyping operations. The considerable variety of metal, plastics, and cable supplies leads to the rapid differentiation of work processes. Significant sectors of skilled industrial work emerge, such as the maintenance of injection-molding tools.

Globally uniform work procedures and instructions throughout the companies have become a characteristic of contract manufacturing. These practices are also designed to ensure that factories of the same company appear uniform to the customers, encouraging the idea of global "one-stop shopping" in manufacturing services. During the 1990s, Solectron became a pioneer in this field. The company twice won the prestigious Malcolm Baldridge Award for quality manufacturing from the US Department of Commerce. It used the criteria from quality audits and certification procedures to create so-called common processes for work and management practices in Solectron facilities around the world. Many of those factories had been taken over from other companies with disparate management systems. Flextronics developed worldwide work standardization through a concept of material flow and quality control known as *demand flow technology* (DFT).

Quality management in electronics contract manufacturing is typically organized through quality teams on the shop floor, controlled by higher levels of management. Quality teams implement concepts of management and workplace discipline adapted from Japanese multinationals by Western consultants, such as the well-known Six Sigma system. Teamwork concepts based on autonomous decision making among workers do not exist in contract manufacturing. Assembly lines in contract manufacturing do not even practice the limited forms of job rotation in the Japanese "Toyota model," except for a few cell-based work concepts in final assembly.

Work in contract manufacturing is shaped by the service orientation in this type of production. It includes the following characteristics:

Relatively low wages: Particularly in emerging economies, wages and benefits are low, typically below the existing national standards for assembly work in older segments of the electronics industry. Bonuses and other performance-related pay, including profit-sharing schemes, are designed to ensure "customer orientation" among workers. Low base wages provide a strong incentive for overtime work.

Flexible employment: Frequent and often abrupt changes in production contracts and volumes require extensive employment flexibility. Such changes often produce precarious and insecure conditions for many production workers. Temporary and contract labor has become a common form of employment in low-cost locations such as Mexico and Eastern Europe and increasingly is being used in the United States and Europe.

A high proportion of women, migrant, and ethnic minority workers: In most areas of electronics assembly in industrialized and developing countries, most production workers are women. Contract manufacturers and most other new manufacturing companies in the IT industry (Lüthje 2001) tend to hire workers who are immigrants and racial minorities for lower-wage and insecure jobs. This is the case for Latin and Asian immigrant workers in the United States. In most low-cost locations, the employment of a workforce with these characteristics is possible because of complex systems of labor migration and ethnic, religious, and cultural division and discrimination.

Despite the fact that work is highly standardized, diverse work practices exist to varying degrees in many contract manufacturing companies. This is mostly a result of the rapid expansion of the industry during the 1990s, driven by a wave of acquisitions and mergers among the emerging industry leaders (see chapter 2). North American contract manufacturers in particular had to integrate the work practices of the numerous factories they took over from traditional electronics manufacturers that had entrenched corporate cultures (for details, see Lüthje, Schumm, and Sproll 2002). The stereotype of contract manufacturing as a "McDonald's strategy in production," often heard in industry circles, has to be viewed with caution. In fact, contract manufacturers continually try to integrate various production "philosophies" and "cultures" in the different locations of transnational production systems. The companies have accumulated considerable expertise in the integration of different employment systems.

MEXICO: HIGH-TECH PRODUCTION BEYOND *MAQUILADORAS*

Mexico, with its center of IT production, the city of Guadalajara, was a typical low-cost location when contract manufacturers started production in

1997. Within a very short time span, a number of large-scale factories were built, each with several thousand employees, producing for the North American market. Compared with other locations in this study, the swift construction of factories and the subsequent downturn of production and employment following the global recession 2001–2002 were particularly extreme. Contract manufacturing facilities in Guadalajara and other Mexican locations have been highly unstable. Factories expanded rapidly between the two recessions of 2001–2002 and 2008–2009. During that period, massive competitive pressure from rapidly growing factories in China eventually forced EMS factories in Mexico to upgrade and to rapidly expand production and employment.

Systems for controlling labor and employment mirror diverse economic and social conditions in Mexico and the country's integration into the North American market under NAFTA. The liberalization of the Mexican economy increased its dependence on the capitalist world market, creating problems and contradictions in labor policies. Mexican labor laws, historically a relatively strong framework regulating the workplace, were hardly enforced with multinational corporations, including contract manufacturers. Modern conditions of production were therefore accompanied by low wages, highly flexible employment, and oppressive labor policies. Mexican NGOs and grassroots labor groups have tried to challenge multinational contract manufacturers. Their influence on labor standards has been limited, but their initiatives have raised international awareness of labor issues in the electronics industry.

Regime of Work

Contract manufacturers in Mexico established highly modern facilities with state-of-the-art production equipment. Before the crisis of 2001, standard products of less complexity, such as PCs and printers for mass markets, were manufactured in large volumes. For this kind of production, relatively little engineering work was needed. Product development happened elsewhere, product changes were relatively infrequent, and the basic programming of assembly machines often were usable for several weeks.

This situation changed when large quantities of production were shifted to China, a development provoked by the downturn of 2001. High-volume standard products, such as cell phones, were still manufactured in Mexico, but they were augmented by products of higher complexity and value. Along with classical IT and telecommunications products, such as servers, routers, switching equipment, set-top boxes, cell phones, scanners, card readers, and copiers, the diversified product portfolio also included automotive, medical, and industrial electronics. This pushed the development of highly integrated and diversified production, including the capacity for product introduction, printed circuit board assembly, systems integration, logistics, repair services, and manufacturing of enclosures, cables, and backplanes (completely cabled and connected racks of equipment, such as servers).

This upgrading required a steep learning process within Mexican manufacturing sites and produced a broader use of information technology and improved quality management. The profile of the workforce changed, and the proportion of engineers increased. Data exchange during the early years of the 1990s was mostly carried out in traditional ways, by telephone and fax. Later, contract manufacturers rapidly adapted to the standards of global brand-name companies. They introduced higher-integration *electronic data interchange* (EDI) systems and data-network-based inventory systems such as VMI (*vendor-managed inventory*). In this system, components and parts used for manufacturing remain under the ownership of the suppliers, which take responsibility for managing inventories at the manufacturers' facilities. This optimizes use of the supply chain and enables just-in-time manufacturing.

Flextronics initially created a technology center in Guadalajara, which supports the specification of manufacturing processes, technologies, and materials at early stages of product development as well as the development of testing procedures. For Guadalajara, this was an important step beyond its status as an "extended assembly line," although the design of products was still performed in other locations. Product design capabilities do exist in Mexican contract manufacturing facilities but are not used because of strategic decisions by multinational brand-name customers, who prefer to use existing networks in their US locations or the design capabilities of ODM companies.

Significant learning has also taken place in quality management. Contract manufacturers use standardized quality-control methods in their Mexican facilities, which are models, according to the audits of major brand-name customers. Audits are performed on a regular basis, sometimes every two weeks. Our investigations in 2003, however, saw a considerable number of problems. It was reported, for instance, that in many contract manufacturing facilities supervisors still recorded production data by hand, while major brand-name companies in Guadalajara, such as IBM, use automated systems. Managers explained that it was difficult to convince employees to note production figures accurately on boards (2003 interview data). Production workers also reported big quality problems. Many faulty circuit boards had to be reworked because they had been handled during assembly without antistatic protection. Production workers made comments such as the following:

> What the auditors get to see when they come to the factories often is a lie. Usually we work without protections. Everybody is talking to each other. People make jokes. Everything is dirty, material supplies are a mess. Then the

supervisor comes, and we stop the lines and start cleaning, disposing of gar-
bage, tagging inventory. They tell us "put a label on this," "put this away,"
"clean this," "brush your hair," "use your safety glasses," and "put your smock
on." That's what happens when the inspectors come. (2003 interview)

During later fieldwork in 2005, we observed significant improvements in
quality control, particularly under the impact of requirements from higher-
value production segments, such as automotive electronics. Declining profit
margins led to greater attention to quality issues in local manufacturing facilities, driven by massive competition among different locations. Comprehensive certification following the ISO 9001 standard helped to improve production yields. An engineer described the result of such a process, during which
the existing ISO norms in place since 1998 were systematized after 2004
under the concept of total quality management and Six Sigma:

> Now, we are using this in projects, and that has helped us to achieve a higher
> level of problem analysis. Now we can tackle problems at their roots. . . .
> Before, engineers did not understand what a median value was, what a stan-
> dard was. These are very simple things, but you need them. . . . Before, I used
> to stop the line when the company told me, and looked for whatever I could
> find. Now, I first analyze the data and try to locate the cause of the problem.
> We used to have lots of faulty products. Now this has stopped. Since there was
> no automatic recording of quality data, people did not tell the truth. When five
> printed circuit boards were faulty, they only reported one. This has changed.
> (2005 interview)

However, the upward trend in quality control did not engender a management strategy that would involve production operators in the basic aspects of
quality programs. Contract manufacturers are using modern US-style management concepts, such as open-door policies, employee involvement, and
continuous improvement schemes to encourage employees' suggestions. In
fact, contract manufacturing plants resemble those of many multinational
export manufacturers in other industries. They are modern worksites, compared with their rather conservative indigenous Mexican counterparts, and
use new production concepts, such as just-in-time, lean production, or total
quality management (see de la Paz Hernández Águila 2002, 138; de la Garza
Toledo 2002).

It has to be said, however, that such management concepts have been
combined with work organization that contains strong features of Taylorism.
There are hardly any elements of teamwork. Only in final assembly have
some factories introduced work cells, but without any job rotation within the
work groups. Since work in contract manufacturing is organized along project lines with high flexibility, employees are "automatically" placed in different jobs and accordingly acquire multiple skills. This does not lead to
higher compensation, however—a major point of conflict in Mexican EMS

factories. Managers report the beginnings of a team culture, which does not traditionally exist in Mexico, through project groups designed to discuss production problems. To our knowledge, though, front-line operators have not been integrated into such groups. The teams consist only of line leaders, supervisors, and engineers. The dominance of authoritarian and paternalist styles of leadership, inherent in both contract manufacturing and indigenous Mexican traditions, prevents the recognition and improvement of production workers' skills and knowledge.

Mexican EMS workplaces are typical of contract manufacturing factories in low-cost locations around the world. They offer a relatively acceptable work environment, usually in clean and air-conditioned buildings. However, basic aspects of occupational safety and health are often disregarded. In the course of our studies we received numerous reports of such problems, which have also been given international attention by publications such as the "Report on Working Conditions in the Mexican Electronics Industry" by the Centro de Reflexión y Acción Laboral, CEREAL, a well-known NGO in Mexico (2006). Measures to ensure physical work safety are often absent. Workers often wear only their smocks and have no protective gear, such as work shoes, gloves, and safety glasses. Hand injuries are commonplace in work with sharp metal parts, such as enclosures for servers. Chairs on production lines often do not meet basic safety standards. Usually the factories have a medical department providing basic first aid in case of injuries. The doctors, however, seem mainly interested in keeping downtime due to health-related absences low. They frequently send workers with medical ailments back to work. Several workers reported that injured employees were threatened with dismissal for visiting public hospitals belonging to the government-run social insurance system, IMSS. The success rate of so-called zero accident programs set up by several local contract manufacturers is obviously artificially inflated.

Exhaust systems and air filters were installed to remove toxic fumes, especially around wave soldering equipment. However, the equipment is often insufficient to guarantee an environment free of pollutants. Efficient exhaust systems are missing in workplaces using manual soldering. Many employees complain of mucosal irritation and dizziness. In some cases, toxic fumes cause serious accidents with permanent injuries. No financial compensation is offered in such cases. Workers often do not know the hazardous substances to which they are exposed and the kind of health damage those substances can cause, even ones that present a high risk for cancer. Mexico is among the locations in the electronics contract manufacturing industry where soldering substances containing lead and tin are still being used. However, the Mexican electronics industry has adopted the relatively strict norms established by the European Union, such as RoHS (Restriction of Hazardous

Substances). In recent years this has succeeded in substantially reducing the use of toxic substances (see CEREAL 2009).

Regime of Employment

Wage Policies

In spite of diversifying and upgrading production, wages in manufacturing have not changed much in recent years. Contract manufacturing in Mexico is still low-wage production. In Guadalajara, the daily base wage for assembly line work was around ninety pesos during 2005 and 2006. This makes a monthly wage of 2,745 pesos, equal to US$240, based on June 2006 exchange rates. In some factories, the entry-level wages were only fifty-six to seventy-five pesos per day, and in others around a hundred pesos.[1] These wages are above the legal minimum in Mexico, which is between 45.81 and 48.67 pesos per day, according to the Comisión Nacional de los Salarios Mínimos (as of December 26, 2005). However, they cannot cover the cost of living for a family of four. In northern Mexico, the average cost of living is very high by Mexican standards because of proximity to the United States. Here, even relatively high minimum wages still produce living conditions worse than in other parts of the country for many migrant workers. In Tijuana in 2003, wages were not much higher than in Guadalajara. Even in first-tier brand-name companies, such as Sony, the base wage was between seventy-five and one hundred pesos per day. The crisis in the electronics industry caused lower wages in the wake of the declining demand for labor.

In Guadalajara, the rapid construction of new factories increased the competition for labor in the electronics industry before the crisis in 2001. Contract manufacturers had to pay wages comparable to those of international brand-name firms. In the wake of the crisis, average wages at temporary labor agencies dropped below those at brand-name companies. Many workers said the situation in brand-name firms was significantly better than at contract manufacturers because well-known multinational companies provided better benefits. At the same time, more secure employment was normal at brand-name companies, while most contract manufacturers used temporary labor agencies as recruiting agents. This system of employment and the consequent reduction in wages existed throughout contract manufacturing in this region. IBM, however, began using contract labor in the early 1990s. Eventually, most brand-name companies stopped manufacturing in the area. Wages have hardly improved in recent years. With the expansion of contract manufacturing plants after 2005, wages rose slightly, but they dropped again in the wake of the global financial crisis in 2008. According to CEREAL (2009), daily wages in the industry were around ninety pesos in 2009, roughly equal to the level of 2005.

In most cases, the base wage was complemented by varying components, including performance-related pay. Some companies pay bonuses for productivity, skill, or timeliness and attendance. Absenteeism is a widespread problem in many contract manufacturing plants. Performance pay also varies widely among companies and factories. The crisis caused the general reduction or elimination of variable pay. In spite of the improved economic situation after 2004, this trend was not significantly reversed. Many employees were laid off and rehired at reduced pay, especially with lower bonuses. Bonuses were paid at longer intervals, usually once a month, with a similar effect. A one-day absence resulted in the loss of the attendance bonus for four weeks. Previously the attendance bonus was paid on a weekly basis. Workers reported that on average, their bonuses amounted to 100 pesos per week in addition to a weekly base pay of 600 pesos (2005 interview data).

In addition to company-provided performance bonuses, Mexican labor law requires companies to distribute 10 percent of their annual profit to employees. In 2009, workers directly employed by contract manufacturers usually received between 500 and 1,000 pesos, significantly lower than before the crisis. Agency workers received almost nothing. This brought about growing discontent over the implementation of profit sharing. Workers began to criticize the unequal treatment of regular and temporary workers and the lack of transparency in determining the amounts paid, and they collected signatures to protest. Some contract manufacturers in Guadalajara conceded additional payments. Others dismissed workers identified as "troublemakers" (2009 interview data).

Wages are also supplemented by a number of fringe benefits, usually food stamps (called "food baskets" in Mexico), factory canteens with subsidized food prices, and transportation in company buses. Extra pay for Christmas, vacation days, and paid holidays are required by law. Many workers, however, reported that vacations were not provided or were given only in times of slow demand. Christmas pay must be prorated for workers on short-term contract, but this obligation was often not met by many companies. Various tactics were used to further depress wages, sometimes in violation of existing Mexican labor laws, which provide relatively comprehensive individual and collective rights for workers. Illegal practices are used in spite of the fact that contract manufacturing does not represent informal sector employment. Employees must be insured under Mexico's public pension and health insurance system (IMSS) and are fully eligible for benefits.

The situation of technical and clerical workers is somewhat different. These groups enjoy considerably higher salaries, sometimes above the local average in comparable companies. Salaries for engineers, for instance, are several times higher than those of production workers, although engineers are not top earners in the local labor market. Typically, a testing engineer starts his career as a junior engineer at a contract manufacturer with a monthly salary of 4,000 pesos (approximately US$350 at 2006 exchange rates). The engineer can reach 10,000 pesos per month after several years of work. Moving to another company can bring a leap in income. Engineer salaries have improved from 10,000 to as much as 18,000 pesos monthly through mid-career job changes. The relatively strong position of skilled employees is caused by strong demand from contract manufacturers. For many higher-skilled jobs, including administrative positions, employees are recruited from competing companies with the help of headhunters. Clerical workers with permanent employment receive much better benefits than production workers, including extra pay for Christmas, company savings plans, supplemental health insurance, life insurance, and performance-related bonuses, including stock options.

In spite of the fact that production workers in contract manufacturing are paid below the prevailing average, many workers see work in the industry as relatively attractive. High-tech manufacturing has a modern image and a relatively clean and air-conditioned environment and also provides services and benefits such as company-provided canteens and transportation, not usually found in Mexican companies.

Recruitment and Employment Policies

Contract manufacturing companies try to remedy insecurity and risks with flexible production concepts. Their manufacturing workforce in Mexico is very flexible. The creation of a large number of jobs was linked to new forms of recruitment. Multinational temporary labor agencies, such as Adecco, Manpower, and Kelly Services, set up shop in Guadalajara along with contract manufacturers. After IBM began using temporary workers in the early 1990s, this practice spread with the expansion of contract manufacturing. This expansion exposed the lack of adequate definitions for the status of temporary workers under Mexican labor law (see Fressmann 2004). In spite of legal uncertainty, contract manufacturers relied heavily on temporary labor agencies, which also provided recruitment services for skilled administrative and technical workers. Those workers, however, usually receive a permanent labor contract after a probationary period.

Employment policies for production workers are quite different, and the majority are contract employees. In some cases, temporary labor agencies run so-called *in-plant operations*, or branch offices inside contract manufacturing companies. They handle personnel-related affairs such as hiring, control of working hours and absences, wage payments, and layoffs. In spite of the booming labor market in the early years of contract manufacturing in Guadalajara, workers were rarely employed for periods longer than three to six months, often only for a month or fifteen days. Temporary labor agencies often dispatched workers after the end of one contract to the same manufacturer on another contract, creating permanent short-term employment. Outsourcing human resource management to temporary labor firms was convenient for contract manufacturers. Some companies, however, did not use temporary labor or used it only to a relatively limited extent. These companies also used short-term labor contracts to maintain employment flexibility, with employment periods between a few weeks and a year.

These practices undermine basic employees' rights, codified in Mexican labor law, which defines employment status mainly by seniority. Severance payments based on seniority can be extensive, along with vacation days and holiday pay. For shorter employment contracts of more than a month, prorated holiday pay and paid vacation days still have to be provided. But these requirements are often not fully met by employers, and workers have increasingly sued them over such issues in local labor courts. Although illegal, the practice of using consecutive short-term contracts of less than twenty-eight days is motivated by employers' desire to avoid paying legally stipulated benefits. Employment contracts are often not written, although the law requires it, or written contracts are signed by employees but not made available to them (2003, 2005 interview data; see also CEREAL 2006). When the demand for labor rose after 2005, the average duration of labor contracts increased, often up to one year. However, in the wake of the global financial and economic crisis, this trend reversed, and short-term contracts of twenty-eight days have become the rule again (2009 interview data).

Flexible working hours go along with the limited duration of employment. In accordance with Mexican law, most factories formerly had six workdays per week, with three eight-hour shifts per day. In times of high demand, especially during the early boom years of electronics contract manufacturing in the 1990s, overtime was frequent. Sunday was usually a seventh weekly workday, and extra shifts on regular workdays often resulted in sixteen-hour days for individual workers. In some factories, shift plans were based on twelve hours of daily work, which was a violation of Mexican labor law. These practices indicated that enforcement of existing legal standards was notoriously weak.

For workers, the flexible working hours also severely affected their wages. Late-night and weekend shifts had to be compensated with one-half hour's extra pay per late shift, one hour's extra pay per night shift, and double pay on weekend shifts. Overtime pay therefore made up an important part of workers' incomes. With flexible employment, this extra income was often reduced substantially, since workers were dismissed when production fell, were sent on vacation without pay, or were not paid overtime (see CEREAL 2006). Among clerical workers, excessive working hours were also normal, usually six workdays per week and peak daily shifts of twelve hours and more.

Temporary labor agencies not only perform workforce recruitment and administration, they also gather and provide important information about the local labor market. When the initial boom in contract manufacturing produced labor shortages, some contract manufacturers, such as Solectron and Flextronics, extended workforce recruitments into the rural area around Guadalajara. Temporary labor agencies cooperated with local governments in recruiting mostly female workers and organizing transportation to the factories. However, the overwhelming majority of workers in contract manufacturing came from the urban areas of Guadalajara and adjacent communities, where a pool of experienced industrial workers was available. Contract manufacturers provided temporary labor agencies with profiles of desired workers, including age, gender, and skill. Applicants had to submit to an assessment procedure, which was increasingly criticized for discrimination and illegal practices.

Apart from the usual personal data, such as name, address, age, sex, school education, work experience, and so on, workers were assessed using psychometric tests. They were questioned extensively about their socioeconomic situation, and their personal appearance and habits were analyzed, including their family situation, child-care needs, and potential use of drugs. The purpose of these background checks was to determine whether workers would live in stable social relationships, seen as a prerequisite for reliability and good performance at work. In particular, companies demanded to know whether a female applicant was pregnant, refusing to hire pregnant women. The last steps in these procedures included blood and urine tests, which are not allowed under Mexican law.

These recruitment procedures became the basis of strong public complaints by workers about discrimination. Many workers reported that they had been questioned about their sexual relationships and inclinations as well as their menstruation cycles. Tattoos were another criterion for excluding an applicant. Many applicants were asked to undress and complained about humiliating physical examinations by doctors. Applicants were questioned about membership in trade unions or whether they had lawyers in their families. Both were considered signs of potential troublemakers. Reports we received in our interviews are consistent with eyewitness statements in the publications of CEREAL. In these reports, some companies announced guidelines to prevent discriminatory hiring practices by temporary labor agencies or the companies' own HR departments (CEREAL 2006). Many recruitment practices are the result of the fact that 70 to 80 percent of production workers are women. Most of them work in assembly with a high proportion in manual labor, such as visual inspection of printed circuit boards. Male production workers usually work on wave soldering equipment and repair workstations on SMD lines. Assigning work functions by gender contributes significantly to wage differentials between male and female workers.

During the initial period when contract manufacturing plants were expanding in the late 1990s, they hired mostly young women, often eighteen to twenty years old, as production workers. This pattern changed significantly in the wake of the crisis of 2001, when recruitment shifted to workers over twenty-five. The main reason for the shift was to reduce workforce turnover. Companies started looking for workers who would see employment in an electronics factory as a permanent rather than transitional job. This led to increased employment of single mothers, who in many companies made up 40 percent or more of the workforce. The large number of workers in this situation reflects the increasing instability of established family structures, driven by a massive migration of male workers to the United States. Young women often are abandoned by their husbands when they become pregnant, resulting in a growing number of families depending on a single mother's income. According to figures from the Mexican Federal Statistics Office, INEGI, 23.7 percent of households in Jalisco were led by single women in 2005, a slightly higher number than the national average in Mexico of 23.1 percent (INEGI n.d., 10).

From a management perspective, these women are heavily dependent on a stable source of income and therefore are more reliable workers. A big problem for single mothers was the lack of child-care facilities. Companies did not provide them, and there is no affordable public childcare. Therefore, workers' mothers or grandmothers usually have to care for the children, and many workers are even forced to leave their children by themselves.

The proportion of women among manufacturing workers in Mexico has been decreasing again in recent years, after the growth of the *maquiladora* industries propelled a steep increase in women's employment during the 1970s and 1980s. At the national level, this trend reflects changes in the *maquiladora* industries, which have been shifting from traditional labor-intensive "women's industries" to technologically more sophisticated production (Barrientos, Kabeer, and Hossain 2004; Braig 2004; Salzinger 1997). This development is visible in the electronics industry. The proportion of women workers in electronics manufacturing, including brand-name and contract manufacturers, is roughly about 50 percent. This reflects an increase of higher-skilled jobs in technical and engineering work, usually performed by men. Contract manufacturers, however, still have a significantly higher proportion of women workers, although it has decreased from 80 percent to 70 percent in recent years. In administrative departments, such as purchasing, the proportion is about 60 percent men and 40 percent women, while in technical areas such as engineering, men are the majority. Most are young and were hired as trainees directly from universities (2003 interview data).

Skill Development Policies

The large number of well-known institutions of higher education and research in Guadalajara has often been cited as a major advantage over locations near the US border. In 2004 alone, three new universities started educating engineers. Among contract manufacturers, a distinctively American company culture prevails, heavily relying on training "on the job." Higher-skilled workers in areas such as engineering, finance, and purchasing are taking responsibility and making decisions early on, including participating in negotiations with suppliers. Training often includes short-term assignment to the facilities of contract manufacturers or their customers in the United States. At the same time, Mexican engineers support US-based customers ramping up production in Mexico.

Contract manufacturers rely on high-quality universities and schools to supply more highly skilled workers and support the development of job-specific skills through comprehensive training programs. In contrast, requirements for manufacturing workers are much lower. In Guadalajara, junior high school graduation is the standard qualification for entry-level workers. In the north, only six years in Mexican schools is required. Workers have to acquire their technical skills directly on the assembly line after basic orientation classes lasting one to three days. For new recruits with previous work experience, technical skill training is often skipped. When temporary labor agencies organize placement of workers on short-term contracts, many have already worked in several contract manufacturing plants. This enables companies to minimize expenses for entry-level training.

Training for special skills, such as wave soldering and repair work, is documented with certificates. Higher skills obtained through company training or previous education and experience are not rewarded with higher pay. Many workers reported that after several years of employment they were still receiving the entry-level wage for assembly work. In some cases, certificates were at least included in the calculation of bonus pay. There are no policies for skill and career development that would reward training with promotion into higher-paid positions. Under this authoritarian and paternalistic style of management, many workers do not feel their performance is recognized—a major reason for job-hopping and high turnover rates. In general, the shift to more complex products of higher value enhances skill development opportunities for engineers, but not for production workers. This creates a continuing polarization between higher- and lower-skilled work.

Regime of Control

In Mexican contract manufacturing plants, the Taylorist assembly-line organization of production shows a pattern of hierarchic control and an authoritarian and paternalistic style of management. Workers are usually addressed by supervisors and management using the personal form of "you" (*tú* in Spanish) or their first names, while workers are required to address their higher-ups with the formal form of "you" (*usted*) or their family names. Many employees are treated arbitrarily and yelled at by their supervisors and managers. Along with the denial of better pay for skilled and more experienced workers, most workers feel their personalities, skills, and performance are not recognized. This mode of control clearly does not rely on employees' motivation and self-control and does not mobilize their initiative and creativity, often advertised in concepts of teamwork and lean production. Because of the hierarchic segmentation of the workforce, self-directed work and decision making is encouraged only for engineers and other higher-skilled workers and supported through training programs.

Production relations and labor policies are shaped by a complex institutional setting. The government's policies of industrial, technological, and educational development play a role in this context. But production relations are also shaped by Mexican labor law, often described as one of the most developed in Latin America (Boris 1990). It includes relatively far-reaching rights for workers and provides the basis for a corporatist and authoritarian system of trade unionism, incorporating unions into government and party politics. Thus, the major Mexican locations of contract manufacturing are not union-free environments. However, those regions are dominated by trade unions that are not independent and active representatives of the workforces. Rather, the existing trade unions negotiate so-called protection contracts (*contratos de protección*) with employers, designed to prevent the emergence of independent trade unions. The historically established trade union system lost its social base under the impact of the massive restructuring of the national economy during the 1980s and needs fundamental reform.

The Mexican Revolution from 1910 to 1917 and the national-populist government of Lázaro Cárdenas in the 1930s shaped the governmental policies that gave considerable institutional strength to trade unions. A system of industrial relations was established that was not based on direct bargaining between capital and labor but that always included the state as third actor, controlling and regulating the process. Under the import substitution policy for industrialization, led by the government (see chapter 3), the role of trade unions was to "supply the production system with a disciplined workforce," as Rainer Dombois and Ludger Pries (1999, 73) have expressed it. Although considerable bargaining over contracts and political influence took place under this system, trade unions did see themselves as an organizing force that would control labor markets but not intervene directly into the process of production.

Mexico's trade unions still operate under the Federal Labor Law of 1931, which regulates individual rights of employees in a comprehensive and detailed way. Seniority in age and length of service is the basic principle for hiring, termination, and wage determination. Flexible employment achieved through temporary work, limited-term contracts, and discrimination against young and female employees, therefore, severely undermines this foundation of trade union influence. Stable bodies of workers with accumulated seniority rights are becoming less common (see Bouzas and Alfonso 1999; Zapata 2001).

Collective labor rights are also regulated under the Federal Labor Law, shaping the trade union system of craft and industrial unions. Normally, only one trade union represents workers in a workplace. The union is registered with the Federal Department of Labor and can negotiate collective bargaining contracts biennially, which also have to be registered with the Department of Labor and the local arbitration and conciliation bodies (*Junta de Conciliación y Arbitraje*; Bouzas and Alfonso 1999). The biggest official trade union confederation is the CTM (*Confederación de Trabajadores de México*), followed by the CROC (*Confederación Revolucionaria de Obreros y Campesinos*) and the CROM (*Confederación Regional Obrera Mexicana*). These organizations were structurally incorporated into the Party of Institutionalized Revolution, the PRI, which had ruled for seventy years. These federations survived that party's fall from its monopoly position in 2000. There are also a number of smaller or independent trade union confederations. Individual trade unions have diverse political orientations and play different roles at the local level. In some industries, such as the automobile sector, some official trade unions have achieved considerable success in representing workers' interests. But the Mexican trade union system in general is increasingly losing its base because of the development of today's export-led model and conflicts over democratization.

The existence of active trade unions at the local level is a major factor influencing the attractiveness of certain regions for multinational capital. Economic development agencies on both sides of the border advertise peaceful and harmonious labor relations as a major factor contributing to the favorable investment climate in Mexico (Guadalajara interview data, 2003, 2005). In Guadalajara and the state of Jalisco, trade unions report that companies receive information from the state government about various options for choosing union representation, including recommendations of certain trade union confederations. Based on this information, companies contact the respective trade union and negotiate a collective agreement. With the registration of such an agreement with the local government, no other trade union can claim jurisdiction over the workforce at that location (2003 interview data). Like many other regions of the country, Jalisco is dominated by trade unions that sign protection contracts designed to avoid the emergence of independent trade unions. Such employer-oriented contracts basically simulate the existence of collective bargaining. They are a manifestation of the widespread corruption existing under the declining corporatist and authoritarian regime of industrial relations (see Bouzas and Alfonso 2001; Wittmütz 2004).

Many contract manufacturers in Jalisco have contracts with the CTM and CROC. In the 1970s and 1980s, several attempts were made to establish independent and democratic trade unions. Those initiatives were vigorously opposed by the official trade unions and finally could not overcome their opposition (see de la O Martinez 1999). Factories often sign agreements with an official trade union, although most workers do not know that the agreement exists. Workers are even registered as union members without ever having signed a membership card or paid union dues. "Because of the low wages," a CTM representative explained in an interview, "we cannot put this burden on our members. Therefore, the employers have to take care of union dues" (2003 interview data).

Mexico continues to have a reputation for providing favorable conditions to multinational investors, including cheap and relatively skilled labor and weak labor rights and environmental laws and regulations. This does not mean that Mexico has no viable system of labor laws but only that those laws are not strongly enforced. Jalisco shows the interconnection between development-minded local governments, eager to attract multinational investment, and state-corporatist trade unions. The regulation of work always has been a key point in relationships between the United States and Mexico. However, a binational labor policy does not exist. Instead, the border between the countries is being protected in specific ways—from the Mexican side by labor policies preserving Mexico's status as a low-wage location, and from the United States through restrictive immigration policies. NAFTA's side agreement on labor, the North American Agreement on Labor Cooperation (NAALC), has been ineffective, according to the overwhelming majority of experts (see Constantini 1999; Dombois 2002).

On a global level, the traditional labor, social, and environmental standards are increasingly replaced by voluntary codes of conduct among private actors (see Sproll 2005). In the electronics industry, a campaign by the UK-based Catholic Agency for Overseas Development (CAFOD) denounced violations of basic labor rights in electronics contract manufacturing in Mexico, China, and Thailand. That resulted in a code of conduct, which the major contract manufacturers from North America as well as Foxconn promised to honor (see CAFOD 2004). However, the Electronics Industry Code of Conduct (EICC) represents only a set of rules unilaterally established by the respective companies and is legally nonbinding. Many of its elements do not even meet the core labor standards of the International Labor Organization (ILO). The freedom of association in particular is at least partly denied to Mexican workers. The EICC nevertheless inspired some initiatives by NGOs to improve labor relations in the global electronics industry, and the activities of the Mexican NGO CEREAL are among the most important (see chapter 5).

MALAYSIA: NEO-TAYLORISM, WOMEN WORKERS, AND ETHNIC SEGMENTATION

Work organization and labor policies in electronics contract manufacturing factories in Malaysia reflect the dynamics of the country's rapid development. Today it is one of the most important locations of electronics manufacturing worldwide and experiences many social and political contradictions because of its underlying model of development. The large-scale operations of contract manufacturers exemplify the transformation of Malaysia's electronics industry. It started as the back end of the global assembly line under the "new international division of labor" (Fröbel, Heinrichs, and Kreye 1977; McGee 1986) and evolved into highly integrated post-Fordist mass production. The social structures of this production model show remarkable continuity, reflecting an authoritarian-paternalist system of political regulation under the ideological and cultural auspices of a moderate version of political Islam. This has made Malaysia a favorite destination for manufacturing investment by multinational corporations.

Still, electronics production in Malaysia—and contract manufacturing in particular—depends on a regime of low wages, long working hours, and noncompliance with internationally accepted standards of collective bargaining and trade union rights. The ethnic and gender segmentation of the workforce is based on the large-scale employment of women workers of Malayan ethnicity and Islamic religion. This has not changed since the trend emerged in the 1970s (see Aihwa Ong 1987). Relations of production in Malaysian EMS factories are structured along ethnic, religious, and gender lines to a degree beyond all other cases in this investigation. This characterizes the model of development adopted under the *New Economic Policy* in the wake of Malaysia's political crisis in 1969 (see chapter 3). It has been further transformed with the rise of Wintelist mass production and its crisis in the years 2001 and 2008–2009.

Regime of Work

The organization of work and production in EMS contract manufacturing in Malaysia is shaped by state-of-the-art technology and specialization. The industry manufactures high volumes of printed circuit boards and components for computers, network equipment, and peripherals, as well as performing the final assembly of such devices in a large variety of configurations. It also produces audio, video, automotive, and medical electronics devices and, to a lesser degree, cell phones. In recent years, mass production of these systems has been complemented by relatively specialized products, more mechanically complex and in lower volumes, including high-end medical and measuring devices and precision printers. Still, assembly of printed circuit boards and box build form the backbone of contract manufacturing in Malaysia. Production of plastic and metal enclosures and, therefore, tool and die making have remained relatively limited, along with the need for skilled labor.

Generally, work is relatively homogenous within and among factories. This reflects the high-volume character of production and its focus on a relatively limited spectrum of products. Large and fairly modern factory buildings are part of this picture, as well as modern urban surroundings with the infrastructure for traffic, communications, and logistics. In Penang, the center of EMS production in Malaysia, factories are located in large industrial parks with tens of thousands of employees in each one. In Kuala Lumpur and the southern province of Johor, factories are located in large suburban industrial areas with a relatively developed living environment. The working conditions at contract manufacturers are not very different from those at brand-name firms in the same location. All the factories hire and compete for the same workforce.

Malaysian EMS factories have relatively few production areas with massive safety and health hazards, such as those manufacturing raw printed circuit boards or plastics and metal enclosures. Working conditions in the factories seem relatively favorable. In particular, the use of air-conditioning in most factories improves the working environment in the tropical climate. This picture seems to confirm the "clean" image of electronics manufacturing. But many problems result from heavy workloads and long working hours. Stress, repetitive motion injuries, and back and eye problems caused by poor ergonomics on assembly lines are widespread among Malaysian electronics workers. The methods for disposing of manufacturing waste are inadequate. In the industrial parks of Penang in particular, discharges of industrial waste, including toxic substances, are still visible, the heritage of the early years of industrial development in the 1970s and 1980s (see Wangel 2001, 20ff.).

Production work in Malaysian EMS factories is highly segmented. Automated assembly takes place on long lines—a textbook example of neo-Taylorism. This pattern is typical of the mass assembly of PCs and printers, where segmentation is particularly widespread. The manufacturing of printed circuit boards is mostly performed on high-volume SMT lines with manufacturing technology comparable to that in industrialized countries. Optical inspection, manual assembly, and rework are also common processes. The automation of computer-controlled SMT equipment is often not used to its full potential due to the abundance of cheap manual labor. In some areas with more flexible and specialized mass production and with frequently changing

product configurations (such as business PCs or network servers), more integrated work structures also exist. In areas with low-volume manufacturing of
highly specialized products, such as credit card printers, workers perform
complex mechanical assembly. Skilled craft labor is found only in equipment
maintenance and—to a very limited extent—in the manufacturing of mechanical parts. According to our observations, the upgrading of the product
portfolio in recent years has produced only a very limited upgrading of
assembly work. In most of the big mass-production factories, the norm is
line-based production with extensive segmentation, short work cycles, and
usually no rotation of tasks.

The Taylorist division of labor extends to the highly automated segments
of printed circuit board production, including operating the sophisticated
computer-controlled SMT machinery. Integration of jobs does not exist, such
as material handling or process control on computer screens, with more
complex tasks in preventive maintenance, repair, or basic programming. This
separation of skilled and unskilled work is reinforced along gender lines.
Equipment operators usually are Malayan women. Maintenance and programming remains the preserve of men, mostly ethnic Chinese or Indian
engineers and technicians.

In the newer configurations of flexible-volume manufacturing developed
in the wake of the 2001 recession (see chapter 3), the rigid, line-based organization of production has been partly replaced by work groups or cells. In this
environment, individual workers perform more complex work processes,
with relatively frequent changes of tasks. However, simple assembly work
still prevails. The integration of more conceptual tasks (such as the organization of material flows) or repair and maintenance into the activities of work
teams is not recognizable. The extremely short cycles of manufacturing
contracts severely limit learning on the shop floor. We studied one case of a
final assembly operation for high-end business PCs for corporate customers
in Penang. There, work-cell-based production was developed, with ten work
groups of eight workers each, and production ramped up within just a few
weeks. The remarkably fast learning process among workers and engineers
was not rewarded, however, since the factory lost the manufacturing contract
after six months in the wake of a sudden restructuring of the brand-name
customer's global manufacturing network (2003, 2005 interview data).

Work organization different from the highly segmented work in mass
assembly developed only in specialized low-volume manufacturing, which
gained significance in Malaysia after 2001. Those operations are organized
either as line- or cell-based manufacturing with relatively long work cycles
and a high amount of individual work processes or as craft-type, single-
workplace assembly with a high variety of discrete work steps. These environments require a relatively complex learning process among workers since
the quality of the product essentially depends on the proper performance of

manual assembly. However, in the cases we studied, the greater requirement for skill and experience did not translate into significantly higher wages. In a manufacturing shop for high-value precision printers in Penang, for instance, wages were barely higher than in mass manufacturing in neighboring factories. Yet individual workers had to perform between ten and fifty single work steps per product (2002 factory visit data). In the case of a single workplace production of credit card printers, one worker assembled about two hundred mechanical parts under changing assembly manuals for different types of devices. The exact wage of this group of workers was not even known to the factory management since these older and highly skilled women were foreign-country contract workers. It is common for factories to import both low- and high-skilled workers from neighboring Indonesia (2005 factory visit data).

Regime of Employment

Wages and Benefits

Malaysia's status as a low-cost location is fundamentally related to its prevailing level of wages and benefits, which has remained relatively low in spite of the country's remarkable industrial development in recent decades. Malaysia is internationally known as a location with significantly lower labor costs than the four Asian tiger countries of Singapore, Hong Kong, Taiwan, and South Korea. It is still relatively expensive, however, compared with other countries in Southeast Asia—the Philippines, Thailand, and Indonesia. During the foreign investment boom of the 1990s through the so-called Asian financial crisis in 1997, wages in Malaysia's industrial sector increased relatively quickly, with annual overall growth rates of 8–10 percent per year. In Kuala Lumpur and Penang they were even higher (Anna Ong 2000, 7ff.). Among Malaysia's modern industrial sectors, electronics manufacturing is at the lower end of the wage and salary scale. According to data from the Malaysian State Bank, wages and salaries in the electronics industry in most job categories were 30–50 percent lower than in the chemical and steel industries, the highest-paying industrial sectors, and just above the lowest-paying industry, textile and garment work. The low wages in electronics and in the textile and garment industry are related to the high proportion of women workers in these industries (C. Edwards 1999, 238).

Wage standards in electronics manufacturing are derived from figures provided by the Malaysian Industrial Development Agency (MIDA), which publishes figures annually for multinational investors. According to this data, salaries for various functions of factory management in the manufacturing sector were between US$1,000 and US$1,500 per month in 2002, excluding benefits and calculated at current exchange rates.[2] For engineers in electronics, the respective salary levels were between US$750 and US$1,500; for production supervisors, US$310–360; for maintenance technicians and other skilled workers, such as welders, US$210–480; for semiskilled production workers, US$143–337; and for unskilled production operators, US$127–373. These figures show a strong polarization between wages of production workers and salaries of engineers and management personnel. Engineers can earn three times, and upper managers five times, as much as semiskilled or skilled production workers. However, salaries for engineers in Malaysia remain relatively low in international terms, particularly in relationship to Singapore—an important factor for Malaysia's increasing attractiveness as an investment location (MIDA 2002).

Fringe benefits comprise company payments to the government-run pension system (the Employees' Provident Fund) of 11 percent of the total wage (workers have to pay an additional 9 percent of their incomes), the government-run industrial injury insurance scheme of 2.25 percent of the total wage (with no payment from workers), and the Human Resources Development Fund (HRDF), a government program for professional education and training, of 1 percent of the total wage. Unemployment insurance does not exist in Malaysia (Wangel 2001, 11). In addition, most multinational companies offer health insurance with different levels of copayment by workers, and shift premiums of US$0.50 for the first shift, US$0.50–1 for the second shift, and US$1–1.50 for the night shift (MIDA 2002). Common benefits such as company-provided bus transportation to the workplace, dormitories, and free meals in cafeterias are uncommon in Malaysia.

Such official benchmarks, however, are the upper limit on the wages and salaries actually paid in the electronics sector. Although we could not obtain official data from contract manufacturers on their wages (as in the other cases we studied), the figures cited by local managers clearly were at the lower end of the wage bands published by MIDA. "Four hundred dollars in all" was a commonly cited figure for low-skilled operators. In Kuala Lumpur, the capital, wages were still somewhat higher than in Penang and in the relatively new industrial area of Johor. This reflects the fact that in the metropolitan area of the capital, trade unions have a presence in some large factories of leading electronics multinationals. In the sole major electronics factory with union representation in Penang, Sanyo, the collective bargaining agreement provides for wages of operators in the higher skill and seniority categories of US$130–380 and for skilled workers and technicians of about US$180–450. According to local trade union experts, this is roughly the same as the wages paid at contract manufacturers. Only the top wages for high-seniority workers are higher under the union contract (2003, 2005 interview data).

In general, the wage system heavily promotes long working hours among workers with relatively short periods of training. In the biggest EMS factory in the country in Penang, the starting monthly wage for an unskilled operator was around US$60, and for more experienced ones around US$100. After an initial period of on-the-job training of one or two months, monthly income can reach US$200–250, including shift allowances, attendance bonus, and extra pay for weekend work. Wages rarely increase greatly because of a longer period of employment. The base wage for an assembly worker with four to five years of work experience is around US$130–150, about one third higher than for a recently hired worker (2003 interview data). The flipside of such wage policies is high turnover rates. During years of favorable economic conditions, an annual turnover of 30–40 percent of the workforce was seen as relatively low (2003, 2005 interview data).

Recruitment and Employment Policies

During the 1990s, labor market development in the Malaysian electronics industry was shaped by the largest exporting boom in the country's history. The number of jobs in the industry increased annually by 10 percent during that period. Turnover rates were rising, too (Hobday 1999, 78). At the end of the 1990s, the total number of electronics workers was around 200,000, out of which 117,000 were employed in Penang, the largest location (SERI 2002). These figures clearly reflect the industry's character as a mass-production sector. In the wake of the crisis, this changed dramatically, particularly in Penang. In this area, the number of electronics workers fell to around eighty thousand in 2001 (SERI 2002; Toh 2002). A significant proportion of the job losses occurred at contract manufacturers. According to our investigation, EMS firms in Penang employed around fifteen thousand workers in 2004, in Kuala Lumpur, three to four thousand, and in Johor, approximately ten thousand. Those figures, of course, are subject to the large short-term employment fluctuations typical of contract manufacturing.

The structure of the workforce in contract manufacturing in Malaysia is shaped by high-volume PCB and system assembly. There are relatively few development and design engineers in the factories but large numbers of production engineers educated at Malaysian universities and colleges. Among these highly skilled employees, the largest number are ethnic Indians and Chinese, almost all of them men. Those engineers have a local orientation and lifestyle; only a few have international university degrees or work experience. The small numbers of ethnic Malays in higher positions are mostly in human resource management or in government and public relations. There are relatively few foreign engineers because of immigration restrictions on skilled personnel (2003, 2005 Penang government interview data).

Production operators are almost exclusively Malayan women. Malays have played a growing role in the urban population and industrial workforce since the 1970s. This historic trend is a result of the export-oriented New

Economic Policy after 1969 and the related changes in the political system (McGee 1986, 50). The recruitment procedures for production workers, however, differ widely from region to region.

Kuala Lumpur, the most developed region, has relatively stable metropolitan labor markets and social environments, a result of its history of urbanization and suburbanization dating back to the 1960s. Recruiting procedures here are similar to those in developed industrial countries. Women workers employed by electronics firms are often secondary earners in households dependent on wage income, similar to the situation of some women in industrialized countries. In the case of Malaysia, this is reinforced through Islamic religious beliefs and family structures. Employers have to cater to the reproductive needs of workers' families in an urban environment, particularly women's double burden of work and child care. Since most female workers are of parental age with family obligations, many everyday workplace conflicts arise from this role (interview data, Electronics Workers Industrial Union—EIWU).

In Penang and southern Malaysia, workers are recruited from rural environments, which are becoming suburban because of massive and rapid industrialization. Women workers here are significantly younger than in the capital, usually between eighteen and twenty-five years of age. In Penang, production workers are usually hired through the drivers of company buses carrying young women to work from their villages, often commuting up to a hundred kilometers every day. In Malayan village communities, the bus drivers, who are exclusively male, enjoy considerable social status because the heads of rural family clans "entrust" to them personally their daughters sent to work in factories. The bus companies assume the status of informal recruitment agencies and are extensively used by electronics companies, especially during labor shortages.

The former HR director of a large EMS factory in Penang describes the advantages of this system as follows:

> A lot of workers here are actually from the countryside. It is possible to commute here from remote villages. And there are real recruitment drives, done by the transport company. You see, it makes sense for the bus owners to help us recruit, because they get what they call their trips. It is their business, so they bring in a team of people, they go into a particular village and maybe one or two of our people will go with them and say: "We are from a legitimate company, this is what we do, we are looking for X number of people to work for us.". . . . For someone like me to go into the village, I am Chinese, and it may be difficult to get an audience with them. But if I bring somebody with me who is Malay from there and knows them, no problem. (2003 interview)

Such methods of recruitment, established in Penang since the beginning of export-led industrialization in the 1970s, changed significantly in the wake of the 2001 recession. Suddenly, the companies no longer had to confront the problem of labor shortages but instead of downsizing the labor force. Large-scale layoffs took place, especially in Penang, with its vast production complex for computers and computer-related components, and most dramatically at the large manufacturers of hard disk drives, such as Seagate. The total number of layoffs in Penang was estimated at a minimum of twenty thousand by local trade unions (2003 interview data). All contract manufacturers reduced employment on a large scale. The biggest reductions took place at Solectron, where two thousand of nine thousand employees were affected. The high number of layoffs was a result of the relatively few limited-term or temporary workers employed in Malaysian EMS factories. The bigger factories tried to reduce the number of layoffs through so-called voluntary separations, for which they offered severance pay (2003 interview data).

The employment crisis of 2001 and 2002 made a deep impact on workforce recruitment. Contract manufacturers started to work with temporary labor agencies, a method for creating a more flexible workforce uncommon in Penang up to that time. All EMS factories we investigated in Malaysia began to hire temporary workers, who then made up between 10 and 30 percent of the workforce. One factory in Penang reduced the number of its workers, who had all been employed on unlimited-term contracts, from 1,200 to 650. Several months later the workforce was increased again, to one thousand, in order to meet a new large-volume manufacturing contract. However, 30 percent of the new hires were temporary workers and another 30 percent, contract workers from Indonesia. Temporary labor offered an advantage over the previous informal mechanism of recruitment because it was more flexible and it reduced dependency on the bus drivers (2003, 2005 interview data).

The employment of foreign contract workers, mostly from Indonesia, is the second important element of flexible employment. These workers are recruited through contract labor firms in the much larger but poorer neighboring country. The system of contract labor has emerged from the labor practices of agricultural plantations in Malaysia. The recruiting agencies are the direct employers of the workers (Standing 1999, 65ff.). The wages of the workers they recruit are considerably lower than those of regular employees. The contract labor company is also responsible for handling visa requirements and for housing the workers. EMS contract manufacturers began to hire these completely unprotected workers during the boom period of the 1990s, often with contracts of one year or longer. Because of labor shortages, extended employment terms enabled the manufacturers to keep a stable, low-cost workforce. During the crisis, the duration of labor contracts was reduced drastically, however. Contract laborers are used now as a short-term reserve workforce.

Such mechanisms to flexibilize the workforce were also used widely to mitigate employment reductions during the 2008–2009 downturn. As in

2001, the manufacturing sector in Malaysia was hit hard by the crisis. By midyear in 2009, the general rate of registered unemployment reached 4 percent, a high level by Malaysian standards. Eight percent of the manufacturing workforce was shed, and more than 120,000 workers lost their jobs, with foreign workers taking a disproportionate hit. In the electronics sector, about five thousand jobs were lost during the last half of 2009 in the electronics sector (World Bank 2009). Contract manufacturers resorted to temporary plant closures. Flextronics shut down its Penang facility in December 2008 and January 2009 and permanently closed its operations in Shah Alam, near Kuala Lumpur, laying off 1,382 workers from this plant. Jabil and Sanmina-SCI, along with a number of brand-name electronics companies, avoided layoffs during the crisis but reduced pay by 50 percent and rescheduled work shifts. The number of temporary workers laid off in such cases, however, is not known.

Skill Development and Quality Management

Since the 1990s, Malaysian industrial policy has emphasized skill development of the national workforce in both rhetoric and practice. The relatively low skill level of workers has been depicted as a key obstacle to helping Malaysia become a successful economic player in global technology markets (Rasiah 1999b, 186–87). Malaysia's school system produces a low illiteracy rate, and people have a relatively widespread education in basic English (the only common language of Malays, Chinese, and Indians).

During the 1990s, industry representatives increasingly complained of a shortage of skilled workers, however, particularly for medium-skilled and highly skilled technical professions. This shortage was blamed on shortcomings in the country's system of universities and professional colleges. Only 7 percent of high-school graduates go to university, a low rate compared with those of the more successful emerging economies in Asia, such as Taiwan and South Korea. The labor shortage was also seen as a negative effect of the government's increasing orientation of its policies toward advancing ethnic Malays, highlighted by the replacement of English as the first language in school education by Malay and the related Islamization of the education system (Ismail 1999, 30–31).

The transition toward more capital-intensive electronics production after the end of the 1980s coincided with the increased employment of ethnic Malays in medium and higher positions in management and engineering (ibid., 24ff.), which the government strongly favored. The framework for these policies was defined by the *Action Plan for Industrial Technology Development* (APITD) of 1990 and the *Second Industrial Master Plan* (IMP2) of 1995. In 1992, the *Human Resource Development Act* (HRDA) was enacted—the key legislation for developing professional education. It required companies with more than fifty employees to pay 1 percent of their total wages to the *Human Resource Development Fund* (HRDF) run by the government. The plan for the education of skilled workers included increased efforts by foreign organizations in this field, such as the German Society for Technical Co-operation (GTZ) (Rasiah 2003, 7ff.).

Significant differences exist among the various locations of the IT industry in Malaysia, reflecting divergent industrial policies. Company-external skill development has a relatively limited role in Kuala Lumpur. Penang created a strong network of semigovernmental institutions for professional education and training, including the *Penang Skill Development Center* (PSDC). Vertically integrated multinational electronics firms, such as Sony and Bosch, as well as chipmakers such as Intel, National Semiconductor, and NEC have had a heavy presence in Penang. They have well-developed internal systems for skill development and therefore make relatively little use of external training organizations. Contract manufacturers, along with companies in the PC and hard disk drive industries, with their ultralean corporate organization, strongly rely on local programs for professional education. For most of them, PSDC was their chief partner for professional education in Penang (2003, 2005 interview data).

Increased efforts in skill development after the 1990s accompanied the use of advanced systems of quality management such as the Japanese-inspired *total quality management* (TQM) in electronics manufacturing. European electronics firms such as Osram, with its large factory in Penang, led in this effort (Hobday 1999, 80). At the beginning of the twenty-first century, all major electronics companies in Malaysia were using such programs (Rasiah 2003). At EMS companies, TQM was integrated with global quality management systems and company-wide benchmarking of best manufacturing practices. The internal training systems of the EMS factories in Malaysia follow their company-wide practices. Newly hired production operators receive an orientation of one to three days, followed by on-the-job instruction in assembly operations. For specialized work processes, training courses of several days or several weeks are offered—partly inside the company and partly in external training centers. Temporary and contract workers, especially those from foreign countries, are usually not eligible for such training.

The focus on skill development reflects changes in production, as David O'Connor aptly describes:

> One reason for this is that the average production worker is now responsible for operating sophisticated—and expensive—automated machinery whose downtime must be minimized. This implies not only that operators must be able to supervise the equipment effectively but also that they should be able to handle at least some of the routine maintenance and repair of that equipment, freeing up technicians for more serious problems. It also suggests that compa-

nies must be more careful to select operators skilled and knowledgeable
enough not to cause serious damage to equipment. (O'Connor 1993, 229ff.)

At the beginning of this discussion, we pointed out that enhanced diversity of the product spectrum and the higher complexity of production equipment have not substantially upgraded production work in recent years. Improvement of the skill base and related efforts by local and national governments remain precarious. In contract manufacturing in particular, upgrading
of work is limited by the notoriously frequent changes in manufacturing
contracts and the seasonal cycles of many products—factors out of the control of local actors. At the same time, skill development has been decoupled
from pay for industrial workers. As in most other countries we studied,
workplace-related learning processes in electronics contract manufacturing
are rarely awarded with higher wages. Institutionalized standards for determining wages at a plant or industry level are mostly absent. In Malaysia, the
ethnic and gender segmentation of the workforce is a particular impediment
to upgrading work and excludes both women of Malayan origin and foreign
contract workers from advancement into higher-skilled production jobs.

Regime of Control

There is a huge mismatch between the relatively modern production environment and the Taylorist organization of work, with its strong elements of
authoritarian control. Our investigations in EMS factories confirm the analysis of critical social scientists in Malaysia that labor relations in the country
barely include forms for worker participation, in spite of the significantly
increased technological and organizational complexity of production. Labor-
management cooperation is also absent from innovation processes (Rasiah
1999b, 193–94). Workers' interests on the shop floor are usually unrepre-
sented. Employee grievances are mostly handled through corporate HR departments. This situation is the result of the protracted suppression of trade
union representation rights at the shop floor and industry level. In Penang,
the most important location, as well as in Johor and Melaka, all EMS factories are union-free. The only factory with a rudimentary trade union, owned
by Flextronics, is located near Kuala Lumpur.

The practices for shop-floor control in EMS factories are not very different from those at brand-name electronics firms. Relatively uniform sociopolitical conditions are developing throughout the tightly integrated production
networks of the global electronics industry in Malaysia. Multinational electronics firms pursue a relatively homogenous version of TQM tailored to
local conditions. The national traditions of the respective multinationals do
not play a significant role, although Japanese and European companies seem
to accept a company union more easily than their US counterparts do (see

Bhopal and Todd 2000). In Penang, working conditions, pay, and employment policies in the sole major factory that has a company union are not very different from those of North American contract manufacturers. The degree of the Taylorist segmentation of work is by no means lower than in EMS factories. However, this one factory at least had a contract-based grievance procedure (2005 interview data).

Only a small number of indigenous Malaysian contract manufacturers provide a different picture. At the biggest company of this kind, which produces handheld VHF radios for a known US brand, work organization and the workforce are similar to those of foreign contract manufacturers. However, employment is remarkably more stable. Workers are recruited from nearby locations without intermediaries such as bus drivers or other recruitment agencies. At the time of our investigation, most workers had been working for the company for more than two years. Even during major downturns, the company tried to keep most employees. Such relatively stable employment is part of a paternalist management style, designed to present the company as a role model of indigenous enterprise. However, because of its close connection to the government, the company is strictly antiunion.

The absence of institutionalized forms of interest representation on the shop floor is particularly visible in occupational safety and health. It is well known that stress-related injuries and illnesses occur in electronics manufacturing in Malaysia, but there is currently no valid medical data on the relevant symptoms. Comprehensive statistical research has been successfully blocked by the companies (2005 interview data). Some legal regulations exist for occupational safety and health, but governmental enforcement is notoriously inefficient. Employees cannot enforce the regulations because of the absence of shop-floor representation (Wangel 2001). A substantial improvement of health protection would require fundamental changes in work hours and organization.

Oppressive labor policies and discrimination against women workers have a long history in Malaysia that dates back to the founding years of the modern Malaysian state in the 1950s and the suppression of the Communist Party, which had a leading role in the struggle for independence from the British colonial regime. Malaysia's current restrictive labor legislation continues that of the British colonial regime and places the establishment of trade unions under strict government control. The key component of this system is a complicated registration procedure through a government agency called the *Registrar of Trade Unions* (Jomo and Todd 1994).

With the growth of the electronics industry during the 1970s, these mechanisms were used against trade unions in the factories of multinational enterprises. They were particularly directed against attempts to set up an industry-wide trade union in the electronics sector. The legal vehicle for this policy was separating the "electrical" and "electronics" industries, put forward by the *Registrar of Trade Unions*. In the older "electrical" industry trade unions, some of them with industry-wide organizations and bargaining power had already been established. In the newly emerging "electronics" industry, the emergence of trade unions was suppressed. "Electrical" products were defined as finished devices, such as household appliances, radios, and telephone sets. "Electronics" was defined as components, especially semiconductors (Grace 1990, 15). This distinction obviously catered to the interests of multinational chip makers, who were setting up shop in Malaysia during the 1970s.

These policies emerged in the wake of the political unrest of 1969, during the creation of the free trade zones that were designated as protected areas for foreign capital (see chapter 3). Part of the hidden agenda of the accelerated industrialization strategy under the New Economic Policy was the large-scale hiring of young Muslim women, exempt from existing labor protections. With the rapid emergence of an industrial working class of Malay origin, the country's ethnic majority group became a potential force in social conflicts between capital and labor. Government labor policies, therefore, tried to prevent the emergence of industrial unionism in the new exporting industries (Grace 1990, 6ff.). With the rapidly growing numbers of electronics workers, conditions developed for forming an industry-wide organization, particularly since the existing trade union for electrical workers, EIWU, actively promoted new organizing strategies in the electronics industry. The union based its strategy on a distinctively multiethnic approach that targeted women workers as trade union members, then a rare phenomenon in Malaysia (ibid., 44ff.).

In the face of mounting social tensions in the new industrial zones, restrictive government policies against trade unions were eased to a certain extent during the 1980s. A change in the trade union law in 1988 permitted trade unions in the "electronics" industry—but only at the factory level. This limited policy shift occurred during the expanded effort for industrial upgrading through human resource development that had begun in the 1980s. It reflected the increased orientation of Malaysia's governing elites toward Asian industrial policies, especially those of Japan.

> The state has not been able to eliminate trade unions per se, but incorporates and accommodates labor and ensures regime legitimacy as embodied in its "Look East" policy and promotion of in-house unions. Such a union structure is seen as representing a model for the advancement of national and enterprise interest, while an anti-Western and, in particular, pro-Japan, rhetoric has been used to try and mask labor exploitation and ensure control at the level of the factory and nation. (Bhopal and Todd 2000, 201)

This development, however, led to a deep split within the trade unions. The Electrical Industry Workers Union (EIWU) continued to target industry-wide trade union organization. However, the Malaysian Trade Union Council (MTUC), the umbrella organization of trade unions in Malaysia, was ready to accept company trade unions as a "lesser evil." At one point, even an electronics workers union was established to coordinate company unions in some of the bigger electronics factories in the Kuala Lumpur area. Multinational electronics firms, however, continued to pursue hard-core antiunion policies after 1988. Coordinated through the Malaysian American Electronics Industry association (MAEI), companies such as Motorola, AMD, and Hitachi repeatedly dismissed employees who tried to set up trade unions at a company level (Bhopal and Todd 2000, 199). Harris, a chip maker from the United States, tried to break a company trade union established under the trade union law of 1998, and the labor conflict lasted from 1990 through 2005. With union-busting tactics based on lawsuits and repression against individual employees, the company finally succeeded in exhausting the core of trade union activists (2005 interview, Harris Advance Union).

The labor policies of North American contract manufacturers in Malaysia reflect the same orientation (2003, 2005 interview data). Flextronics, a company usually emphasizing liberal and employee-friendly labor policies, took the lead. In a factory acquired from Ericsson in 2000 in Shah Alam, near Kuala Lumpur, the company tried to eliminate the branch organization of the EIWU, organized in the factory in 1974. After some key collective bargaining provisions were cancelled, the company challenged the legal existence of the trade union in litigation before the Labor Department. Based on the distinction between the "electrical" and "electronics" industries, the company questioned the legitimacy of an industrial trade union in "electronics" (2002, 2003 interview data). In spite of significant resistance among workers, the company finally prevailed. The authorities did not bother to evaluate the antiquated distinction between "electrical" and "electronics" in the age of integrated digital information technology. In the case of another factory taken over from the Japanese multinational Casio at the same location, Flextronics accepted the existing company union—showing that EMS companies are particularly opposed to industry-wide trade unions (2005 interview data). However, with the closure of the Shah Alam factory in 2009, the only remaining company union in Malaysian EMS factories was eliminated.

CHINA: MASS PRODUCTION, MIGRANT WORKERS, AND POSTSOCIALIST COMPANY PATERNALISM

The mass-production character of electronics contract manufacturing is very visible in China, where a large new industrial workforce has been created. The latecomer among the low-cost locations today boasts the highest number of production facilities and by far the largest number of workers. This development was propelled by the massive relocation of manufacturing after the year 2000 and by low labor costs, known as the "China price" (BW, December 5, 2004). Contract manufacturing factories and industrial parks in China are vertically integrated to a very high degree. A large spectrum of diversified labor processes has emerged which exceed the scope of production activities in most of the other locations examined in this book. At the same time, increasing regional differences in industry structure and labor markets has developed between major locations for electronics manufacturing. Segmentation along the chain is developing between large-scale EMS and ODM factories and small and medium-sized component producers and assembly shops.

The hallmark of industrial mass work in Chinese contract manufacturing is the massive employment of young, mostly women workers from rural areas. These migrant workers (a somewhat misleading term for industrial workers) shape the face of new exporting industries in an industrial society emerging at a very fast pace. Electronics contract manufacturing combines wage labor from poor and undeveloped areas with highly modern work and living environments in world-market factories. The system of labor migration in China discriminates against this workforce because the legal status of workers is still determined by the system of household registration (*hukou*) developed during the Mao period.

The labor policies in IT contract manufacturing represent the special case of a non-union environment at the center of China's new capitalism (Lüthje 2006). Official Chinese trade unions have hardly been able to gain a foothold. The institutional framework is different in the various locations. Labor laws are usually unenforced by local governments because of competition among regions. Companies have a relatively free hand in setting working conditions and employment policies. Because of mounting social tension, however, especially in the wake of the global financial and economic crisis of 2008, the central government is making increased efforts to stabilize labor policies. Significant changes have occurred in recent years, prompting companies to advertise and promote corporate social responsibility, compliance with labor laws, and limited acceptance of trade unions.

Regime of Work

In the key industrial regions of China, large complexes of electronics contract manufacturing have emerged, with modern production capacity and work organization. High-volume production uses standardized work processes. Specialized manufacturing at lower volumes, with new product introduction, is also growing but still appears relatively small compared with the enormous scale of mass manufacturing. Diversified production is a result of integrating the manufacturing of plastics and metal enclosures, cable assemblies, raw printed circuit boards, and other electronic and nonelectronic components in the operations of contract manufacturers. This is taking place especially in the industrial parks of large EMS providers such as Foxconn and Flextronics or in similar operations by leading ODM companies from Taiwan. With this diversification, skilled industrial work is also growing in maintenance, tool and die making, and mechanical engineering.

Like the other locations we examined, production technology in China is similar to that in industrialized countries and uses standard PCB-assembly and soldering equipment from a small number of global vendors. And like other low-cost areas, the potential for automation in manufacturing in China is not usually pushed to its limit because of the abundant availability of cheap labor. The work in Chinese contract manufacturing plants typically uses large-scale assembly lines. In no other country we studied did we observe lines of comparable size and volume. This is also true for manual assembly of printed circuit boards and systems. Production engineers and managers in China often emphasize the flexibility of manual labor and its economic advantages in the face of frequent ups and downs in manufacturing volume.

The organization of work inside the factories reflects diverse regional conditions in the major locations discussed in chapter 3. In the Pearl River Delta (PRD) in South China, simple mass production is the norm (high volume, low mix). More complex production is mainly found in the manufacturing of plastic parts and metal enclosures. In South China, this takes place primarily in the industrial parks and large factories of the leading EMS providers Foxconn and Flextronics. EMS factories in the greater Shanghai region are mostly located in modern industrial parks, where there is a higher proportion of flexible mass production of lead products using relatively complex assembly. Products include various kinds of telecommunications equipment, such as base stations for mobile communications, which incorporate relatively complex printed circuit boards and a high content of customer-specific configuration. However, a large amount of volume production also goes on in this region in the assembly of notebook computers and cell phones at the large ODM providers from Taiwan. Production of plastic and metal enclosures plays a minor role, mostly concentrated in smaller, specialized facilities with fewer than one thousand employees (2002–2009 interview and factory visit data).

Improved skills in manufacturing usually result from flexible-volume production and large amounts of maintenance and repair work, less so from specialized low-volume manufacturing. Chinese workers or production engineers perform most of the repair, maintenance, and programming of production equipment in China. Unlike in Malaysia, such work is usually not done by experts from external locations (such as Singapore and Taiwan) except for some highly complex processes such as printed circuit board manufacturing.

Shop-floor quality management is designed to support the Taylorist organization of production. Except for some areas of flexible mass production, cell- or group-based work organization is rare. Quality and the speed of work are usually checked via personal supervision by line leaders and foremen. Most areas in PCB and systems assembly have one supervisor per line and a number of shift leaders and managers in charge of work assignments, organization, and discipline. Experiments with technically and organizationally more sophisticated methods of work measurement, such as methods-time measurement (MTM), in some of the factories under investigation were aborted because of high costs and organizational problems.

Managers believe the high degree of work segmentation is adequate for the presumably low skill level of most workers. Direct personal control also seems to fit Chinese work culture, which is characterized by hierarchical thinking and the traditions of a planned economy. In relatively limited areas with higher work integration (such as the final assembly and configuration of telecommunications network equipment), complex and frequently changing process configurations, with a limited autonomy of task execution, were successfully introduced. However, the wages in such areas were not higher, in spite of higher skill and experience requirements. The jobs were seen as attractive by many workers since they were less monotonous and stressful (2002, 2003 interview data and factory visits).

The widespread use of Western or Japanese systems of quality management contributes to the picture of top-down organization. A system used globally by Flextronics to organize material flows (called demand flow technology) contains detailed rules for the design and organization of each workplace and a standardized description of work procedures. Basically, every worker has to check on the quality of the previous work step before beginning the next. Another system of this kind is Six Sigma, originally developed in Japan. This consists of a simple set of basic rules for workplace behavior, especially orderliness and timeliness. Individual employees can earn awards and degrees—in China, mostly limited to foremen and management personnel.

In the modern large factory environment of electronics contract manufacturing in China, the structure of work within and among major companies is relatively homogenous. Working conditions are similar to those at large multinational brand-name firms. The level of pay, however, is significantly lower. In South China, work in contract manufacturing compares favorably with small and medium electronics parts suppliers and other light manufacturing such as garments, shoes, and toys, which employ more than ten million people in the region (T. Chan 2005). Work at electronics contract manufacturers is comparable to work at the large, vertically integrated mass-production factories of Taiwanese first-tier contract manufacturers in the garment and shoe industries that produce for famous multinational brands such as Adidas, Nike, and Reebok. The smaller electronics parts factories we studied in Guangdong are dominated by rigid forms of Taylorist assembly-line work but at a much lower level of technology than at EMS firms. Sometimes the representatives of major customers exercise direct control of work processes (2002, 2004, 2005, 2009 interview data).

Systematic data does not exist for occupational safety and health in Chinese IT contract manufacturing factories. Working conditions seem to be relatively good, especially in comparison with smaller electronics parts suppliers. In the subtropical climate of South China, the use of air-conditioning in manufacturing plants contributes significantly to favorable working conditions. However, air-conditioning is rare in dormitories. In PCB and systems assembly, safety equipment, rules, and procedures are largely up to international standards, favored by globally uniform production equipment and concepts. The same can be said for the high-tech sections of supply production. At a major US-based EMS contract manufacturer in South China, the highly toxic and environmentally hazardous processes of printed circuit board manufacturing are performed in closed systems, using the highest safety standards developed by a subsidiary of the company in Germany. Volume manufacturing of plastic parts is automated, often to a higher degree and with lower exposure of workers to noise and hazardous fumes than in comparable plants in North America or Eastern Europe. However, the production of simple plastic parts (e.g., for computer mice) and paint spraying is often performed with methods and equipment that are highly hazardous to workers' health, frequently with no or insufficient protective gear (2002–2005 factory visits). Major health hazards include stress, repetitive motion, and extremely long working hours (see Brown and O'Rourke 2007). The high demand for external medical advice from doctors' offices, hospitals, and NGOs on these issues illustrates the need for occupational health education and services—especially among young migrant workers from the countryside (2002–2005 interview data from hospitals and NGOs in Shenzhen, Hong Kong, and Guangzhou).

Regime of Employment

China has become a magnet for assembly industries of all kinds because of its low wages and salaries. In the EMS factories in the Pearl River Delta, the monthly wages in the years between 2002 and 2004 hovered around 500 and 800 renminbi (RMB) (about US$60–100 at that time), including overtime. The monthly wages of unskilled or semiskilled operators are near the legal minimum fixed by local governments at the city and township level. In 2000 this was usually around US$60 in the PRD area. In the face of a growing labor shortage in the area during 2005 and 2006, minimum monthly wages were raised substantially to around 800 RMB in most locations (about

US$100). The 2008–2009 economic crisis and massive layoffs in the region have stopped the rise of minimum wages, however. Many factories in the region often do not pay the full minimum wage, and enforcement by local authorities has been lax, particularly prior to 2004.

In Shanghai and Suzhou, the comparable wage rates were about 20–30 percent higher, one of the reasons why many migrant workers preferred to leave the PRD and seek work farther north during the boom before 2008. There are vast differences between locations in the greater Shanghai area. In the internationally well-known industrial parks in Shanghai's Pudong area, monthly wages for assembly workers at international electronics firms were around 1,200–1,500 RMB (US$150–185 in 2005). In Suzhou, they were 1,000–1,200 RMB, and in neighboring Kunshan, a city dominated by Taiwanese companies, they averaged 800–1,000 RMB. The highest operator wages paid by contract manufacturers were found in Beijing, around 1,200–1,500 RMB per month (2002–2005 interview data).

The salaries of skilled workers and engineers are considerably higher but still very low by international standards. In South China, engineers were hired as recent graduates from major universities during 2003 and 2004 at 2,000 RMB per month by major contract manufacturers from Taiwan. Technicians earned around 1,500–1,800 RMB. At North American contract manufacturers, salaries and wages were about 25 percent higher, especially because of the English-language proficiency required by these companies. Engineers' salaries tend to rise rapidly with tenure and experience, and after two years of work, most engineers can double their salary. Pay for skilled personnel is about 20–30 percent higher in the Shanghai region than in South China, and in Beijing, about 50 percent higher. In and around Shanghai, the differences among various locations are considerable. In Kunshan, at the lower end of the regional pay scale, an experienced engineer in contract manufacturing earns 3,000–4,000 RMB per month, but in Shanghai, the same engineer will earn twice that. As we explain in more detail below, these variations reflect the differences between the local labor migration systems in the various locations.

In general, wage hierarchies are strongly polarized. Skilled workers and supervisors often make three to five times more than operators. Skilled workers and administrative personnel have had a strong upward trend in pay during recent years (before 2008), especially for employees with good English skills. This reflects the massive shortage of skilled workers, particularly in the industrial areas of the Pearl River Delta with their unattractive living conditions. On the other hand, the wages for operators have risen only modestly, even during the "labor shortage." The increases between 2004 and 2008 were mostly a result of increases in the minimum wage and the central government's policies for improving the living conditions of migrant workers. Minimum wages were increased by around 20 percent during that period, but companies continued to pay base wages at, or even below, the minimum (2004, 2005 interview data).

Employees of all kinds work large amounts of overtime. In South China in particular, production workers, and often technicians and engineers, are housed in factory dormitories, with no family life or other personal interests and duties. Migrant workers in assembly have to compensate for their low wages with extensive overtime on a regular basis. At the same time, a substantial portion of wages is sent to families in workers' rural home communities. Most factories run two or three shifts, five to seven days per week. The legal workweek in China is forty hours, and thirty-six hours of overtime work are permitted per month. In almost every contract manufacturing facility, overtime is part of regular shift plans. The extra pay legally required for overtime is often not paid.

Such practices have been publicly reported and documented for Foxconn in Shenzhen, the biggest electronics manufacturing facility in the world. Here, a fourteen-hour workday is the rule, with no extra pay for overtime (*DC Ribao*, June 22, 2006; *BBC News*, August 18, 2006; 2004, 2005 interview data).[3] After a series of negative media reports, the company began to pay overtime and shifted to a much-publicized policy of compliance with labor laws. However, overly long working hours are still part of normal work organization because of an exemption from Chinese labor law granted by the Labor Bureau of Shenzhen. This practice was upheld even during the recession in 2008–2009, when the company laid off about sixty thousand workers in a few months (2009 interview data).

In all the factories in our investigation, the wage system for operators is based on hourly pay. Piece rates or output-related wage incentives could not be found. The situation in the big EMS and ODM factories differs markedly from that in smaller component assembly shops, where piece rates are widespread. Piece rates are often used to push the regular base wage below the legal minimum (2008 interview data). Contract manufacturers in China do not pay individual or group bonuses to meet quality or productivity targets. Wages are also not linked to "customer satisfaction," as they are in many other locations around the world. The only form of bonus payments are quarterly profit-sharing payments provided routinely by North American EMS firms. Thus, productivity control and incentives in China seem to rely more on traditional means of direct control and work segmentation than in most other locations we studied.

The pay systems of contract manufacturers in China barely provide incentives for operators to accumulate seniority, even during permanent labor shortages. Seniority-related wage increases do not exist for operators. Some EMS factories in South China pay attendance bonuses while other factories in the same region do not, since they see regular attendance as a basic element of work performance. Attendance is usually achieved by strict control. In one North American EMS company in South China, workers are dismissed without further notice if they report late for work three times. In Taiwanese companies, attendance is additionally enforced by the widespread practice of group appeals and joint physical exercise at the beginning of each work shift (2003, 2004 factory visits).

A key part of the production system in Chinese contract manufacturing plants is housing for workers in factory dormitories, which provide food and other services on company premises. In the facilities studied, dormitory rooms for operators usually housed eight to twelve persons. More highly skilled workers lived in rooms with two to four beds. In Taiwanese companies, many mid- and high-level managers also stay in dormitories of higher standards. The quality of the dormitories for workers varies widely. The better ones have recreational facilities, such as gyms, group rooms, and cafés. Lodging and cafeteria food is usually provided at company expense. The cost per worker is usually one third to one half the monthly wage. For higher-skilled employees, it is proportionally lower. Company-provided food, lodging, and recreational facilities usually cover an operator's basic living expenses. The quality of dormitories and food is thus a key factor determining the attractiveness of a particular workplace, often more important than the quality of the work. In the absence of seniority-based wages, better-than-average housing and food are key incentives for staying with a particular company or factory.

Recruitment and Employment Policies

The massive concentration of electronics contract manufacturing in China is reflected in employment figures. In 2005, the total number of employees among EMS contract manufacturers in China was estimated at 250,000–300,000, according to data obtained from companies. At that time, Foxconn alone employed two hundred thousand workers in China. Before the global crisis of 2008, employment saw another surge, especially at Foxconn. In 2008, the company reported 700,000 workers all over China, fully 320,000 of them at the giant Shenzhen Longhua facility ("Foxconn City"), another 80,000 in other facilities in Shenzhen, and the remainder in about a half-dozen newly built industrial parks in other parts of China, such as Kunshan, Hangzhou, Nanjing, Yantai, and Wuhan (Lüthje 2008). For ODM firms, there are no figures available for overall employment in China. According to the Taiwan Labor and Education Center (TLIEA 2006), twenty-one thousand employees worked for Taiwanese ODM companies in Suzhou and Kunshan. A similar number are estimated to have worked in Shanghai and other locations in the region in 2006.

Contract manufacturing factories have the employment profile of typical manufacturing facilities. In most of the sites in our investigation, 70–80 percent of the workforce was classified as *direct labor*, that is, workers in assembly, maintenance, inventory, and other manufacturing-related areas. The overwhelming majority of these workers are migrants from other provinces. Local workers are employed only in some upper-category industrial parks in Suzhou, Shanghai, and Beijing. Migrant workers usually are recruited through government or private recruitment agencies in densely populated provinces in inland areas such as Sichuan, Hunan, Jiangxi, Henan, and Yunnan. Many provincial and city governments in rural areas maintain relationships with city governments at the locations of contract manufacturing, providing for a relatively regulated system of workforce recruitment (for an extensive analysis of such mechanisms, see Hsing 1998, 84–85). Some of the facilities we studied received several busloads of new workers every day. Most of them have to travel several hundred or thousand kilometers and therefore return to their villages or hometowns only once or twice a year, usually around the Chinese New Year festival in January or February. The majority of the workers are very young women, usually between eighteen and twenty-five years of age. Sometimes it cannot be verified that the workers are really at least eighteen, the legal minimum age for industrial work (2003, 2004 interview data).

Indirect labor comprises engineers, administrative personnel, and sales personnel, as well as supervisors, technicians, and line leaders. The number of engineers and technicians has been rising rapidly. Most engineers work in production or the development of components such as printed circuit boards, plastics, and metal parts. Bigger factories often employ several hundred engineers, a majority of them Chinese, recruited from better-known universities and colleges in the country. At Foxconn in Shenzhen alone, five thousand engineers were employed in 2004 (interview data). Foreign or overseas Chinese engineers occupy only the top levels of their departments. These expatriates earn several times more than their Chinese colleagues. A considerable number of engineers come from other developing economies in Asia, such as India, Malaysia, and the Philippines. The salaries of these employees rank somewhere between those of foreign and native Chinese employees.

In South China, engineers are almost exclusively hired from other provinces, not through mass recruitment like operators, but from universities and career fairs. In the Shanghai area, the proportion of locally recruited engineers is much higher, between 30 and 70 percent. All companies complain about the lack of skilled personnel for such positions. Among supervisors and technicians, labor shortages also spur external recruitment. Training and promotion of skilled production workers into such positions are rare. Technical workers are usually men, but in China the gender stratification at these levels is not as rigid as in most other countries we studied. Women are a minority among skilled workers and supervisors in Chinese factories, but they are not exceptional (2002–2005 interview data).

The recruitment strategies of contract manufacturers and the regulation of labor markets in the industry is heavily shaped by the Chinese labor migration system. In postrevolutionary China, urban workers enjoyed much better living conditions than the rural population did. Compared to the countryside, urban environments offered a low but relatively secure standard of living and comprehensive social services provided through the workplace (*danwei*). The relatively privileged situation of urban industrial workers reflected the social cleavages in the Soviet model of industrialization that was practiced in China between 1955 and the late 1970s. This model was based on the transformation of economic surpluses from the countryside at the expense of peasants. The division between urban and rural population was rooted in the system of household registration (*hukou*), introduced immediately after the foundation of the People's Republic in order to control the large-scale migration of peasants suffering from war and warlord government during the preceding decades. The *hukou* system is based on the principle that individuals must be registered at the place of their native family household and can enjoy their civil and social rights (including welfare, health care, and school education) as well as their party membership only in this community. Transferring one's *hukou* from a rural location to a city is very difficult. Migrant workers, therefore, have a guest worker status in the location of their employment, with no citizenship or social rights. Until recently, they were not even allowed to join trade unions. This position and its related social, ethnic, and cultural discrimination define the conditions of existence for about 150 million migrant workers in China (Solinger 1999).

In recent years, the *hukou* policies of local governments have contributed to an increasing social differentiation among the migrant workforce in major urban regions. In most cities of the Pearl River Delta, for example, skilled technicians, managers, and engineers can obtain permanent residence with no major problems. But production workers cannot transfer their *hukou* from the countryside to the city, even after many years of employment. In other regions, skilled employees are privileged in similar ways. In these locations, however, production workers have some options for gaining permanent residence and access to social services and education after several years of work in the city. Such differences in migration patterns and local labor market policies are reflected in the composition of the contract manufacturing workforce. In South China's Guangdong Province, EMS factories almost exclusively employ migrant workers. In Shanghai, Suzhou, and Beijing, the proportion of migrant workers is much lower. In Suzhou Industrial Park (SIP), migrant workers are only about 10 percent of the production workforce of major EMS contract manufacturers, mostly from nearby rural areas in the province. In this area, workers' housing is not provided by the companies. Instead, the city builds dormitories of relatively decent standards and rents them out to companies or workers directly (2005, 2006 interview data). Migrant workers can also become members of a special social insurance scheme modeled after Singapore's social insurance and housing credit system, with relatively decent benefits. It has to be said, however, that in outlying areas of the same city, which house mostly Taiwanese ODM manufacturers, living conditions are much worse. The companies here employ mostly migrant workers as operators (2009 interview data and factory visits).

In every region—including the Pearl River Delta—it is becoming more and more evident that the large-scale migration of workers into these areas is no longer a transitional phenomenon. A relatively stable urban working class is emerging in spite of restrictive migration policies. Many migrant workers today have worked for ten years or more in the area. Even during the crisis of 2008–2009, workers tended to return to their home provinces only temporarily (2009 interview data). This trend reflects the massive industrial development the region underwent during the past two decades, which cannot be reversed even as a result of enforced restructuring. During the labor shortage between 2004 and 2008, the companies hired more and more workers from the local labor market, that is, migrant workers in the region who had previously worked for other electronics companies. Job ads at factory gates, newspaper and Internet advertising, and job fairs organized by local labor bureaus and private agencies are the main channels for finding workers. Because labor markets have become increasingly localized, temporary labor has played a relatively limited role in the recruitment strategies of contract manufacturers in South China and other locations.

The hallmark of this development has been extremely flexible labor markets, reflected in high, sometimes extreme turnover rates among the workforces of South China contract manufacturers. In the factories we studied between 2003 and 2005, the lowest turnover rate was 25 percent of the workforce per year, and 30–40 percent could be considered the standard rate, including at the largest factories. In the Shanghai area, turnover appeared to be lower, mostly due to a more stable labor market in some of the top locations (2003–2005 interview data). The flexible labor market became particularly visible during the crisis in 2008–2009. Contract manufacturers reacted to the crisis with large-scale layoffs of tens of thousands of workers. Foxconn publicly announced in 2008 that it would reduce its workforce of seven hundred thousand in China by 15 percent. In the Shenzhen Longhua facility, sixty thousand workers were laid off in late 2008 and early 2009 or did not return from their home villages after the Chinese New Year. In Shanghai and Suzhou, layoffs were smaller. Some factories tried to retain at least their more skilled workers during the crisis—a policy encouraged by some local governments in the area.

Skill Development

Skill development figures prominently in the rhetoric of economic modernization in China. However, conditions in the major locations and factories of
electronics contract manufacturing tell a different story. The skill level of
migrant production workers is generally low. In 2003, the Labor Bureau of
the City of Dongguan estimated that the proportion of academically trained
individuals among the five million rural workers in the city was less than 10
percent (2003 interview data). Academic studies, however, reveal that the
level of education of workers in the Pearl River Delta is generally higher than
the terms "migrant workers" or "floating population" would suggest. About
two-thirds of migrant workers in coastal areas have graduated from China's
nine-year general high-school system, and many hold higher degrees, making
them eligible for university studies (Hsing 1998, 36–37). In the contract
manufacturing factories we studied, a high-school diploma is a general requirement for hiring.

Government training centers and vocational schools offer few skill development opportunities for operators in electronics manufacturing. This is particularly true for the migrant workers of cities in South China but also holds
true for Shanghai. Only in Suzhou is the picture different. Here, close collab-
oration between major contract manufacturers and other electronics companies with local high schools and technical colleges is used to recruit local
workers (2005, 2009 interview data).

The absence of skill development opportunities for migrant workers reflects the orientation of local governments, which use large-scale exploitation of low-wage labor as a tool for economic development. The Labor
Bureaus in Dongguan and Shenzhen explicitly count on the fact that most
employers look for only cheap, unskilled labor. They therefore see training
and skill development provided by local government as unnecessary (2003
interview data). This situation is reinforced by the gender structure of labor
markets. Many managers, as well as the Chinese public, view simple assembly work as adequate employment for young women from rural areas (Lee
1998). This is a stereotype well known in other developing industrial countries, such as Mexico and Malaysia, and even in the European and US electronics industry of former decades.

The skill and training systems of contract manufacturers in China are
usually designed along globally uniform company guidelines. Training is
mostly done on the job. North American contract manufacturers offer two or
three days of orientation on the workplace and company values. For more
specialized tasks, new employees can receive up to eight weeks of training.
Contract manufacturers from Taiwan usually have a longer orientation of one
to two weeks in order to promulgate company philosophy and rules of behavior in the workplace. Administrative and technical employees receive a rela-

tively broad spectrum of training and career development programs. Often training courses are integrated into company-wide programs called the "company university," offering distance learning and video instruction through the Internet. The main function of these programs is to disseminate a globally uniform image of the company and the behavior of its employees, especially in interaction with customers. In countries such as China, these programs also launch international careers in the company. At all levels, the training programs of contract manufacturers focus on workplace and company-specific skills. In spite of these limitations, skill development opportunities at major contract manufacturers are much better than in most small and medium-sized component suppliers and assembly service shops.

Regime of Control

The low-wage contract manufacturing factories in China do not exist in a political vacuum. Labor policies have been shaped by massive changes in the regulation of wage labor over the past two decades. The reforms of labor laws and the trade union system and the politics of labor migration are major elements in this scenario. So, too, is the client relationship between local governments and party organizations and domestic and international investors, a relationship based on the far-reaching fiscal and political autonomy of cities and provinces (Hsing 1998, 110ff.) Chinese labor laws created after the 1990s provide a relatively well-defined framework for regulating wage labor and follow the norms of developed capitalist countries (for details, see Taylor, Chang, and Li 2003) as well as the traditions of state-corporatist interest mediation (A. Chan 1993). The rule of law established through this historic process marks a fundamental change in Chinese labor relations, which were shaped by the nonantagonistic traditions of the socialist factory community (*danwei*) (Lee 2002, 197).

The laws are directed at harmonious regulation of rapidly unfolding antagonisms between capital and labor. But they are controlled and enforced in very selective ways. Relatively favorable institutional conditions for law-based labor regimes can be found in state-owned enterprises (SOE) and Chinese-foreign joint ventures. In contrast, laws are weakly enforced in the exporting industries in coastal provinces, especially in former special economic zones and areas with high proportions of overseas Chinese capital. In these areas, trade unions are almost completely absent, and the workforce has no tradition of trade union and social organizing (Taylor, Chang, and Li 2003). As already explained in chapter 3, the "flexibility" of local governments in interpreting existing laws is a major mechanism of competition between locations in China.

Electronics contract manufacturing is an example of this. In Guangdong Province, the industry's most important location in China, the nonenforcement of labor laws by local governments is standard practice. Although the law provides a stable framework for setting up trade unions in foreign-invested enterprises, until recently the progovernment All China Federation of Trade Unions (ACFTU) barely had a presence in contract manufacturing plants in the Pearl River Delta. In all of the factories in our investigation, the legally mandatory collective contract, which defines the framework for management-employee relationships on the shop floor, did not exist (2003–2006 interview data). There were no efforts to establish official trade union organizations in electronics manufacturing plants of foreign and overseas Chinese investors until 2006, although some local trade union officials saw this as a problem. In the only EMS factory in our investigation that had a company trade union at that time, the union was represented by a line leader selected by the company. There is no systematic analysis of workers' grievances, lawsuits, and labor conflicts in Chinese electronics factories. Massive protests and labor conflicts remain the exception, although their number and scope had been rising under the impact of the labor shortage between 2004 and 2008 (C. Chan 2008). At the same time, local NGOs and law experts report a rising number of grievances and lawsuits over violations of labor laws (Lüthje 2008).

Against this backdrop of mounting social tensions, contract manufacturers have been experimenting with various policies to stabilize workplace relations. Most of these concepts mirror the modern company paternalism that is dominant in non-union IT companies in the United States, particularly in Silicon Valley (Lüthje 2001). These policies reflect a continued emphasis on "company values," the ample use of quality management programs, the extensive recreational facilities and activities in large factories, and the involvement of clubs and associations of migrant workers in managing social affairs in dormitories and cafeterias. The largest EMS factory in South China offers a wide range of shops and fast-food restaurants on its premises. Fitness centers, movie theaters, and recreational facilities, including sophisticated computer game rooms and a cybercafé for clerical workers, are designed to give a metropolitan feel to the lives of migrant workers from urban areas.

Obviously, such practices reflect the fact that migrant workers, young women in particular, are seeking wage labor not only because of economic need but in hopes of a better urban lifestyle in cities and factories (Hsing 1998, 99). Modern company paternalism can also draw on some of the traditions of the socialist *danwei*, with its cradle-to-grave care for workers organized through the factory (Li 1996). The permanent advertising of company values aims to produce a kind of social identification despite an environment of low wages and weak regulation of working conditions and employee rights. That environment hardly offers workers any long-term opportunity for professional and personal development.

Paternalism in EMS companies and workplaces, however, is only one element in the complex regulation of wage labor in a situation in which workplace, social, and government institutions in postsocialist China have become fragmented, which Ching Kwan Lee (2002) describes as "disorganized despotism." This concept refers to tacit or open alliances between the local party and the government apparatus on the one hand, and the companies on the other. These alliances are driven by a joint interest in maintaining the weak enforcement of existing labor, health and safety, and environmental regulations, which creates a legal vacuum for capitalist development and unintelligible and personalized power relations between investors and government officials.

In the PRD region, this system creates massive competition between cities and townships to deregulate labor relations. It results in significant differences in the level of local minimum wages, which, according to the law, should be determined by consultations among local government, employers, and trade unions. In Shenzhen, for example, the minimum wage in 2004 in the two city districts with the highest concentration of electronics manufacturing was 595 RMB (approximately US$73 at that time) in one area and 460 RMB in the other. Minimum wages were raised under pressure from the so-called labor shortage in the PRD after 2004, but enforcement mechanisms remained weak.

Regulation of living conditions in dormitories also differs widely. Most local labor bureaus maintain rules that have gradually become stricter in recent years in response to bad publicity and workers' protests. However, in Dongguan, for example, a guideline published in 2003 prohibited occupancy of a single dormitory bed by two or three workers working on different shifts—a big improvement, according to government representatives (2003 interview data).

Workers in EMS factories are relatively powerless because they lack collective contracts and representation that could pressure for labor relations based on negotiation. Due to the absence of collective bargaining, it is almost impossible for workers to claim even the simplest social norms and individual rights in the workplace, even though they exist in labor law. The weakness of collective rights and collective bargaining is a general feature of Chinese labor relations, even in workplaces where the official Chinese trade union has a presence (see Taylor, Chang, and Li 2003, 155ff.). In the non-union environment of large-scale contract manufacturing plants, the institutionally disorganized politics of production makes labor relations unstable. The number of lawsuits is increasing, a hallmark of frequent violations of individual workers' legal rights. Guangdong Province has had the highest per capita number of officially registered labor conflicts (i.e., petitions to labor bureaus or lawsuits in labor courts) in China for many years (Sun 2000, 168ff.; Lee 2007, 160ff.).

Recent sociological studies have analyzed in detail the way daily shop-floor conflicts can produce a rising tide of court and arbitration procedures and even promote worker activism and self-organization (A. Chan 2001; Lee 2002, 2007; Pun 2005). Contract manufacturing fits this pattern. There are hardly any collective labor lawsuits by groups of workers at major contract manufacturers in the PRD (2003, 2005 NGO interviews). The labor legislation of recent years and media coverage of related social issues have raised workers' awareness of their rights in the workplace. This became particularly visible after the introduction of the Labor Contract Law of 2008. A large number of worker protests and lawsuits against unfair dismissals and non-payment of wages followed the global economic crisis in 2008 (2009 NGO interviews). Large and modern electronics contract factories offer an example of the most widespread form of individual resistance to intolerable working conditions—changing one's job and employer. Turnover rates between 30 percent and 60 percent of the workforce among contract manufacturers in the PRD show that even relatively good benefits in housing, food, and recreation do not significantly stabilize the workforce.

In some major contract manufacturing plants, tragic incidents have highlighted the often desperate situation of individual workers who seek to escape the permanent pressure of management control and workplace stress. At Foxconn in Shenzhen in June 2009, a younger technical worker killed himself by jumping off a high-rise building inside the factory after he had been blamed for leaking prototypes of Apple's famed iPhone to parties outside the factory (Xinhua, June 17, 2009). In the first half of 2010, a series of suicides of ten young migrant workers at "Foxconn City" shook the Chinese public and, for the first time, triggered massive discussions about the production regime at Foxconn and the need to change the model of economic development in China's exporting industries.

In 2006, the situation in Foxconn's giant industrial park in Shenzhen also gave rise to the first major public debate in China about the working conditions at contract manufacturers and subsequently caused significant changes in labor relations. A report in a British tabloid exposed the working conditions in the production of Apple's iPod music player at Foxconn. Chinese media then ran numerous stories about ultralow wages and extremely long working hours in Foxconn factories in Shenzhen and other locations around the country. The company's extensive control system could not prevent workers from reporting to Chinese media that violation of labor laws was a common practice at Foxconn. The company sued three journalists from *First Financial News* in Shanghai, the country's most respected business daily, for US$3.5 million for what was called "inaccurate reporting." A storm of protest erupted in Chinese media and on websites, including the central organ of the Communist Party of China. As a result, a local Shenzhen court injunction was quickly repealed, and the All China Federation of Trade Unions announced that it would establish a trade union at Foxconn (Xinhua, September 1, 2006). This process coincided with the widely publicized organizing of a trade union at Walmart in China, in which Shenzhen was also a major focus. In the case of Foxconn, however, the ACFTU did not mobilize rank-and-file workers, although it did at Walmart (Feng 2007).

The trade union at Foxconn has become integrated into the company's HR management—mirroring common practices in many Chinese and multinational first-tier companies. Foxconn also changed its attitude toward labor laws. Company chairman Terry Guo appeared in the Chinese media at the end of 2007 and declared full support for the newly enacted Labor Contract Law and for related government efforts to improve the enforcement of labor standards. This attitude reflects the increasing difficulty multinational contract manufacturers have in controlling the social and political costs of their despotic low-wage regime. It also reflects the increasing sensitivity of labor relations in Taiwanese factories in the context of economic reunification and political détente between the People's Republic and Taiwan. Major contract manufacturers from North America and Europe have adopted similar attitudes in recent years. At Flextronics, labor unions have been established in every major factory in China under a general company policy adopted in 2008. However, most of these trade unions are weak and seem to be completely controlled by the company (2009 interview data and field research).

The term "corporate social responsibility" (CSR) is frequently used when multinational electronics companies deliberate about working conditions in China. Apple, Hewlett-Packard, and Nokia are among the major global brands that have pushed this idea in China in recent years, through the *Electronics Industry Code of Conduct* (EICC) and its implementation in Chinese EMS and component manufacturer operations. These efforts have focused on Foxconn in particular, in response to public concern over the labor situation in the company's megafactories, but also in response to the generalized discourse about a "harmonious society" in China's current political leadership. The trade union at Foxconn is also actively promoting CSR. It sees cooperation with EICC compliance auditors from multinational customers as one of its major tasks—a channel of communication happily accepted by multinational companies well known for their non-union attitudes around the world. Nevertheless, many of the "flexible interpretations" of Chinese labor laws at major contract manufacturers, such as the regime of permanent overtime at Foxconn, continue with cooperation from local governments. At Foxconn, the trade union refers to the EICC-defined limit for working hours of sixty per week as an internationally accepted standard for working hours in electronics manufacturing (Lüthje 2008; 2009 interview data). In the wake of the suicide series at Foxconn in 2010, it became publicly known that the chairman of the Foxconn trade union was also a personal aide to Foxconn chairman Terry Guo. Chinese labor experts publicly criticized the trade union at Foxconn as a "fake" trade union that would not fulfill its legal role to represent the interests of the workers (Caijing, June 4, 2010). Obviously, the tragic events at Foxconn marked the total failure of the Electronics Industry Code of Conduct.

EASTERN EUROPE: LOW-COST PRODUCTION AND FORCED COOPERATION

Until the crisis of 2001, only relatively simple mass-produced products, such as computers, telephones, printers, modems, and disposable cameras, were manufactured in EMS factories in Eastern Europe. After precarious upgrading in 2001, the product spectrum became broader and more diversified, including telecommunications networks, radio equipment, and measurement equipment. In the area of higher-end consumer products, smaller volumes of printers, cell phones, card readers, and copy machines were added, accompanied by non-IT products such as toys, washing machines, irons, and ATMs, as well as automotive, medical, and industrial electronics. Printed circuit board assembly, systems assembly, and related logistics were still at the center of activity. The logistics component changed as well. Large-scale delivery operations for high-volume products, which were dominant before 2001, disappeared after the global downturn, replaced by a host of smaller delivery and repair centers for smaller volumes.

Regime of Work

As in the other regions, working conditions in Eastern Europe are characterized by relatively high levels of technology and organization. PCB assembly is performed mostly by automated placement machinery. Equipment is state of the art, and working environments are well lit with relatively little noise and fumes. In addition, there are relatively large areas performing manual soldering. Compared with other electronics manufacturing facilities in the region, manual assembly of components is less tedious at contract manufacturers. Exhaust for soldering fumes is better, and well-lit factory buildings reduce the strain on workers' vision. Work is dominated by repetitive and line-based hand assembly, however. Workers in manual assembly and inspection typically are women, although some factories in Europe have a mixed-gender workforce. More complex testing work, usually separated from assembly lines and performed with automated equipment, is dominated by men. Men also make up the majority of workers manufacturing nonelectronic supply parts, which occupies an important position in the product spectrum of Eastern European EMS factories. In plastic injection molding, male and female workers are employed in varying proportion, although paint spraying is performed almost exclusively by men. Working conditions in these areas often recall a traditional large factory environment with a lot of noise and fumes. Significant technological innovations were introduced in recent years, such as fully automated paint spraying in separate cabins. Higher-skilled production work, tool and die making, and maintenance are also dominated by men. In these areas, classical craft work involves steady work schedules and substantial control by workers over the work process.

Engineers are employed both in production areas (in testing, quality management, and process development) and in nonproduction-related design and logistics. Although most EMS companies have promotion policies for women, the proportion of women in engineering is only 20 percent (2002 interview data). Employees are usually rather young, in their early thirties on average. Management of Eastern European EMS facilities is mostly local. The number of expatriate managers and specialists dispatched from lead factories in Western Europe has dropped significantly, although general managers and supply-chain managers are still mostly from Western European countries. Employees are usually categorized as "direct" and "indirect" labor. Indirect labor includes not only white-collar employees not directly involved in production, but also production and service workers in areas such as inventory, cleaning, and cafeteria services, whose jobs have been outsourced to external providers.

Manufacturing facilities, most of them built at greenfield sites, feature modern, open architecture. Manufacturing areas are visible from most offices, as are resting and smoking areas. Many offices have glass walls, including those of top managers. In many factories a relatively relaxed atmosphere prevails, and workers display considerable self-confidence. Music from radios can often be heard, employees often enjoy opportunities for short conversations, and the work style is cooperative. Team-oriented work practices are reinforced by the shift of production from standardized mass manufacturing to smaller volumes of more highly specialized products with varying customer requirements. Some degree of spontaneous communication and team building has become necessary to support flexibility in the workplace, typical of low-cost mass production in Eastern Europe.

As a model for production "without product," contract manufacturing faces special challenges. Motivating, identifying, and retaining employees is a challenge reinforced by continuously unstable market demand and production volume. From a shop-floor point of view, massive competition among contract manufacturers for customers imposes enormous pressure on quality and timeliness of delivery. Not surprisingly, complaints by management about the limited motivation of employees is common (2003, 2005 interview data). Managers routinely explain this behavior as a heritage of the socialist planned economy of former decades, which they allege limits the development of factories and companies.

Constantly promoting customer satisfaction is a key strategy in meeting these motivational challenges. On posters in manufacturing buildings, in visual displays of production targets along assembly lines, and in group sessions, workforce meetings, and award ceremonies, the customer is portrayed as the person on whom everybody in the factory depends, operator and general manager alike. Joint efforts to maximize customer satisfaction are declared everybody's "job number one," including by reducing costs through deferring wage raises (2003, 2005 interview data). Customer satisfaction is also measured in mathematical terms, as a customer satisfaction index that is displayed to workers in various ways. This service culture is accompanied by permanent competition between and within factories, a tactic taken from textbooks on lean management. Factory departments, such as inventory, logistics, and assembly, are organized as profit centers, and operating profits are constantly compared among business units.

Production is generally organized as teamwork in very restrictive forms. "Customer focus teams," in charge of communicating with one or several customers, exist at upper levels. Organization of customer-specific teams continues all the way down to manufacturing. Regular meetings between group leaders and workers evaluate the achievement of production targets and discuss improvements. The growing number of low-volume manufacturing contracts with higher complexity makes this kind of organization desirable. But production teams also exist in areas where high-volume production predominates and semiskilled women workers perform highly Taylorized work on long assembly lines. Here, competition is organized between groups of workers on different assembly lines or between shifts. It focuses on manufacturing yields, attendance rates, cleanliness, and proposals for improvement. Teams have to monitor the quality of the work performed by the previous team and report any defects or failures. Each failure and unreported defect detected at later stages is counted as a loss of quality points. Points cause a reduction in the variable portion of the wage (2003 interview data).

Comprehensive competition among employees is enforced by strict control of individual work performance. Almost every site under investigation introduced the scanning of bar codes on work pieces and parts at the beginning of each work step. That scanning is a standard method for tracking assembly defects down to individual work steps. Besides punishing individual workers with wage loss in the case of frequent failures, the identification of failure sources is the basis for a continuous improvement process by production teams.

In spite of the promotion of teamwork, team values, and jointness, this highly competitive form of work organization does not substantially involve workers in decision making. Managers routinely explain that workers are not mature enough for self-directed work groups or codetermination. The mentality in Eastern Europe is different from that in Western European countries such as Germany. In Eastern Europe, strict management directives are considered necessary, and managers believe that otherwise people would be disoriented. Strong identification with the company is expected from workers, especially given higher quality and flexibility requirements. But work organization remains competitive and hierarchical. Personal dependence on supervisors and managers is not replaced by market-style workplace relations, but reinforced.

Regime of Employment

Employee recruitment is usually based on minimum skill standards, which vary from country to country and have changed substantially in recent years. In most locations, contract manufacturers required above-average education and skill credentials during their initial years and lowered their requirements in subsequent years. In Hungary, Poland, and Estonia, a ten- or twelve-grade high-school diploma or an apprenticeship were the general prerequisites for recruitment. In recent years, only an eighth-grade high-school diploma has been required. These recruitment standards reflect the situation in local labor markets. Where skilled labor is in ample supply, the standards are kept high. In Romania, a twelve-year high-school diploma is still required, even for production workers (2005, 2007 interview data).

Usually, companies conduct recruitment in close cooperation with local labor offices. These government agencies provide customized services to contract manufacturing companies. Data banks are assigned to each company, with data on potential recruits and former workers who may have been laid off. In one case in Romania, the company laid off 650 workers and rehired 500 of them through the local labor office after nine months, saving on complicated recruitment procedures and job interviews. In recent times, however, temporary labor agencies have increasingly taken over recruitment services for flexible employment.

Hiring is usually preceded by extensive tests lasting two weeks and then a three-month probation period, during which workers acquire the skills for their respective jobs. There is no general, classroom-based education. Training is completely on the job, limited to instructions for procedures for the respective tasks. Production workers can advance from simple operator to "butterfly" operator, able to perform various tasks along the line, and to "trainer," instructing new assembly workers. In addition, lower-level factory management, including supervisors and line and shift leaders, are recruited from the ranks of production workers. Some contract manufacturers also offer free English classes, an opportunity that production workers use. Language instruction has a special feature in Estonia. Here, many workers in EMS factories are recruited from the eastern part of the country, where unemployment is high, most of them women of Russian nationality. Since citizenship status for ethnic Russians in Estonia is contingent on the acquisition of language skills, classes in Estonian offered by companies along with English classes are highly popular among employees (2005 interview data).

Generally, managers in Eastern European contract manufacturing locations complain about a lack of skilled workers. Large numbers of skilled personnel immigrated to Western countries when many technical colleges and universities in Eastern Europe closed during the 1990s. In Hungary, technical colleges cancelled programs in tool and die making, a profession needed for retooling complicated machinery in plastic injection molding. Management tries to overcome shortages in this field through partnerships with local professional colleges. In Hungary, companies must pay a tax of 1.5 percent of their profits for education, which they can avoid by investing in cooperative projects with local educational institutions. Through this practice, the scale and scope of professional education is increasingly tailored to the specific needs of companies.

In contrast to the common image of foreign-owned factories as islands of high wages in Eastern Europe, our research shows that contract manufacturers tend to pay wages below prevailing national averages. The development of wages in EMS sites in Eastern Europe follows a pattern similar to that in many factories in Western Europe. In factories established during the early presence in a country or region, compensation was above the average national or regional level but then declined in subsequent years. This is the experience of older locations in Eastern Europe, such as Hungary and Estonia. Newer locations, such as Romania, are still at the beginning of this cycle.

In *Estonia*, the basic wage in electronics contract manufacturing is roughly equal to the national minimum wage, approximately EUR175 per month. In addition, there are variable bonus payments, usually adding up to a similar amount. Thus, the regular monthly wage before taxes is about EUR340, before the income tax of 24 percent is deducted. In *Hungary*, the wages vary considerably among companies. Regular total wages (base wage plus overtime and bonuses) in contract manufacturing average between a maximum of EUR500 before taxes and a minimum of EUR300. In *Poland*, for many years considered to be the "high-wage country" in Central Eastern Europe, monthly wages for contract manufacturing workers are no higher than EUR300 (2004 interview data). In Poland and Hungary, those wages are considerably below the regional average for comparable industrial work of EUR400 and 450, respectively, contrary to what management tries to make outsiders believe. In Poland, some employees make as little as just above the legal minimum wage of EUR175 per month. Here, extra pay for overtime is also below the prevailing regional level. The legally mandatory surcharge of 20 percent for overtime work is paid only for night shifts, not for weekend work (2003 interview data). This situation has not changed much in recent years. In 2006, after-tax wages between EUR200 and 300 could be achieved only with substantial overtime (Seibert 2007). Finally, in *Romania*, wages in EMS factories equal the national average. The monthly base wage is about EUR120, and overtime work carries an extra pay of 25 percent for night shift, 175 percent for weekends, and 200 percent for holidays. However, extra pay for overtime has been reduced in practice, since the regular average workweek, which is subject to plant-level agreements, has been extended, for example, by including Saturdays in normal work schedules (2004, 2005 interview data). This situation has not changed much in recent years. In 2008, the average starting wage for a line operator was between EUR192 and 219. The average variable portion of wages has hovered between 20 percent and 40 percent of the monthly total. Wages in contract manufacturing are therefore significantly below regional average pay for industrial work. Base wages are not much higher than the national minimum wage of EUR130 (Plank, Staritz, and Lukas 2009). Engineering salaries in these countries are around EUR1,000 before and EUR600 after taxes, causing widespread dissatisfaction among engineers. "You certainly know why they cannot find enough skilled people," an engineer commented in an interview.

In fact, wages are among the most controversial issues in Eastern European EMS workplaces. As in other regions, companies were not willing to provide official data on their wages and salaries—a practice sometimes vehemently justified by managers on grounds of confidentiality and competition. Yet low wages were among the key reasons for protracted dissatisfaction among workers and for trade union activity. From the point of view of employees, below-average wages do not compensate for the rapidly rising cost of living, especially skyrocketing housing costs. In most of the relevant cities in Eastern Europe, the rent for (usually very small) apartments typically takes up two-thirds of after-tax wages. Massively inflated housing costs are also criticized by national governments (e.g., Hungary Department of the Economy 2000, 15). Everyday consumer goods are very expensive in relation to disposable income, with the exception of basic food items with regulated prices. Prices for many consumer items are often about 75 percent of those in the most developed countries in Western Europe, such as Germany. But wages are only a fraction of those in the West. According to many studies, manufacturing wages in Eastern Europe are below subsistence levels. Only two-income households can pay for their basic cost-of-living expenses (Seibert 2007). A bizarre consequence of low wages is the extensive security measures Eastern European contract manufacturing plants employ to prevent theft. Security services are present in many factories, particularly those manufacturing mass consumer goods such as mobile phones, where access to factory buildings is strictly controlled. Electronic body scanning at factory exits (similar to that used at airports) is mandatory, often leading to long lines of workers during lunch breaks or shift changes.

In spite of the popular perception that wages in Eastern European coun-tries are too low (making high-tech goods produced for Western markets unaffordable to most local workers), managers are constantly justifying wage restraint. They cite the unstable economic situation in Eastern Europe and competition among countries in this low-wage zone. In Estonia, for instance, managers raise concerns that rising wages will trigger the relocation of pro-duction to Russia, especially to contract manufacturing facilities in nearby St. Petersburg (2005 interview data). In Hungary, wages in Romania and Ukraine are cited as a threat. Trade union representatives in Hungary, Po-land, and Estonia insist that their countries can no longer be classified as low-wage locations because workers are under pressure from low-wage countries farther east. Similar patterns can be observed within each country. In Tab, a small town in southern Hungary, for instance, management tried to block union demands for higher wages by pointing out that the location lost a large number of jobs. Many orders were relocated to another factory in eastern Hungary, where wages are lower (2005 group discussion).

Another common phenomenon in first-generation locations of contract manufacturing in Eastern Europe was the reduction of benefits offered in early years. In Hungary and Poland, company-provided bus service, bever-age vending, and medical services were discontinued in the wake of the crisis in 2001–2002. With some exceptions, food services became so expensive that only better-paid clerical workers and engineers could afford to eat in company cafeterias (2003, 2005 interview data).

The problems of low wages and wage flexibility are intertwined. The variable proportion of the wage—paid in addition to base wages, often at the level of the legal minimum wage—consists of overtime pay, allowances for night and weekend work, and other components related to the particular job. In addition, there are so-called bonuses, a "soft" component of the wage related to the quality of production and the personal attributes of individual workers. These include "team orientation," "work attitude," suggestions for improvement, and absences due to medical, family, or other personal rea-sons. In most of the workplaces, bonus payments alone contributed 20 to 30 percent of the monthly wage, and only 10 percent in some rare cases. The proportion of bonus payments varied somewhat by country, with Hungary and Estonia at the high end and Poland at the low end (2002, 2005 interview data; see Seibert 2007). Only in Romania was the situation fundamentally different. Here managers conceded that wages were so low that it was hard to convert parts of it into a variable pay. The same companies had introduced variable wages tied to company performance and employee attendance in its factories in Hungary just months before (2002, 2005 interview data).

From the perspective of management, bonus wages are incentives for high work performance. Workers should not only provide quality work but also identify with the factory environment. Trade unions were critical about bonuses, particularly since they were exclusively assigned by management (i.e., department supervisors and team leaders). Distribution of bonuses was arbitrary, contributing to massive irrationality in company wage policies. According to our own investigation, bonus payments are part of a hierarchical and personalized system of control. Criteria for allocating bonuses are often defined by factory or department managers. The same people or their subordinates at lower levels determine bonus payments to individual workers. At the same time, criteria for bonus payments are rigid. In one case investigated in this study, three customer complaints would result in nonpayment of the company's "quality bonus" (representing about 5 percent of the monthly wage). Similarly, more than three days' absence per month would cause the loss of the "attendance bonus," resulting in a 5 percent reduction of monthly pay. Bonus systems are highly unpopular among employees since payments seem to be constantly lowered. A trade union representative in Hungary said in an interview: "We don't like the bonus. In the beginning, it was paid regularly, now it is less and less" (2005 group discussion).

In addition to the flexibility of wages, the flexibility of employment in Eastern European contract manufacturing facilities is also very high, reinforced by changes in labor and trade union laws enacted between 2001 and 2004 in the course of negotiations over admission to the European Union. The common contents of these changes were easier dismissal of employees, reduction of requirements for payment of night and weekend work, and inclusion of weekends in regular work schedules. All these measures, introduced in the name of "adjusting" national regulations to EU standards, caused a de facto lowering of historic labor standards. Generally, the legal standard workweek now is forty hours, but work time "corridors" that can last up to a year allow de facto extension of regular working hours by forty-eight hours per month. In Hungary, the "corridor" period is only two months, but extensions of up to one year can be negotiated with trade unions at the shop-floor level. Such extensions are usually not a problem for management, given the weakness of trade unions in the country.

The reform of labor laws, and flexible employment in particular, was pushed through under enormous pressure from the EU and the IMF with little public attention. The case of Estonia provided the precedent after the European Commission rejected the country's new labor law, enacted in 2003, as incompatible with basic EU standards. The commission criticized low labor flexibility, substantial restrictions on overtime work, and too much participation from trade unions. According to the EU, more than two hundred hours of overtime work per year must be possible without negotiation with trade unions, the standard workweek should be extended to forty-eight hours, and the compensation period for overtime should be extended from three to eight months (EIRO 2004). After these changes were finally accepted by the Estonian government, similar developments took place in Poland. In each case, the associations of foreign employers exerted massive pressure behind the scenes. In Romania, the primary source of pressure was the IMF, which pushed for a "return to Europe" and "adjustment to EU guidelines" as part of a major financial restructuring package in the wake of the country's economic collapse in the late 1990s. A new national labor law approved in 2003 was dubbed "incompatible with a free market economy" and repealed, as foreign investors and the IMF complained about exaggerated limitations on working hours and too much trade union influence (Ciutacu 2003; Preda 2004; 2004 interview data).

Liberalization of legal standards for working hours is evident in a myriad of factories. In the factories under our investigation, a "rolling workweek" with a three-shift system integrated the weekend as a fourth shift if needed. This is a widely used pattern, often based on four-day workweeks with twelve-hour shifts. Factory managers are experimenting with a variety of models, often changing from product line to product line. Often, these models combine reductions in the workweek with extra work on short notice, which is not paid as overtime. Such schemes often entail income reductions and are therefore unpopular among workers. Overtime on short notice is also very common, as well as short-time work without compensation for several days. In these situations, employees usually stay at home, sometimes losing vacation days. In Hungary, for instance, the law stipulates that 75 percent of annual vacation days can be allocated "in accordance with company needs" if employees agree. Under conditions of massive unemployment, consent from employees is not difficult to obtain. In Estonia, "sending employees home" is also a standard practice, often for a few hours per day. However, under Estonian law, such time off cannot be counted as vacation days (2005 interview data).

Another form of employment flexibility is short-term and temporary work, greatly expanded by the above-mentioned changes in labor and trade union laws. Temporary labor firms became legal after 2002. New laws and government policies created options for the almost unlimited renewal of limited-term labor contracts without any mechanism for employees to become permanent. To be sure, limited-term and contract labor did exist in the countries and companies under investigation before, but such practices gained formal legal status under the 2002 legislation (2005 interview data). One consequence of this development in Eastern Europe is the increasing role of multinational temporary labor firms such as Manpower or Adecco, which have been taking over and eliminating smaller local temporary labor agencies. The implementation of such laws was slower only in Romania, and the relevant guidelines were not published until 2006. However, managers assumed that the use of temporary labor would not be a problem in the absence of such regulations.

Contract manufacturing factories underwent a rapid expansion of limited-term and temporary labor, although its pace and scope were uneven. In the companies under investigation, the ratio of temporary workers was between 25 and 50 percent. Only in one location was temporary labor used to a very limited extent, affecting only fifty out of three thousand employees (2005 interview data). The proportion of limited-term workers was even higher, usually around 50 percent. The duration of limited-term contracts was two to four months, in some cases up to a year. At one site, only 100–200 workers out of 1,400 were employed permanently (2002 interview data).

From the point of view of management, the key reasons for using limited-term and temporary labor are cost (no bonus, vacation, and severance pay) and easier dismissal. In Romania, for example, mass layoffs of regular workers must be announced forty-five days in advance. Together with a negotiating period of fifteen days, dismissals require sixty days' advance notice. "Temps," however, can be laid off in two days. In Hungary, the timeline for dismissal of individual regular workers is twenty-one days and for mass layoffs, three months. But work assignments for "agency people" can be cancelled in a week (2005 interview data). The high number of flexible workers in foreign companies is not limited to electronics contract manufacturing. In two Czech subsidiaries of Siemens, the German electronics multinational known for its tradition of stable employment and decent wages, the portion of limited-term employees is between 60 and 75 percent (Bluhm and Dörrenbächer 2003, 104ff.). Nevertheless, contract manufacturers are clearly at the forefront of this development. Factories with no temporary or limited-term workers could not be found in our sample.

Divisions within the workforce between "core" and "peripheral" workers are further complicated by segmentation along ethnic lines. As most Eastern European countries are rather small in territory and population, this may seem surprising. However, ethnic cleavages arise both from regional differences between richer and poorer regions as well as from labor migration among countries. In Estonia, the majority of workers is made up of young women of Russian ethnicity, most of them from the east of the country. Some of them live in dormitories subsidized by the companies, a situation often inducing jealousy among local workers who have to pay high rent for housing. In Hungary, workers from Slovakia are frequently used as temporary laborers, an issue of particular concern for Hungarian trade unions.[4] In the town of Komárom, Nokia and its EMS contractor Foxconn, both located in Nokia's industrial park, use temporary workers from Slovakia in large numbers, transported daily in buses across the nearby border. Many workers from the Ukraine are employed in eastern Hungary, most recruited from the Ukraine's Hungarian minority. These workers receive only the legal minimum wage in Hungary, which is more than half the average industrial wage in the Ukraine (2002, 2005 interview data).

Foxconn's operations in the Czech Republic are linked to massive labor shortages there. The Czech Republic's accession to the EU allowed Czech workers to seek better-paid jobs in Western Europe and created a growing shortage of industrial labor, filled by migrants from farther east. In 2007, Skoda, the Czech carmaker owned by Volkswagen, was actively recruiting workers from Vietnam as labor markets in Slovakia and Poland were also affected by workers' migration to Western Europe (Buckley 2007). In 2008, 57,660 Vietnamese were living in the Czech Republic, making up the country's third-largest ethnic minority, most on temporary or permanent visas (Pechová 2009). Foxconn hires migrants as well as Czech workers with the help of labor agencies. Around 58 percent of its staff is recruited through agencies. Although workers from Vietnam are the majority, Lucie Studnicna (2009) reports that twelve different nationalities are working at Foxconn's operations. During the recession following the 2008 crisis, migrant workers not only were exposed to increased racist pressure from their coworkers (Pechová 2009) but were also the first to lose their jobs.

Regime of Control and Labor Relations

As in other regions of the capitalist world market, contract manufacturing in Eastern Europe severely restricts trade union organization. The industry implements a highly flexible model of production based on precarious employment and management policies designed to enforce internal competition, put pressure on wages, and increase dependence on personal decisions by supervisors and managers. In most countries, high unemployment exists alongside increasing poverty in large sectors of the population. Not surprisingly, the locations of foreign-owned companies, especially those on greenfield sites, are usually union-free environments, although some research points to increasing variation in this picture (Bluhm and Dörrenbächer 2003; Gardawski 2002). In spite of such adverse conditions, workers aspire to better wages and working conditions, and trade unions have emerged in some locations. In most factories we investigated, some form of trade union representation exists. This is true even for those companies that are explicitly antiunion. The Jabil factory in Poland, for instance, is represented by Solidarność, and an "autonomous trade union" exists in Szombathely, Hungary (2005 group discussion).

In most Eastern European countries, the former official trade unions maintained a dominant role in spite of competition from the "autonomous" and "free" trade unions that emerged during the transition years after 1989. The exception is Poland, where a dual system of trade union representation emerged. The reform trade union Solidarność and the reconsolidated ex-communist trade union federation OPZZ are the main organizations, roughly equal in strength. Almost everywhere, trade union membership dropped after

1989. In Poland and Estonia, unions represent about 15 percent of the overall workforce, in Hungary, 20 percent, and in Romania, roughly 30 percent. Collective bargaining, contracts, and most labor conflicts are confined to the plant level. Industry-wide bargaining is almost nonexistent. However, the dynamics in individual factories should not be underestimated. A new generation of trade union organizations is developing in Eastern European contract manufacturing sites. In most cases, activist cores are very young, with pragmatic political orientations. Nevertheless, they show considerable militancy.

In *Estonia*, a trade union was established in a contract manufacturing facility in 1995, which since then has had its ups and downs. With eighty members out of a workforce of three thousand, the union has remained too small to conduct collective bargaining. Under existing laws, unions must represent a minimum of 30 percent of the workforce in order to negotiate. Workers, therefore, have individual work contracts. The trade union is trying to compensate for its weak influence at the workplace through public pressure on the company, although management claims a good and cooperative relationship with the trade union as part of modern company culture. According to management, it has provided facilities and some free working hours to the trade union. The trade union reports grievances in regular meetings. This is confirmed by the trade union, although effective trade union work is impossible while the company does not allow free communication among union members at the workplace, according to union activists. The union used public pressure in 2005, when it informed the public that there had been no wage raises in eight years. The company reacted with a highly visible media campaign, claiming that the pay level would exceed the regional average by 60 percent. In the ensuing public debate, the union insisted that the company was using the country's small sweatshops as the benchmark and its wage estimate was therefore too low. In another conflict of this kind, the union appealed to the ambassador of the company's mother country to push for collective negotiations. The company complied with this demand but delayed the beginning of the negotiations (2005 interview data).

The recognition of the trade union became a difficult issue when the union supported the formation of a company-wide European works council that conformed to the relevant laws and guidelines of the EU. In the election of the works council, management proposed a list of candidates. According to the union, the company nominated only supervisors and line leaders, no operators. The elections were conducted like those "in Soviet times." Workers' ballots listed their names, showing who had voted for the candidates proposed by management or the trade union (2005 interview data). The election was organized by a company-appointed committee called the "social affairs council," which usually dealt with workplace safety and health. Management tried to promote this committee as an alternative to union-based representation.

In *Poland*, managers emphasize the importance of trust-based relationships with employees. However, in one important case, a trade union formed when workers saw a massive breach of trust by management. Managers sent letters to half the workers urging them to sign new highly flexible limited-term employment contracts. If they refused to sign, they would be dismissed. This caused overwhelming resentment among workers, particularly since it happened shortly after a highly visible event celebrating the values of the "company family." In 2003, a factory branch of the Solidarność trade union emerged from this experience. The union has many younger pragmatic activists who describe themselves as apolitical and company oriented, in contrast to the tradition of Solidarność as a strongly political movement. Cooperation with management is seen as a basic principle. However, since management on several occasions departed from the path of cooperation, the union turned to more adversarial tactics, particularly using lawsuits in labor courts to achieve its demands. The demands of the lawsuits included discontinuation of limited-term contracts, severance pay for laid-off workers, and ending the resolution of jurisdiction disputes by a management-appointed employee representative. The suits had mixed success for the trade union. The union viewed the company-controlled representative in particular as a violation of basic principles of mutual trust. That spurred shop-floor activism by the union and produced a considerable growth in union membership (from one hundred in the winter of 2003 to eight hundred in the summer of 2005). The conflict has continued (Seibert 2007). A representative of the trade union in this factory was elected president of a newly created company-wide network for the formation of a European works council. The union does not hesitate to resort to more militant rhetoric in the traditions of Solidarność.

The key issues for the union are the simplification and systematization of the wage categories seen as arbitrary by workers, resistance against temporary labor agencies (Adecco opened an office on company premises in 2005), and low wages. The union believes wages should be raised to the regional average at least (2003 interview data; 2005 group discussion). For this purpose, the trade union is pushing for a collective bargaining agreement at the factory level, but it has not made much headway. Management was able to delay this process through 2007, and negotiations had to be restarted three times after being interrupted due to changes in the factory's management (Seibert 2007).

Trade unions in electronics contract manufacturing sites in *Hungary* mostly belong to the national union of electronics workers, VASAS. It is part of the "old" but now reformed trade union federation that was formerly government controlled. In spite of the small size of the country, trade union activities are remarkably broad and diverse.

In one company, located in a former coal-mining area with strong trade union traditions, the union represents over 30 percent of the five thousand employees and displays remarkable self-confidence. Soon after the acquisition of the factory by a major EMS multinational, the union was able to force the company to negotiate a collective agreement. It had relatively decent wages, lunch-break rules, and overtime allowances substantially above legal standards. For an extended period, the union also succeeded in limiting temporary labor. The proportion of contract workers, however, has increased substantially in recent years. The union also had setbacks around flexible work. According to union activists, negotiations became much more difficult after the management began to involve the works council, which is much more management friendly. Hungary has a system of dual representation by trade unions and works councils, somewhat similar to the German model. However, in Hungary both the trade union and the works council can negotiate over workplace and compensation issues at the plant level, so competition often occurs between the two bodies.

In contrast to this relatively militant trade union, the factory union in other major locations of this company defines itself primarily as a partner with management. Leading trade union representatives see their main function in the distribution of company-provided benefits, an orientation very typical of the tradition of government-controlled trade unions during the socialist era. In another site of the same company, however, workers have a more militant orientation. Here, the union developed from a group of rank-and-file activists, critical of the "cozy relationship" the incumbent trade union leadership had with management in spite of the company's frequent legal violations. As these problems could not be solved in negotiations with the HR manager, the union filed a lawsuit and won (2002 interview data).

Here, as in other factories in Hungary, the number of young trade union representatives is remarkable. Their orientation is usually not adversarial in principle. Trade union activists oppose management behavior they perceive as "abnormal" and violating commonsense standards of fairness. Trade unionists therefore see themselves engaged in "orderly" trade union work directed at securing "orderly" behavior of management toward workers and the union (see Hürtgen 2003). Regular collective bargaining is seen as part of such "normal" relationships, which are often disrupted or delayed by contract manufacturing companies. In particular, trade unions demand regular and timely information on the situation of the factory, especially during economic downturns such as those in 2001–2002 or 2008–2009. With support from the European Metalworkers' Federation, several factory trade unions in Hungary are involved in projects to establish company-wide European works councils.

The trade union situation in *Romania* is difficult to understand even for insiders. A host of company trade unions exist in industries such as electronics contract manufacturing, favored by legislation under which any group of workers with more than fifteen members in one factory can be recognized as a trade union. Many factory trade unions are independent from the country's three trade union federations. Each federation has a different relationship with the government and business elites, but all of them have a corrupt reputation. Academic analysis proposing a particularly high degree of militancy among Romanian workers (Kiduckel 2001) could not be confirmed in the factories we investigated. The militancy and aggressiveness that the Romanian coal miners and other workers in former state-owned enterprises displayed in the massive protest movements of 2005 (see EIRO 2005) are nowhere to be found in the newer industries dominated by foreign multinationals.

In the country's major contract manufacturing site, a trade union was formed by rank-and-file employees, demanding higher wages and better working conditions, particularly better safety and health standards for hazards such as soldering fumes (2002 interview data). According to management, this trade union had thirty members at the time of the investigation, although the union claimed eight hundred. The union was not recognized by management, although managers claim not to be hostile to unions. Instead, the company established a promanagement employee representative, called the employee council, and proposed to negotiate a collective agreement with it. The plan was derailed by the independent trade union. Two years later, managers said neither of the two groups was a legitimate representative but that they would cooperate with one of them in regular meetings concerning day-to-day problems such as the quality of cafeteria food. Independent information could not be obtained about legal and court procedures involving the recognition of trade unions in this case (2002 and 2005 interview data).

In spite of important differences among Eastern European countries in their traditions, labor policies, and labor movements, some common observations are possible about the system for control and the social contradictions in contract manufacturing facilities:

- First, trade unions did develop in most factories in spite of adverse conditions of highly flexible employment and massive competition among workers. Generally, trade union representatives are receptive to the interests of company management, including the constant concern about customer satisfaction. However, there are massive contradictions between the concept of jointness proposed by management and its underlying philosophy of quality management and service orientation and the reality of low wages, very insecure employment, and a lack of real codetermination in the workplace.
- Second, low wages are the key problem in the system of work, employment, and control, and they contribute to the spread of poverty among workers in most areas under investigation. There is a contradiction between the high-tech work environment and the perception among most

workers and trade union activists that they perform high-quality work at Western standards at a fraction of Western wage levels. Many workers and trade unionists are aware that their low wages are used as a major "competitive advantage" over locations in Western Europe and other developed industrial countries.

- Third, trade union and management relations seem to develop in a certain uniform way among countries and factories. Trade unions develop from activities of rank-and-file workers. They are then confronted with "alternative" employee representatives set up by management in order to control communication with employees and to prevent collective bargaining and the contractual regulation of wages and basic working conditions. Such policies are also directed at complying with basic EU regulations on workplace representation and fending off potential confrontations with workers on this issue (see Kluge and Voss 2003).
- Fourth, these management strategies have limited success. For different reasons, trade unionists are not willing to give up their pragmatic aspirations for "real" representation of employee interests. On the contrary, merely formal acceptance by management and bargaining relations with no substance trigger resentment and motivation for union activism.
- Fifth, initiatives by international labor organizations to form company-wide European works councils and networks of employee representation are of strategic importance. They provide legitimacy and a structure of material and moral support to factory trade unions and works councils.

NOTES

1. Companies in Guadalajara did not provide information about the wages they pay. Government statistics relate to the manufacturing sector only as a whole, allowing no conclusions about the wages in contract manufacturing. Therefore, our data are based on our own investigations. According to the above-cited report by CEREAL, the employers' association for the electronics industry, CANIETI, lists an average daily wage of 112 pesos for the electronics industry in Mexico for May 2006. Our investigations are consistent with CEREAL's conclusion that the average daily wage is ninety pesos (CEREAL 2006).

2. The Malaysian currency, the ringgit, has been pegged to the US dollar in a fixed relation of 1 to 3.8 since 1997. Therefore, the following figures have not been subject to currency fluctuations in recent years.

3. These observations were confirmed by the extensive media reports and academic investigations in the wake of the series of suicides in the Shenzhen factory compound in 2010.

4. In some cases, trade unionists in Hungary expressed a great deal of prejudice against workers in eastern Hungary, especially those recruited from Ukraine. One of our interviewees gave an example of that sentiment: "Some workers from eastern Hungary came to job interviews with a shepherd's cane. They smashed the food vending machines. They didn't find the flushing in the toilet. They were in a factory for the first time in life. Some dropped printed circuit boards on the floor and left the factory after two days" (2002 interviews).

Chapter Five

From Silicon Valley to Shenzhen

Network-Based Mass Production, Industrial Development, and Work

In the three preceding chapters we traced the changes in the IT industry's production networks from sectoral and global perspectives. We examined the emerging international division of labor and the new forms of industrial work in the major low-cost locations in Asia, North America, and Europe. We explored the relationships between the globalization of production and the profound economic and social transformations in a core area of capital accumulation, that is, the production process of a key high-technology industry. We further examined the changes in the organization of companies and industry networks and in the socialization of labor, which in this industry has become global in the real sense of the word. The resulting picture is complex. Its elements are shaped by the social and political conditions in the respective locations, which sometimes may appear hard to understand to Western readers. The title of this book, *From Silicon Valley to Shenzhen*, marks two geographical locations that have been central to this transformation, but it does not fully cover the economic, social, and political multipolarity of the process.

The reader who has followed us up to this point will ask for the theoretical and political consequences of this analysis. For a concluding discussion, we refer to the theoretical considerations developed in chapter 1, in which we characterized contract manufacturing in the IT industry as a new model of network-based mass production. It emerged in the context of ongoing competition and conflicts over the norms of production and technology in post-Fordist capitalism. We summarize our findings in relation to our proposals in chapter 1, in particular to the divergent dynamics of industrial development in various countries. In conclusion, we describe some implications of our study for future issues in research on global production networks and draw political conclusions about global labor standards and the social and political organization of the new workforce in the low-cost locations of global IT production.

GLOBAL PRODUCTION NETWORKS BEYOND WINTELISM

The first part of our empirical analysis, chapter 2, dealt with the emergence and transformation of electronics contract manufacturing as a production model in the context of the changes in the IT sector during and after the period of the so-called New Economy of the 1990s. In particular, we focused on the changing relations between brand-name companies and on their strategies "to get rid of manufacturing," which spurred the growth of contract manufacturers into large multinational corporations. In describing the division of labor within the industry and among companies, we used the term "production networks" in relation to the companies' strategies of reorganization and relocation, examined in chapter 3, as opposed to the production systems of and within individual companies.

Both aspects, however, are deeply intertwined. They represent elements of a broader restructuring of the norms of production in the IT sector, resulting in massive changes in the patterns of capital valorization and accumulation. Restructuring in this industry in two recent decades has focused on the disintegration of production systems. Manufacturing has been separated into highly specialized segments of single products and systems, such as chips, software, computers, communication equipment, and key components such as hard disk drives (Ernst and O'Connor 1992; Borrus and Zysman 1997; Lüthje 2001). Contract manufacturing, or electronics manufacturing services (EMS), emerged as an industry segment of its own, with specific norms of surplus production. This was a manifestation of industry-wide changes, essentially propelled by financial markets and their profit expectations. The struggles and conflicts over the division of labor between brand-name firms and contract manufacturers and the resulting definition of contract manufacturing as a complex portfolio of manufacturing and manufacturing-related functions formed an essential element of these industry-wide changes.

Although the new production model has been termed a "service" model, our observations confirm the importance of manufacturing and manufacturing work in network-based models of innovation and capital accumulation. Post-Fordist forms of production cannot be adequately described as "information based" or "immaterial" (see Hardt and Negri 2000). Rather, the restructuring of material production and industrial work continues to be a core element of the global movement of capital, as this pillar industry of the information society demonstrates. Our analysis of industry-wide production networks in the age of Wintelism illustrates the complexity of this development and its highly contradictory nature. Network-based mass production, therefore, is a strategy to cope with the structural problems of post-Fordist capitalism caused by the overaccumulation of capital and industrial overcapacity. Meanwhile, technological innovation takes place at an extremely rapid pace, along with struggles over norms of production and technology. This strategy includes the massive inclusion of new labor forces in developing industrial countries into global production networks on a scale not known under the Fordist capitalism of past decades.

As explained at length in chapter 2, the transformation of the IT industry does not proceed in a smooth and linear fashion. Rather, it is characterized by the ongoing fragmentation of industry segments and production and the simultaneous centralization of production networks and corporate organization (Ernst and O'Connor 1992). Within the production networks of the IT industry, this contradiction appears in the relationship between vertical disintegration and specialization of production by brand-name firms and vertical reintegration among contract manufacturers. Such dialectics of decentralization and recentralization of capital constitutes the basic dynamics of network-based mass production. It can also be found—in different ways, of course—in other industries with global networks of outsourced production, such as automobile, garment, and footwear manufacturing. The older and newer flagship companies of the IT industry focus on relatively narrow but fast-growing and highly profitable production segments.

Meanwhile, contract manufacturers have grown at breathtaking speed, interrupted by massive downturns with unprecedented job cuts during global recessions. Our empirical analysis demonstrates that this development is driven by massive overaccumulation of capital and declining rates of profit due to exploding capital intensity in key sectors of the IT industry and massive conflicts among the various industrial actors. This trajectory cannot be characterized as one of harmonious "coevolution" (Sturgeon and Lester 2002) between various partners in global production networks.

The inherent economic and social contradictions of network-based mass production appeared during the industry-wide recessions of 2001–2002 and 2008–2009. The massive layoffs at contract manufacturers in Mexico, Malaysia, and Eastern Europe and the plant closures in the United States and Western Europe in 2001–2002 resulted from a domino-type chain reaction within the global production networks created under the New Economy of the 1990s. The bursting of the Internet bubble on the financial markets led to a collapse of the highly capital-intensive race for "breakthrough innovations" (Florida and Kenney 1990) among brand-name firms. This shifted the burden of this crisis onto contract manufacturers and their workers. At the same time, the crisis started a new wave of global concentration in productive resources, driven by the massive centralization of procurement and manufacturing networks among large IT brand-name firms such as Hewlett-Packard, IBM, Motorola, and Siemens.

The crisis of 2008–2009 brought about a certain replay of this scenario but with some important modifications. This time, plant closures and layoffs were greatest in China. Yet, at the same time, major brand-name firms from Taiwan and China were among the major beneficiaries of the crisis. Companies such as Acer, Lenovo, and Huawei finally emerged as global network leaders. The further development of the industry more than ever relies on the rapidly developing markets of China and other emerging economies in Asia. However, social stability of these countries emerges as the key problem of more domestically centered growth with higher wages—as revealed by the Foxconn incidents in 2010 and the ongoing conflicts over increases of the minimum wages in China's major centers for export manufacturing.

With the ongoing global concentration of capital in the IT industry, the limits of Wintelism as a model for production and innovation became visible. The strategies of "platform leadership" (Cusumano and Gawer 2002) created by the lead companies of the PC and Internet "revolutions" of the 1990s (such as Apple, Cisco, and Sun) lost their clout, especially in the mass markets of communications and consumer electronics (see Linden, Brown, and Appleyard 2004; see chapter 1). After the crisis of 2001–2002, the combination of fast-growing fabless lead firms with highly specialized technology resources and with contract manufacturers as their agents for global manufacturing were no longer the role model for organizational innovation. Rather, a more diverse picture emerged with various types and strategies of "modular production," some of them resorting to the advantages of vertically integrated models of production from Western or East Asian traditions. Our analysis in chapter 2 illustrates this diversity across various segments of the IT sector.

In the PC industry, the role model of Wintelism—the retreat of the leading brand-name companies from manufacturing—was completed after 2002. Hewlett-Packard and IBM shed their remaining factories and retreated from PC manufacturing altogether. The new big players from the China Circle, Acer and Lenovo, largely rely on contract manufacturing to achieve economies of scale in manufacturing, parts purchasing, and logistics. A large portion of this growth was absorbed by ODM contract manufacturers from Taiwan, especially in the area of smaller computers such as notebooks or subnotebooks.

In mobile communications, the massive shift to Wintelist models of manufacturing, with massive transfers of factories to contract manufacturing, occurred between the late 1990s and 2002. This shift was somewhat reversed by a partial reintegration of production. Major manufacturers such as Nokia and Siemens took back manufacturing activities from contract manufacturers in the wake of the 2001–2002 recession. On the other hand, cooperation with ODM companies from Taiwan was expanded, especially in the area of low- to medium-end mobile phones. Today, the dominant players in the mobile phone industry are vertically integrated companies with "mixed" manufacturing strategies and a relatively broad portfolio of technology resources, such as Nokia, Samsung, and LG. This is also true for the smartphone segment of the industry, although Apple's ascent as the world market leader in this field has given new life to the Wintelist production model based on a strict division of labor between brand-name technology firms and their no-name manufacturers, Foxconn in particular. Apple's need for high-quality manufacturing and logistics and its highly demanding requirements in this field have further strengthened the position of its contract manufacturers, Foxconn in particular. Not only is there extended codevelopment of manufacturing processes, but Foxconn also develops and builds relevant machinery and equipment.

In the game console segment, the traditional market leaders from Japan, Sony and Nintendo, with their strong in-house manufacturing resources, could defend their incumbent positions against their fabless contender, Microsoft, which relied completely on contract manufacturers for hardware production. This example illustrates the vitality of the Japanese strategy of modular production in mass markets for digital consumer electronics. However, the leading companies in this sector have reduced the role of traditional suppliers within their "corporate families" and expanded cooperation with contract manufacturers from Taiwan. They now have longer-term relationships with preferred companies such as Foxconn.

In the course of this development, production models and the corporate organization of contract manufacturers have also become more diversified. Existing forms of cooperation with brand-name firms (for a detailed analysis, see Lüthje, Schumm, and Sproll 2002) after 2001 were expanded by the increased integration of product development in manufacturing services. The driving force was the rapid growth of original design manufacturing (ODM), developed by the leading manufacturers of notebook computers from Taiwan. In this model, the technical design of the final product is almost completely shifted to the contract manufacturer. This practice rapidly gained popularity for a growing variety of products, such as PCs, computer servers, cell phones, digital cameras, MP3 players, and similar devices. In reaction to the growth of original design manufacturing, contract manufacturers relying on the EMS model, especially those based in North America, added new service models that included a variety of product development functions. The rapid growth of ODM companies after 2002 resulted in a division of the contract manufacturing industry into two different models of production, ODM and EMS. Companies primarily offered contract manufacturing "with" or "without" product development. It remains to be seen whether this separation will continue. The new wave of large-scale mergers among contract manufacturers during the recession of 2008–2009 may also lead to an increasing integration of different production models within the new group of "mega–contract manufacturers" emerging as the new top layer of the industry.

The rapid expansion of contract manufacturing in low-cost locations during the 1990s (see Sturgeon 1997) involved the growth of a specific model of production. After the contraction of the global recession of 2001–2002, this model lost its attraction as an engine for the rapid industrialization of newly emerging economies. The relatively open structure of the "commodity-type" production networks of US IT companies (Ernst 1994; Borrus, Ernst, and Haggard 2000) may give a competitive advantage to their flagship companies. But their high volatility to sudden downturns and the restructuring of intraindustry competition creates high economic and social risks for the locations involved. Japanese models of production and internationalization, based on large-scale direct investment and in-house production in developing economies, have proved relatively stable. Korean multinationals have also developed large-scale production in wholly owned factories in countries such as China and Mexico in recent years. During periods of crisis, most of these facilities did not completely stop production, collapse, or shed jobs at the level of the majority of contract manufacturers in 2001–2002 or 2008–2009.

The dynamics of the IT industry, however, remain heavily shaped by the contradictions of permanent fragmentation of production systems on the one hand and their centralization on the other. Under these conditions, the integration of production in large and very large factories and industrial parks in developing economies is progressing, in spite of the massive disruption caused by global recessions, especially the one in 2008–2009. Driven by the profit expectations of financial markets, this process of vertical reintegration "at the bottom" increasingly includes product development. This development takes place either in the large-scale industrial parks of EMS and ODM contract manufacturers or in regional clustering among contract manufacturers, software, and chip design firms, as well as chip foundries and other related manufacturing and service companies. The emergence of such clusters is particularly evident in China. The greater Shanghai region, and to a lesser extent the Pearl River Delta, are developing large-scale cluster structures of this kind, creating the backbone for China's further rise in high-tech industries. Nevertheless, such developments create a high risk of overexpansion. Taiwanese contract manufacturers, with their "global factory strategies" (Ernst 2006c), are an example, similar to their American forerunners of a decade ago.

This development increasingly hollows out the productive and innovative resources of global brand-name firms. The term "modularity trap" (Chesbrough and Kusonoki 2001) describes the loss of innovative capability because of excessive outsourcing of strategic knowledge, and it aptly characterizes the situation among large IT firms with historically established brand names. In the name of shareholder value, companies such as Lucent in the United States and Siemens in Europe gave away their capacity for production and product design. At the same time, they were not able to act successfully as fabless producers according to the Wintel model. Because of structural overcapacity and falling rates of profit, these companies have had to cede market control to competitors from East Asia. These competitors are better able to combine low-cost manufacturing with strong innovative capabilities in rapidly growing vertically integrated conglomerates such as Samsung from Korea, Acer from Taiwan, and Huawei from China.

VERTICAL REINTEGRATION AND INDUSTRIAL DEVELOPMENT IN LOW-COST LOCATIONS

What are the implications of the massive vertical reintegration of production systems for the international division of labor? What are the prospects in emerging economies for developing and upgrading their industrial base? Can we still speak of a complementary division of labor between industrialized and developing countries, where the former keep the more sophisticated elements of global production systems and low-end mass production is performed in developing countries? If this is no longer the case, are there other elements and new forms of hierarchy that maintain the dominance of incumbent high-tech regions and their corporate players over global production networks and systems?

Our empirical data in chapter 3 confirms the general trend toward accelerated vertical integration of production in low-cost locations of global electronics manufacturing. It is inherent in the logic of fragmentation and centralization governing the contemporary IT industry. Locations that offer the best conditions for setting up large integrated manufacturing facilities—including cheap land, developed infrastructure, a large pool of low-wage workers, and their rapid integration into industrial jobs—have a competitive advantage. In addition, access to rapidly growing national mass markets in emerging economies has become another important factor influencing location. The global financial and economic crisis of 2008–2009 seriously affected consumer demand for IT mass products in the traditional core economies of the capitalist world market.

The emergence of flexible high-volume production in low-cost locations is a key trend in the development of contract manufacturers' production systems. EMS production during the 1990s was characterized by the coexistence of low-volume, high-mix production with standardized-volume production. A growing integration of both elements has taken place in recent years. Contract manufacturing has been following trends in older manufacturing industries, such as the auto industry, where flexible high-volume manufacturing was a response to the crisis of traditional Fordist models of production. The adoption of flexible mass-manufacturing concepts, such as the highly advertised Toyota model of lean production by Solectron in 2005, is more than symbolic. It indicates the increasingly sophisticated integration of various product capabilities in large-scale contract manufacturing sites in emerging economies, with serious consequences for the international division of labor.

With the emergence of high-volume, high-mix capabilities in Mexico, Eastern Europe, Southeast Asia, and China, an important argument lost ground against outsourcing and relocating manufacturing from established factories of electronics brand-name firms. Flexibility and quality have been cited as key advantages of traditional manufacturing environments. But the differences between "old" and "newly" industrialized countries in this respect have mostly vanished. Highly sophisticated strategies of production, automation, and logistics, grounded in decades of manufacturing experience, have lost their power to safeguard traditional core factories of high-tech brand-name companies. This lesson was demonstrated by the drastic closure of major production sites for cell phones and telecom networking equipment in Europe in recent years (see Voskamp and Wittke 2008b). Only large-scale synergies and strategic interfaces in research and development between electronics firms and their system customers (for instance, with auto makers and their first-tier suppliers in automotive electronics) remain a viable economic argument for maintaining manufacturing capacity in high-cost locations. However, such strategies are also increasingly vulnerable due to the rapid integration of regional production systems in developing countries, East Asia in particular.

The division of labor in today's global production networks no longer appears as complementary between high-end and low-end production performed in industrialized versus newly industrializing countries. Rather, restructuring in the industry has become increasingly "triangular" (Lüthje 2007a, 2007b). Productive resources are reintegrated among different types of contract manufacturers, contract chip makers (foundries), design and software service companies, and a host of specialized subsuppliers. These include producers of raw printed circuit boards, preassembled motherboards, and nonelectronic parts such as metal casings and frames for notebook computers or cell phones. The locational links between these various segments of global production networks are not primarily vertical, but horizontal. Various types of large-scale industrial clusters exist in a small number of low-cost locations, each with specific dynamics of clustering or de facto integration.

The development of these industrial clusters is not primarily determined by national conditions and policies, a perspective often used in discussions of different varieties of capitalism and their models of development. In the age of network-based mass production, path dependency is essentially defined by global dynamics of development. Certain industry sectors or locations can become increasingly divorced from national economies and their modes of development and political regulation while becoming integrated with similar locations in their specific regions of the world market. The tight interconnection between various contract manufacturing hubs in Asia, such as Penang and Johor in Malaysia, Singapore, Taiwan, and China's Pearl River and Yangtze delta regions (including their specific labor regimes), provide the best example. Similar local, national, and global relations exist in North America and Europe. Industrial development, however, is not progressing in smooth and evolutionary ways but rather in cycles interrupted by plant closures, layoffs, and massive restructuring during periods of economic crisis. Industrial upgrading, therefore, remains highly precarious.

In Mexico, electronics contract manufacturing has been shaped by the country's role as a low-cost production base for the United States and Canada. Production from Asia is exported to North America, Europe, and developed parts of Asia as well, but Mexico primarily depends on one region of the triad of the capitalist world market. It is therefore particularly vulnerable to market cycles in the United States. In electronics contract manufacturing, the division of labor between the United States and Mexico was never complementary. Large-scale integrated manufacturing facilities were built from scratch, directed from the headquarters of big US contract manufacturers such as Flextronics and Solectron in Silicon Valley. The rapid emergence of integrated manufacturing clusters in Mexico in the wake of NAFTA mirrored the decline of the manufacturing base of electronics in the United States. Only during the heyday of the New Economy in the second half of the 1990s did contract manufacturing facilities grow on both sides of the border, in Mexico and the US South (Lüthje, Schumm, and Sproll 2002). But that was followed by an almost total collapse of US plants and industry clusters in California, Texas, the Carolinas, Georgia, and Alabama during the 2001–2002 recession.

After this watershed period, Mexico's contract factories saw remarkable internal upgrading, and their product portfolios became more diversified. Mexico benefitted from its geographic proximity to the United States. It could maintain its position as an assembly and logistics hub for the North American market in spite of immense competitive pressures from China during this period. However, the integration of product development into Mexican sites remained relatively limited. Perhaps even more important, important facilities of original design manufacturing (ODM) were not located in Mexico. The leading companies of this industry segment from Taiwan maintain only final assembly operations in Mexico.

The development in Eastern Europe is somewhat similar, although the area has a very different historical background, particularly the capitalist transformation of formerly planned economies. Integrated factories and industrial parks emerged rapidly during the second half of the 1990s, parallel to the takeover of numerous factories of established electronics brand-name firms by US contract manufacturers. The Western and Eastern European factories coexisted for a short time. The division of labor between "lead plants" in the West and "volume plants" in the East was more pronounced than it was between the United States and Mexico at that time. The 2001–2002 recession was the starting point of an American-style meltdown of manufacturing facilities in Western Europe. Many of the so-called lead factories in countries such as Germany, France, and Sweden were closed, and production rapidly shifted to factories in Eastern Europe, which quickly grew in size and capabilities. Scotland and Ireland were particularly affected by plant closures—they were formerly the preferred low-cost locations for US electronics manufacturers in Europe.

The decline of Scotland's once-sizeable electronics manufacturing base shows that the proliferation of contract manufacturing accelerated the "race to the bottom." That race was not only between high-cost and low-cost locations but even more between low-cost and very-low-cost locations in various regions of the world market. Contract manufacturing plants in Eastern Europe have remained highly vulnerable and subject to massive downsizing in times of crisis. They experience heavy competitive pressure either from newer facilities in second-generation low-cost locations in Eastern Europe or from China. Like the situation in Mexico, the growth of ODM manufacturing did not lead to leading companies locating substantial manufacturing facilities in Eastern Europe. National and local government policies in Eastern Europe are aimed mainly at reducing investment and labor costs for multinational manufacturers. There are few industrial policies for improving the quality of manufacturing, work, and regional clustering of innovative capacities.

The division of labor is different among regions in Southeast and East Asia, the world's primary region for electronics manufacturing. Asia's leading industrialized economy, Japan, does not play a role as a location for lead plants or corporate headquarters for contract manufacturing, mainly because Japanese electronics multinationals did not embrace this production model. Instead, contract manufacturing was established through the vast production networks of US multinationals in the newer segments of the IT industry. They followed companies such as Intel, National Semiconductor, Apple, and Seagate, which had established assembly plants in Southeast Asia as long ago as the 1970s. The main regional hubs for contract manufacturing are Singapore and Taiwan. The latter has clearly emerged as the most important headquarters location for the sector in recent years at the same time as both

EMS and ODM contract manufacturing has expanded enormously in China. As in North America and Europe, the continuing trend is relocating the complex lead functions of product development, prototyping, and ramp-up of manufacturing processes to low-cost locations in the region. These functions are being relocated to Malaysia, and in recent years to China, on a massive scale.

Within the regional division of labor, Malaysia's role is similar in certain ways to that of Mexico and Eastern Europe. Malaysian EMS plants have developed important capabilities for prototyping, product introduction, and flexible-volume manufacturing. Further, enormous improvements in the local supplier infrastructure have been pushed by activist local governments such as the one in Penang. But the rapid growth of China as the preferred location for large-scale assembly plants has had a massive impact on the development of the industry in Malaysia since the year 2000. Contract manufacturing there is rooted in massive production facilities owned by multinational corporations in various sectors of the IT industry, such as facilities for chip making, assembly of PCs and hard disk drives, and production of audio, video, and automotive electronics. But the integration of product development into Malaysian EMS plants has remained relatively limited. ODM manufacturing has not been located in Malaysia. More than any other industry segment, ODM and its supporting infrastructure of design, development, and component supply firms have remained in the China Circle and its major players on both sides of the Taiwan Strait.

China, on the other hand, has clearly emerged as the largest location for electronics contract manufacturing, with the most integrated and comprehensive base of suppliers, development firms, and component manufacturers at both the low and high ends. The massive concentration of EMS and ODM plants and gigantic industrial parks has created a constant pull to locate in China for top multinational electronics component producers. This affects chip makers in particular, but also manufacturers of hard disk drives, motherboards, displays, and the related providers of materials and substances. As a result, China has seen a massive vertical reintegration of manufacturing in factories reminiscent of Fordism but much larger than the biggest factories of that period in developed capitalist countries. At the same time, the state in China is supporting the development of "indigenous technologies" in advanced electronics at all levels. This support is driven by a new generation of Chinese multinationals in key sectors of the IT industry, such as telecom networking equipment; audio, video, and home electronics; and chip making (Liu, Lüthje, and Pawlicki 2007; Ernst and Naughton 2007). This is very different from the other low-cost regions under investigation here. China seems to be the only case where the development of a large-scale manufacturing base can potentially be transformed into a process of indigenous technological innovation with its own brand names.

TRANSNATIONAL NEO-TAYLORISM

Our investigation into a broad spectrum of contract manufacturing facilities confirms the importance of research into the work and labor policies of global production networks. It demonstrates the intimate connection between the changing international division of labor and new forms of control and domination in the workplace. This relationship has been analyzed extensively in older theories of the international division of labor during the 1970s and 1980s. But these questions have not been examined as closely in recent research on global production systems and networks. The enormous dimensions of the reorganization of the labor process and the related recomposition of the industrial working class at different ends of the global economy make further research in this field a key topic for industrial and labor sociology.

The shape of the labor process in the mass-production factories and industrial parks of the electronics contract manufacturing industry displays many characteristics of the assembly line of former periods of Fordist mass production. Massive vertical integration of manufacturing resources and processes accompanies segmented assembly-line work in the tradition of Taylorism. However, this model also integrates many elements of contemporary systems of lean production and "high-performance" workplace management. For this reason, we cannot simply talk of a renaissance of Taylorism. Rather, we use the term "neo-Taylorism" to characterize this system of post-Fordist regulation of work in mass-production factories. It is different from the assembly lines of industrialized countries during the era of Fordism. Neo-Taylorism in newly industrializing countries combines worldwide standardization of work and massive hierarchical control with extreme flexibility of employment based on the large-scale recruitment of mostly rural workers, the absence of trade unions, and the lack of basic social and economic protections by the state.

Neo-Taylorist work organization in contract manufacturing is reviving the polarization between unskilled and skilled labor, typical of the traditional Fordist mass-production factory (Braverman 1974). However, neo-Taylorism adds new forms of polarization, related to the network-based character of globalized mass production. On the one hand, the structure of work and skill is heavily dependent on the position of a particular factory within the production networks and systems. In particular, engineering, design, and other technical work are becoming increasingly separated from production factories. "Mental" and "manual" work are being divided along the chain. The polarization between skilled and unskilled workers within the factories in emerging economies is more pronounced and sharper in many aspects than that in most capitalist countries. In most cases, the difference in pay and working conditions between manufacturing workers and engineers, technical, and administrative personnel is huge. It reflects the companies' effort to attract engineering and technical talent while squeezing labor costs in manufacturing.

Our concept of regimes of production distinguishes among three levels of analysis: regimes of work (the sociotechnical organization of the labor process), regimes of employment (recruitment practices, labor market conditions, and the related patterns of social, ethnic, and gender segmentation), and regimes of control (industrial relations, forms of workers' representation, and related company policies to prevent such representation; see chapter 1). At all three levels, we can find similarities and differences among the various locations in our investigation. This is the result of the complex relationship between "global," "national," and "local" factors in the organization of work and strategies for labor control.

Globalized control and standardization in contract manufacturing production systems is most visible at the level of the work regime. The global division of work between locations includes standardized procedures and equipment, transnational management of material flows, and company-wide "common processes" of work organization, down to the single steps in product assembly. They produce a global unification of labor processes almost unknown in any other industry throughout contemporary capitalism. This standardization puts contract manufacturers in a leading position compared to other industries. Global auto manufacturers also are trying hard to standardize assembly operations through global platforms and benchmarking of best practices. However, their manufacturing practices remain much more confined to established local practices, often reflecting long histories in various countries and their manufacturing cultures. Global brand-name and trading companies in the garment industry rely heavily on global production networks. However, their practices of work standardization on the global level are much less systematic and scientific, and their factories are much smaller and less sophisticated.

This work regime results in highly modern factories in low-cost locations that are at a similar technological level as the production sites in industrialized countries. At the same time, the production capabilities in low-cost sites have developed considerably, resulting in a sophisticated combination of high-volume production with customer- and product-specific flexibility. Automation of production may not be pushed to the greatest extent possible, but the use of cheap manual labor under rigid control provides many advantages over full automation. In all sites and regions in our investigation, assembly work was highly segmented, job rotation was very limited, and meaningful forms of teamwork were almost nonexistent. Technological and organizational upgrading of manufacturing has not produced more sophisticated forms of work organization. Rather, the growing complexity of production is reflected in an increasing hierarchy in skilled technical workers and operators.

Regimes of employment are much more varied in different locations. They have in common a highly flexible workforce with little industrial work experience, recruited from rural or semirural labor markets (Eastern Europe, with its longer history of industrialization, marks a certain exception to this rule). Regimes of employment differ widely in the mechanism of recruitment, local labor market conditions, and the underlying forms of social, ethnic, or gender discrimination rooted in different cultures and societies. However, wage and remuneration policies in the various locations are similar in the sense that wages for manufacturing workers are mostly below the national average for comparable work. Salaries in engineering, administrative, and management positions, on the other hand, compare more favorably to established national standards, as do skill development and promotion opportunities for skilled personnel. The low wages for manufacturing workers, along with almost no pay incentives for improvement of skills and enhanced work experience, are a product of the high flexibility of the workforce. Manufacturing workers bear the burdens of the permanent changes in orders, production volumes, and global market cycles.

Regimes of control show the greatest differences since they are rooted in the systems of industrial relations and state power in the respective countries. Here we also observe the biggest differences between industrialized countries, with relatively established systems of labor relations, and newly industrializing regions. Contract manufacturing is often located in "free trade" or economic development zones, where companies are exempted from existing national standards for wages, employment, and social security. Contract manufacturers, with their global production systems, have proved highly flexible in adjusting to national and local politics. Their challenges are considerable, since the global standardization of work processes leaves relatively little room for experiments with local employment policies and relations with governments, trade unions, or NGOs. Heavy control over workers and the authoritarian-paternalist control regimes inside the factories are a means to cope with the political and social insecurity involved in the rapid buildup of large manufacturing facilities in relatively uncharted sociopolitical territory.

In conclusion, our case studies show that the various dimensions of production regimes are interlinked through common trade-offs. Their lowest common denominator is the connection between a relatively modern neo-Taylorist regime of work with highly flexible employment systems, industrial relations with little institutional stability, and weak labor standards. This relationship defines the character of neo-Taylorism. It can exist only if it is rooted in specific global-local relationships of economic and political power. The political manifestations of these relationships vary considerably. They reflect different sociopolitical settings, such as Mexico's state-bureaucratic labor policies and trade unionism, Malaysia's ethnically based regime of authoritarian development, and the "transformation economies" of Eastern

Europe and China, each with very different trajectories for their transition from centrally planned to market economies.

In spite of these differences, one common element seems to prevail in all locations in newly industrializing countries. There are no institutional mechanisms to establish wage and labor standards beyond individual workplaces and factories. Collectively bargained standards for wages, working conditions, and working hours do not exist at a regional or national level in the electronics industry. The exception to this "rule" is Singapore. But this country clearly has the status of an industrial hub rather than a low-cost location within the global production networks of the IT industry. Only in Eastern Europe are there a few very weak attempts to develop collective bargaining at the plant level and to integrate it with bargaining by national and European trade unions.

The regulation of labor standards in the low-cost locations of electronics contract manufacturing is mostly limited to national labor laws and government policies. The legal standards are very different between countries, as well as the relations between layers of government on the local, national, and even transnational level (for example, the EU's role in deregulating labor markets in Eastern Europe). Enforcement of labor laws through government agencies and local governments is weak in most areas, a notorious problem in China and Mexico. In most of these countries, independent trade unions organized by their members do not exist. The absence of viable social mechanisms and institutions to coordinate basic labor standards such as wages, working hours, seniority rules, and health and safety conditions is one of the key differences between post-Fordist neo-Taylorism and the older regimes of bureaucratic control (R. Edwards 1981) in classical Fordist manufacturing industries.

GLOBAL PRODUCTION NETWORKS AND POST-FORDIST REGULATION

What is the meaning of our analysis in the broader context of the development of contemporary capitalism?

We have already emphasized the importance of manufacturing and industrial work in transforming the production systems of post-Fordist capitalism. Obviously, the traditional basis of surplus value production has not vanished in the age of network capitalism. At the same time, the combination of advanced production technology with low-wage labor, highly flexible working conditions, and hierarchical control is a general element of global production networks in many manufacturing industries. The IT industry is the most dramatic example of a full-fledged conversion from traditional vertically integrated mass production, within large established brand-name firms, toward factoryless production, where manufacturing is entirely carried out by large global corporations that usually remain hidden to the public. This model seemed at one point a potential benchmark for restructuring other technology-intensive manufacturing industries (Sturgeon 2002), the automotive sector in particular. But such projections have not materialized. To be sure, major auto manufacturers have tried to "globalize" and "modularize" their production and purchasing operations by developing global product platforms and large-scale outsourcing to first-tier suppliers, who are also transnational players. Production models in the auto industry, however, have remained differentiated among companies and regions (Boyer and Freyssenet 2003), especially since globalization strategies in this industry have to integrate highly diverse market and production relationships in national markets and regions (Lung and van Tulder 2004).

The diversity of post-Fordist production networks confirms the need to bring "power" and "institutions" back into theories of global production networks and value chains (Sturgeon 2009). This supports our theoretical reflections in chapter 1. It also confirms an older observation by Terence Hopkins and Immanuel Wallerstein (1986), that the degree of vertical integration in global production systems can be highly cyclical in the course of the historic development of capitalism. Our analysis demonstrates that a highly standardized global production model, such as electronics contract manufacturing, has very different outcomes in terms of industrial development in different countries. China, in particular, demonstrates that the potential for developing countries to "upgrade" from mass manufacturing to indigenous innovation is contingent on their model for macroeconomic development, their underlying forms of political power, and the ability of the state to regulate the development of their national market. We therefore have to look again at the macroeconomic and global dimensions of production and its links to national and regional models of growth and capitalist regulation.

As critical theories of political economy have explained, French regulation theory in particular, capitalist restructuring of recent decades has been characterized by an ongoing erosion of the institutional and political mechanisms that had achieved (at least to a certain extent) the parallel development of industrial productivity and mass consumption in the era of Fordism. The political foundations of the post–World War II social contract in industrialized countries, including collective bargaining and the supporting infrastructure of labor and social security laws, has been undermined to a great degree since the 1980s. In some countries, the United States in particular, unionization and collective bargaining appear almost marginalized today. The newly emerging economies generally do not have the social and political institutions that would support a long-term growth of wages and domestic demand. That would be the basis for the emergence of a relatively stable industrial working class with "middle-class" incomes, similar to those of the United

States, Western Europe, and, later, Japan during the period of Fordism. The ongoing marginalization and the continuing low wages in Mexico during the first decade of NAFTA (not even disputed by US business media; see *BW*, December 22, 2003) illustrate this situation, as do the enormous income inequalities in the economic "wonderland" of the recent decade, China.

The rapid expansion of global production networks in industries such as electronics since the 1990s has been propelled by the neoliberal regulation of the world economy. This period has seen continuously declining real wages, job numbers, and social services in industrialized countries and a historically unprecedented shift of industrial manufacturing to a limited number of emerging economies, including some from the former socialist bloc. That cannot be reversed. The extensive use by global corporations of the new industrial workforce at low or very low wages has produced a deflationary dynamic in the global economy. It has driven down the cost of capital and manufacturing and of consumer goods and other commodities in industrialized countries (see Arrighi 2005a, 2005b). Because of this, working people in developed capitalist countries could maintain a certain level of mass consumption, even under conditions of declining real wages and permanent job insecurity (Brenner 2002). The consumer segments of the IT industry, with its vast production networks and permanently declining prices for high-technology goods, have become emblematic of this global mechanism (van der Pijl 2006, 312).

The global financial and economic crisis of 2008–2009 and the ongoing contraction of world economic growth (Wolf 2011) have demonstrated the fragility of this configuration. Originating in the credit squeeze among US home owners and consumers, the largest economic downturn since the Great Depression made clear that global economic growth under conditions of permanently declining mass incomes cannot be sustained. Even the seemingly limitless extension of private household debt and massive trade deficits caused by continuously rising imports of globally produced consumer and industrial goods was insufficient. The crisis has nurtured expectations that some emerging economies with large internal markets, China and India in particular, could "decouple" from stagnation in the capitalist core economies and become the new growth engines of the world economy. Such speculations may indicate the shape of future global regulation. However, in the absence of institutional mechanisms to stabilize consumer demand of large populations of wage earners in developing economies, it hardly seems possible that the new "workshops of the world" can insulate themselves from the boom-and-bust cycles of a finance-driven world economy.

The crisis brutally disrupted the path of export-led industrialization practiced by an increasing number of developing countries as an alternative to older strategies centered on import substitution. It supports the earlier critical analysis of economic and social polarizations caused by export-based industrialization, characterized as "incomplete" or "bloody" Fordism (Lipietz 1987). This concept was used to describe developing economies such as those of Brazil and South Korea, which developed an industrial base in more traditional heavy industries such as steel, petrochemicals, and automobile manufacturing, all Fordist models of mass production. These countries experienced increasing disparity in economic development between rapidly growing new manufacturing sectors that catered to the world market and their "internal periphery" of impoverished agricultural areas that provided cheap industrial labor.

Such disparities are even stronger in the fastest-growing newly industrializing countries of two recent decades, China and Mexico in particular. Rapid industrial development on a historically unprecedented scale is accompanied by social polarization in all sectors of society. Network-based mass production, such as in information electronics, does not offer much economic compensation since it relies on large quantities of cheap labor to an even greater extent than traditional mass-production industries. Only those relatively small economies, such as those of Singapore or Taiwan, that have become regional hubs for global production networks have avoided such social fragmentation, at least to a certain extent. For these countries, opportunities to benefit from global modernization of production have grown significantly. However, the evolving intraregional division of labor between low- and high-cost locations, in Asia in particular, have produced new risks driven by massive competition between them. The relatively skilled workforce of the Asian hub countries is strongly affected by the resulting race to the bottom.

Key differences exist between the industrial catch-up processes of the 1970s and 1980s and today's processes. In today's models of network-based mass production in the main sectors of export-led industrialization, norms of production and technology are not primarily generated in the context of national markets and growth models. Rather, their nature is essentially transnational. This is true not only for distinctively high-tech industries, such as information electronics, but also for industries with lower levels of technological development, such as the shoe or garment industries or related supplier industries in the chemical sector, such as dyes. Under these conditions, the social structure of the newly emerging workforce is changing significantly. The sheer number of agricultural people transformed into industrial workers confirms recent macrohistoric analysis describing the emergence of a large new industrial working class in newly industrializing countries (Silver 2003). A factory like the industrial park run by Foxconn in Shenzhen, with more than three hundred thousand workers, is larger than the biggest mass-production facilities of Fordism in Detroit, Chicago, or Turin of the time. According to statistics revealed by Britain's BBC, Foxconn was the largest private employer in manufacturing in the world in 2011 (*BBC News Magazine*, March 19, 2012). The workforce of these megafactories is overwhelmingly made up of low-paid migrants, most of them women. Heavy legal discrimination (as in China), ethnic-religious discrimination, (as in Malaysia), or gender discrimination (as in Mexico, for instance) keeps the new industrial core workforce of the twenty-first century from entering the ranks of the relatively well-paid working class. Nor do these workers inherit the traditions of industrial unionism as a way to organize and improve their own standards of living.

In spite of the magnitude of this social transformation, one should not stereotype the new industrial workers in places such as Shenzhen, Penang, and Guadalajara as the new global "mass workers" with a strong anticapitalist orientation and the potential for proletarian "autonomy." This, too, was illustrated by the tragic events at Foxconn in Shenzhen in the spring of 2010. The suicides of young migrant workers happened at around the same time as a major series of strikes hit the automotive supply sector in neighboring cities in the Pearl River Delta. Widely reported by Chinese and international media, these strikes were analyzed as a significant social movement of a new generation of migrant workers with higher expectations regarding their standard of living and work and as a potential watershed in the development of industrial relations in China. Local trade unions in the region, lead by strongly reform-minded cadres at urban and provincial levels, made the case for collective bargaining and democratic workplace representation in automobile factories and other industries. However, the massive efforts at Foxconn to control workers' unrest and frustration in conjunction with the company's powerful political machinery in Shenzhen have rendered initiatives for democratic workplace representation and collective bargaining at Foxconn and other major contract manufacturers in the region highly difficult so far (Chen and Lüthje 2011).

Instead of invoking workerist traditions in social theory (Silver and Lu 2009), we should take seriously the ethnic, cultural, and gender differences among these workers. We should look for ways to change the underlying legal and political mechanisms of discrimination and social exclusion. There are many parallels to earlier periods of capitalist industrialization during which women, immigrants, and minority workers played a key role in organizing new mass-production industries. As critical scholarly research on this subject has demonstrated, overcoming social, ethnic, and gender differences within workers' social movements, especially trade unions, has been the key issue in their political development and impact (see, for example, Nelson Lichtenstein's seminal 1995 study on the formation of autoworkers' unionism in Detroit during the 1930s).

GLOBAL POLITICS OF PRODUCTION? APPROACHES TO SOCIAL AND POLITICAL REREGULATION

The prospect does not appear bright for forming broader social alliances that are able to regulate the global production networks of the IT industry in socially, economically, and ecologically more sustainable ways and reform the neo-Taylorist work systems on the shop floor.

In industrialized countries, the ongoing erosion of the social contract of Fordism has not only undermined the ability of workers and trade unions to bargain over basic issues of wages, working hours, and job security. The massive relocation of manufacturing in recent years has also threatened previous efforts to restructure assembly work in the electronics industry and to improve workers' control over workplace operations and skill development, especially for women workers. With increased global competition, sociologists and industrial relations experts have looked for new opportunities for cooperation between management and workers designed to improve work and productivity, in order to assure the long-term survival of manufacturing and industrial jobs in high-wage locations. These strategies focus on trade-offs between the requirements of high-quality manufacturing and innovation on the one hand and modern production concepts with decent working conditions on the other (Kern and Schumann 1984).

In the electronics industry, however, such alliances seem less possible. Joint efforts between management and workers to improve the quality and competitiveness of their factories have become unattractive to multinational corporations—even when unions offer massive concessions on wages, working hours, and benefits. A number of cases mentioned in this study provide examples, such as the closure of Lucent's factory in Massachusetts in 2003 and Siemens's and Nokia's German cell phone plants in 2007. The dire prediction that "shareholder value capitalism would swallow up modern work" (Schumann 2003) seems to have come true in these cases. Longer-term strategies for integrating existing manufacturing facilities into broader clusters of innovation in traditional high-tech regions of the world market have lost their influence. Corporate strategy now emphasizes improving short-term profitability by getting rid of manufacturing or selling off entire businesses with long-standing traditions of manufacturing, research, and development. Siemens did this in telecommunications (for a detailed analysis, see Voskamp and Wittke 2008b).

In developing countries, the neo-Taylorist regimes of production are hardly yet perceived as a problem of economic and social development. Given global competition between locations and accelerated social change in the wake of rapid industrialization, the pressure is enormous to create large numbers of industrial jobs. The argument that work in the factories has to be "simple" in order to absorb large quantities of surplus rural workers has been used extensively by economists, consultants, and government officials. But this cannot hide the fact that much of the integration of the new workforce into the factories of contract manufacturers in electronics and similar industries takes place under repressive conditions. They include the suppression of basic workers' rights, independent trade unions, and democratic workplace participation. Few political leaders and intellectuals in those locations seem to be aware of the vast limitations the neo-Taylorist regime imposes on the development of workers' livelihoods and skills, especially for migrant workers. The long-term social costs are hardly addressed, nor are the limits on industrial upgrading and broader changes in the models for economic development.

Still, are there practical prospects for change, in spite of the massive dominance of corporate interests over the global restructuring of production and work and the long-standing policy of major IT brand-name firms of hiding "the dark side of the chip" (Siegel and Markoff 1985)?

NGOs and grassroots groups have raised key questions about social, economic, and environmental justice. Most have a background in the environmental field and in consumer rights. These questions occasionally surface when media reports make headlines, documenting unsustainable working conditions in contract manufacturing plants. In 2004, reports by the British church organization CAFOD were cited in the *Financial Times* and other major international media. The report described repressive work practices and invasions of workers' privacy in contract manufacturing factories in Mexico, Thailand, and China. In Mexico, this gave momentum to the monitoring efforts by local NGOs and created some mechanisms for regular supervision of working conditions in contract manufacturing plants (see chapter 4). In China, a vaguely researched article in a British tabloid in 2006 described the work practices at Foxconn in the production of Apple's famous iPod. It triggered discussions in China for the first time about the situation of young migrant workers in the factories and dormitories of multinational contract manufacturers. Foxconn's massive lawsuit against journalists of China's most famous business newspaper produced a backlash from the public and the government. This led to the establishment of a trade union at the factory in Shenzhen (see chapter 4). Most recently, the tragic series of suicides among young migrant workers in the same factory in early 2010 provoked unprecedented media publicity in China and internationally. In China, the debate not only focused on the fate of migrant workers but raised profound questions about the need to change the model of economic development based on large-scale use of rural low-wage labor for export production.

Brand-name firms involved in such cases, Apple and Hewlett-Packard in particular, have been highly sensitive. The proclamation of the Electronics Industry Code of Conduct (EICC—later renamed Electronics Industry Citizen Coalition) was mainly the result of the CAFOD report's publication in

2004. As we pointed out in chapters 3 and 4, this code of conduct did not even include some of the core labor standards defined by the ILO. Nevertheless, the concept of corporate social responsibility has been promulgated widely among contract manufacturers and their brand-name customers. This has created a proliferation of monitoring activities by consultants and some nonprofit organizations, often with financial support or under contract from major brand-name companies. In China, CSR has also been promulgated as a voluntary "alternative" to strengthening the basic rights of employees, particularly through the Labor Contract Law of 2008. According to the trade union at Foxconn, trade union representatives regularly consult with representatives of major brand-name companies, such as Hewlett-Packard, Dell, and Apple. However, neither the trade union nor the global brands has challenged Foxconn's overtime policies, although they violate Chinese labor law (2009 field research data). The tragic events in Foxconn City in 2010 underline the failure of industry-proclaimed codes of conduct and their "monitoring" to achieve socially responsible working conditions in this and other contract manufacturing factories.

The results of our study make clear that public scrutiny and control over the global production networks of the IT industry must go beyond mere appeals to the social responsibility of multinational corporations. The bottom line for any substantial change in labor policies in the contract manufacturing sector is the institutionalization of enforceable legal and contractual standards. These standards should govern wages, intensity and quality of work, and skill development based on national labor laws, collective bargaining, and trade union and worker representation independent from employers and the government. The relationships among laws, government policies, and trade unions may vary widely among countries, but some core issues can be identified (Lüthje 2008):

1. The globally standardized regime of work in electronics contract manufacturing makes possible the definition of a global standard for "decent work." Benchmark models for humanized assembly work, based on teamwork and shared responsibility among workers, can be based on earlier experiences in unionized factories in industrialized countries. They might be based on the "humanization of work" program in Germany during the 1970s and 1980s and similar approaches elsewhere. These models could be easily applied to factories around the world since the basic work procedures are uniform within individual companies and well known throughout the industry. Since the technical and organizational base of production in industrialized and developing countries is more or less equal, the often-heard argument that developing countries cannot afford the "luxury" of decent work, according to top international standards, is not applicable in the case of

electronics contract manufacturing. Large-scale operations of contract manufacturers are already role models for local industrial development. They could also be used to disseminate socially and environmentally sustainable work practices. Recent ILO initiatives to enhance the concept of core labor standards by requirements on the quality of work and skill development (ILO 2007) and the organization's concept of "decent work" could serve as internationally accepted guidelines.

2. The highly diverse character of regimes of employment in contract manufacturing includes labor markets, recruitment practices, and ethnic-cultural, legal, and gender differences, requiring different answers for institutionalizing and regulating labor standards in different countries and regions. Those answers have to emerge from the context of each specific country and society (A. Chan 2001; Lüthje 2008). In most cases, standards would be linked to fundamental reforms in the existing political and labor system and its democratization. Such changes certainly cannot be achieved at the level of individual factories and companies. But enforcement of international labor standards against gender, ethnic, and racial discrimination on the shop floor could exert pressure to reform discriminating practices in national labor markets, especially regarding labor migration policies. In the face of the widespread use of precarious employment in contract manufacturing facilities around the world, legally enforceable rules and limitations on temporary labor and short-term employment are certainly needed.

3. A common characteristic of the regimes of control in most low-cost locations of the contract manufacturing industry is the absence of industry-wide labor standards at national or regional levels embedded in collective bargaining agreements or related government policies. Trade unions and institutionalized forms of employee representation at the workplace do not exist in most places. Given the size and scope of the contract manufacturing industry, industry- and region-wide trade union representation would provide a framework for regulating basic wages, working hours, and working conditions. Attempts to establish such forms of representation have been suppressed, as they were in Malaysia and Eastern Europe as well as in Silicon Valley in the 1970s and 1980s. The legal situation looks very different from country to country. In most countries in Eastern Europe, the right of workers to organize in trade unions independent from government and employers is accepted. This is not at all or not fully the case in Mexico, Malaysia, and China. The core labor standards of the ILO provide clearly defined norms regarding the right of employees to organize and have ample scope for implementation in different national contexts.

Securing basic labor standards, however, touches on fundamental problems in regulating global production networks that up to now have hardly been addressed in politics and academic research. The economic, social, and environmental conditions of production are determined by massive price competition and the location of large-scale manufacturing contracts among contract manufacturers and brand-name firms. The practices in this field are not transparent; rather, they are hidden. Although the industry is highly concentrated, the impact of the centralization of manufacturing on competition and market structures has never been investigated. Allocating manufacturing contracts has a massive impact on factories, workers, and communities and requires international regulation of the interface between global production networks, brand-name companies, and contract manufacturers (see Lüthje and Sproll 2002).

One important point of access would be the regulation of telecommunications and data networks and the related IT-product markets. These have been subject to permanent deregulation since the breakup of former telephone monopolies, such as AT&T in the United States during the 1980s. Sustainable standards for consumer protection in this field should include pricing, safety, and the environmental friendliness of products. But they should also include labor standards as a criterion of product certification and market access. Pricing of telecommunications services and their bundling with hardware products is a key issue. In most industrialized countries, telecommunications carriers or service providers give away sophisticated handsets at very low prices or for free, along with service contracts. Profits from high rates for phone calls and other telecommunications services subsidize the price of handsets. At the same time, this kind of subsidy shortens product cycles, drives unnecessary product replacement, and increases the amount of electronic waste. Breaking this vicious cycle would certainly help stabilize production volumes and cycles downstream and reduce the need for ultraflexible employment in contract manufacturing.

Including social standards in market regulation must not be misunderstood as protectionism by "rich" industrial countries against competition from "poor" developing ones. Rather, while the global market becomes saturated, emerging economies such as China and India are among the hottest markets for information and communications technology. In spite of solid prospects for further growth, similar problems of oversupply, "overinnovation," and waste exist in developing as well as industrialized countries. Some countries have implemented more rigorous policies on electronics waste, as China did with its homegrown version of the European Union's recycling guidelines (known as WEEE). Could product certification and perhaps related manufacturing licenses in countries such as China be made contingent on the protection of basic labor standards in production? Significant improvement in working conditions could be the result (Lüthje 2008).

Intellectual property (IP) rights are another key problem in this context. Contract manufacturers often refuse inspection of working conditions by government agencies or NGOs, claiming that they are safeguarding IP of their brand-name customers. Releasing information on manufacturing processes, components, and workplace health and safety would make public proprietary know-how for product design and architecture and create competitive disadvantages for the brand-name companies involved. This, in fact, raises the question of the scope of private control over technology vital for economic and social development. The innovation practices under the Wintel model, as analyzed in chapter 2, point to this question. How "open" are the "open-but-owned" standards of leading companies such as Microsoft or Apple? The massive concentration of manufacturing for competing brands, such as Dell and Hewlett-Packard, in the same factories and industrial parks adds a further dimension to this problem. Greater transparency of product technology in production processes would certainly be in the interest of developing countries and help reduce the "illegal" copying of product designs, trade in counterfeit products, and the resulting price pressure on brand-name manufacturing.

Such questions, however, are not widely asked among the relevant actors in the field of global labor standards. This is particularly true for trade unions, unfortunately. As we mentioned earlier, trade unions in the United States and Europe no longer have a presence in most sectors of electronics production. But this did not lead the unions to search actively for new strategic ways they could play a role in a world of global manufacturing. Rather, trade unions continued "business as usual," even at the price of becoming excluded from the industry altogether. US and European trade unions have never seriously considered broad organizing drives in the contract manufacturing industry, even when economic conditions would have been relatively favorable, as in the United States during the industry's boom in the late 1990s (Lüthje and Sproll 2002). Only a few attempts have been made to establish company-wide coordination among employee representatives at contract manufacturers on an international scale. The European Works Council at Flextronics, supported by the European Metalworkers' Federation, is a notable exception. Recently, the International Metalworkers' Federation has developed cooperation with NGOs that monitor labor standards in the electronics industry and started to study the experiences of trade unions in monitoring the textile and garment industries (Holdcroft 2009). In the wake of the suicides at Foxconn, the International Metalworkers' Federation has joined with relevant NGOs in their criticism of working conditions at Foxconn and Apple's ongoing attempts to evade its responsibility for the situation of young migrant workers in China.

The global financial economic crisis has certainly reinforced the need for a paradigm shift in the labor policies in electronics contract manufacturing and the governing models of production, technology development, and innovation in the IT sector. The massive media coverage of the Foxconn incidents lifted the veil on its "Forbidden City" of global contract manufacturing. Noted British business newspaper the *Economist* aptly stated that "a firm and an industry that has become accustomed to obscurity has to get used to the limelight" (May 29, 2010). In China, a group of nine Chinese sociologists from leading universities took the unusual step of issuing a collective appeal. In their opinion, the crisis at Foxconn reveals deep problems in China's current model of economic development. They challenge the factory regime at Foxconn and call on the Chinese national and local government and the concerned enterprises to allow migrant workers to become "true citizens of the enterprise." We hope this book will contribute to raising such and other challenges in the future.

Abbreviations

AAS	*Austin American-Statesman*
BW	*BusinessWeek*
CO	*Charlotte Observer*
DC Ribao	*Diyi Caijing Ribao*
EB Asia	*Electronic Business Asia*
EN	*Electronics News*
ESM	*Electronics Supply & Manufacturing Magazine*
FT	*Financial Times*
LAT	*Los Angeles Times*
NYT	*New York Times*
SCMP	*South China Morning Post*
SJMN	*San Jose Mercury News*
SZ	*Süddeutsche Zeitung*
WSJ	*Wall Street Journal*

References

Abinee. "Estatísticas: Desempenho Setorial." 2006. Abinee, http://www.abinee.org.br/abinee/decon/decon15.htm (accessed June 16, 2006).

Aglietta, Michel. *A Theory of Capitalist Regulation: The U.S. Experience*. London: Verso, 1979.

Amsden, Alice H. *The Rise of "the Rest": Challenges to the West from Late-Industrializing Economies*. Oxford: Oxford University Press, 2001.

Amsden, Alice H., and Wan-wen Chu. *Beyond Late Development: Taiwan's Upgrading Policies*. Cambridge, MA: MIT Press, 2003.

Angel, Philip D. *Restructuring for Innovation: The Remaking of the U.S. Semiconductor Industry*. New York: Guilford, 1994.

Ariffin, Noriela, and Martin Bell. "Firms, Politics and Political Economy: Patterns of Subsidiary-Parent Linkages and Technological Capacity-Building in Electronics TNC Subsidiaries in Malaysia." In *Industrial Technology Development in Malaysia: Industry and Firm Studies*, edited by Kwame Sundaram Jomo, Greg Felker, and Rajah Rasiah, 150–90. London: Routledge, 1999.

Arrighi, Giovanni. "Hegemony Unravelling, Part 1." *New Left Review*, no. 32 (March–April 2005a): 23–80.

———. "Hegemony Unravelling, Part 2." *New Left Review*, no. 33 (May–June 2005b): 81–116.

Bacon, David. *Illegal People: How Globalization Creates Migration and Criminalizes Immigrants*. Boston: Beacon, 2008.

Bair, Jennifer. "Global Capitalism and Commodity Chains: Looking Back, Going Forward." *Competition and Change* 9, no. 2 (June 2005): 153–80.

———. "Global Commodity Chains: Genealogy and Review." In *Frontiers of Commodity Chains*, edited by Jennifer Bair, 1–34. Stanford: Stanford University Press, 2009.

Barajas, María del Rocío. "Una aproximación al análisis de las redes productivas globales en la Industria Electrónica en la región binacional Tijuana–San Diego." In *Aglomeraciones locales o clusters globales? Evolución empresarial e institucional en el norte de México*, edited by Jorge Carrillo, 161–89. Tijuana, México D.F.: El Colegio de la Frontera Norte, Universidad Autónoma de Ciudad Juárez, Fundación Friedrich Ebert, 2000.

Barajas, María del Rocío, and James Curry. "La participación de las empresas electrónicas de México en las redes globales de producción: El modelo de integración vertical en el Norte de México vs. el modelo modular en el Occidente." Paper presented at el Cuarto Congreso Nacional de la Asociación Mexicana de Estudios de Trabajo (AMET), Hermosillo, Sonora, April 9–11, 2003.

Barber, Tamara. "High-Tech Innovation in Emerging Markets: The Case of Mexico." Master's thesis, Fletcher School of Law and Diplomacy, Tufts University, 2005.

Barrientos, Stephanie, Naila Kabeer, and Naomi Hossain. "The Gender Dimensions of the Globalization of Production." Working Paper 17. International Labour Organization, Geneva, 2004.

Beane, Donald, Anand Shukla, and Michael Pecht. *The Singapore and Malaysia Electronics Industries*. Boca Raton: CRC Press, 1997.

Beckman, David. "The Great Tech Job Exodus: How Microsoft and Other U.S.-Based Tech Employers Are Moving to Offshore as Many Jobs as Possible." Washington Alliance of Technology Workers, 2003. http://archive.washtech.org/news/industry/display.php?ID_Content=441 (accessed April 16, 2013, 2006).

Bengtsson, Lars, and Christian Berggren. "Horizontally Integrated or Vertically Divided? A Comparison of Outsourcing Strategies at Ericsson and Nokia." Working paper, University of Linköping and University of Gävle, 2002.

Berger, Suzanne, Constanze Kurz, Timothy J. Sturgeon, Ulrich Voskamp, and Volker Wittke. "Globalization, Production Networks, and National Models of Capitalism: On the Possibilities of New Productive Systems and Institutional Diversity in an Enlarging Europe." *SOFI-Mitteilungen* 29 (June 2001): 59–72.

Berger, Suzanne, and Richard K. Lester, eds. *Global Taiwan: Building Competitive Strengths in a New International Economy*. Armonk, NY: M.E. Sharpe, 2005.

Best, Michael H. "Cluster Dynamics in Theory and Practice: Singapore/Johor and Penang Electronics." Working Paper 42, Judge Institute of Management Studies, University of Cambridge, 1999.

Bhopal, Mhinder, and Patricia Todd. "Multinational Corporations and Trade Union Development in Malaysia." In *Globalization and Labour in the Asia Pacific Region*, edited by Chris Benson and John Rowley, 193–213. London: Frank Cass, 2000.

Bluhm, Katharina, and Christoph Dörrenbächer. "Systematische Standortpolitik oder emergenter Wandel? Standortentwicklung und Arbeitspolitik des Siemens-Konzerns in Mittel- und Osteuropa." In *Modelltransfer in multinationalen Unternehmen: Strategien und Probleme grenzüberschreitender Konzernintegration*, edited by Christoph Dörrenbächer, 77–112. Berlin: Edition Sigma, 2003.

Bohle, Dorothee. "Der Pfad in die Abhängigkeit? Eine kritische Bewertung institutionalistischer Beiträge in der Transformationsdebatte." Discussion Paper FS 99-103, WZB, Berlin, 1999.

———. "Neo-liberal Restructuring and Transnational Actors in the Deepening and Widening of the European Union." Paper prepared for the conference "Europeanization of Eastern Central Europe," Budapest, June 26–28, 2003.

Bohle, Dorothee, and Bela Greskovits. "Capital, Labor, and the Prospects of the European Social Model in the East." Central and Eastern Europe Working Paper 58, Minda de Gunzburg Center for European Studies, Cambridge, MA, 2004.

Boris, Dieter. *Arbeiterbewegung in Lateinamerika*. Marburg: Verlag Arbeiterbewegung und Gesellschaftswissenschaft, 1990.

———. *Mexiko im Umbruch: Modellfall einer gescheiterten Entwicklungsstrategie*. Darmstadt: Wissenschaftliche Buchgesellschaft, 1996.

———. "Die 'Transition' in Mexico (1986–2000): Neoliberale Kontinuität im Wandel." *Das Argument* 43, no. 241 (2001): 356–62.

Borrus, Michael. *Competing for Control: America's Stake in Microelectronics*. Cambridge, MA: Ballinger, 1988.

———. "The Resurgence of U.S. Electronics: Asian Production Networks and the Rise of Wintelism." In *International Production Networks in Asia: Rivalry or Riches?* edited by Michael Borrus, Dieter Ernst, and Stephen Haggard, 57–79. London: Routledge, 2000.

Borrus, Michael, Dieter Ernst, and Stephen Haggard, eds. *International Production Networks in Asia: Rivalry or Riches?* London: Routledge, 2000.

Borrus, Michael, and John Zysman. "Wintelism and the Changing Terms of Global Competition: Prototype of the Future?" Working Paper 96B, Berkeley Roundtable on the International Economy, University of California, Berkeley, 1997.

Bouzas, Ortíz, and José Alfonso. "El marco legal de las relaciones laborales de jurisdicción local." In *Cambios en las relaciones laborales: Enfoque sectorial y regional*, edited by Enrique de la Garza and José Alfonso Bouzas, 1:11–28. Mexico City: Universidad Nacional Autonoma de Mexico, 1999.

———. "Contratos colectivos de trabajo de protección." In *El sindicalismo en México ante el nuevo milenio: una perspectiva global*, edited by Raquel Partida, Alfonso Bouzas, Patricia Ravelo, and Óscar Contreras, 193–228. Zapopan: University of Guadalajara, 2001.

Boyer, Robert, and Michel Freyssenet. *Produktionsmodelle: Eine Typologie am Beispiel der Automobilindustrie*. Berlin: Edition Sigma, 2003.

Braig, Marianne. "Frauen in Lateinamerika—ein ungenutztes Potential?" In *Macht, Markt, Meinungen: Demokratie, Wirtschaft und Gesellschaft in Lateinamerika*, edited by Dieter Nohlen and Helmut Sangmeister, 147–66. Wiesbaden: VS Verlag, 2004.

Braverman, Harry. *Labor and Monopoly Capital: The Degradation of Work in the Twentieth Century*. New York: Monthly Review Press, 1974.

Brenner, Robert. *The Boom and the Bubble: The US in the World Economy*. London: Verso, 2002.

Brown, Garrett D. "China's Factory Floors: An Industrial Hygienist's View." *International Journal of Occupational and Environmental Health* 9, no. 4 (2003): 326–39.

Brown, Garrett D., and Dara O'Rourke. "Lean Manufacturing Comes to China: A Case Study of Its Impact on Workplace Health and Safety." *International Journal of Occupational and Environmental Health* 13, no. 3 (2007): 249–57.

Buckley, Christine. "Czech Labour Shortage Forces Skoda to Recruit Workers from Vietnam." *Times* (London), November 29, 2007.

Burawoy, Michael. *Manufacturing Consent: Changes in the Labor Process under Monopoly Capitalism*. Chicago: University of Chicago Press, 1979.

———. *Politics of Production*. London: Verso, 1985.

CAFOD (Catholic Agency for Overseas Development). *Clean Up Your Computer: Working Conditions in the Electronics Industry*. London: CAFOD, 2004.

CANACINTRA/UNAM (Cámara Nacional de la Industria de Transformacion/Universidad Nacional Autónoma de México). "Monitor de la Manufactura Mexicana." 5, no. 8 (November 2009).

Carbone, Jim. "Solectron Prepares for the Upturn." *Purchasing*, October 24, 2002.

Castells, Manuel. *The Rise of the Network Society*. Oxford: Blackwell, 1996.

CEREAL (Centro de Reflexión y Acción Laboral). *Report on Working Conditions in the Mexican Electronics Industry*. Mexico City: Centrode Reflexión y Acción Laboral, June 2006.

———. *Third Report on Working Conditions in the Mexican Electronics Industry*. Mexico City: Centro de Reflexión y Acción Laboral, November 2009.

Chan, Anita. "Revolution or Corporatism? Workers and Trade Unions in Post-Mao China." *Australian Journal of Asian Affairs* 29 (1993): 31–61.

———. *China's Workers under Assault: The Exploitation of Labor in a Globalizing Economy*. Armonk, NY: M.E. Sharpe, 2001.

———. "Recent Trends in Chinese Labour Issues: Signs of Change" *China Perspectives* 57 (January–February 2005): 23–31.

Chan, Chris King-Chi. "Emerging Patterns of Labor Protests in South China." Paper presented at Thirteenth International Conference on Alternative Futures and Popular Protest, Manchester Metropolitan University, March 17–19, 2008.

Chan, Thomas. "A Pioneering Model." In *The Confluence of Affluence: The Pearl River Delta Story*, edited by Luisa Tam, 45–54. Hong Kong: SCMP Books, 2005.

Chang, Henry, Larry Cooke, Merrill Hunt, Grant Martin, Andrew McNelly, and Todd Lee. *Surviving the SOC Revolution: A Guide to Platform-Based Design*. Boston: Kluwer Academic, 1999.

Chen, Shin-Horng. "Global Production Networks and Information Technology: The Case of Taiwan." *Industry and Innovation* 9, no. 3 (September 2002): 249–65.

———. *Taiwanese IT Firms' Offshore R&D in China*. Unpublished manuscript, Chung Hua Institution for Economic Research, Taipei, 2004.

Chen, Weiguang, and Boy Lüthje. "Trade Unions and Worker Struggles in Guangdong: Chen Weiguang Interviewed by Boy Lüthje." *Global Labour Column* 55 (April 2011): 3.

Chesbrough, Henry William. *Open Innovation: The New Imperative for Creating and Profiting from Technology*. Boston: Harvard Business School Press, 2003.

Chesbrough, Henry William, and Ken Kusunoki. "The Modularity Trap: Innovation, Technology Phase Shifts and the Resulting Limits of Virtual Organizations." In *Managing Industrial Knowledge*, edited by Ikujio Nonaka and David J. Teece, 202–30. London: Sage, 2001.

Chew, Yoke-Tong, and Henry Wai-chung Yeung. "The SME Advantage: Adding Local Touch to Foreign Transnational Corporations in Singapore." *Regional Studies* 35, no. 5 (July 2001): 431–48.

Ciutacu, Constantin. "New Labour Code Criticized by Employers." EIROnline, http://www.eurofound.europa.eu/eiro/2003/08/inbrief/ro0308102n.htm, 2003.

Constantini, Peter. *NAFTA and After: Unions Test Labor Side Agreement*. Rome: Inter Press Service, 1999. Available at http://www.speakeasy.org/~peterc/nafta/labor.htm (accessed October 6, 2006).

Contreras, Oscar, and Jorge Carrillo, eds. *Hecho en Norteamérica: Cinco estudios sobre la integración industrial de México en América del Norte*. México D.F.: Ediciones Cal y Arena/COLSON, 2003.

Cravotta, Nicholas. "Reference Designs Worldwide: Understanding the IP Imbalance." *Electrical Design News*, November 8, 2007.

Curran, Lawrence J. "An Expanding Universe—The Top 100 Contract Manufacturers." *Electronics Business Today*, August 1997, 20–37.

Custer, Walt. "A Flat Global Trajectory." *CircuiTree*, April 1, 2005.

Cusumano, Michael, and Annabelle Gawer. *Platform Leadership: How Intel, Microsoft, and Cisco Drive Innovation*. Boston: Harvard Business School Press, 2002.

Davis, Mike. *Prisoners of the American Dream: Politics and Economy in the History of the American Working Class*. London: Verso, 1986.

Dedrick, Jason, and Kenneth L. Kraemer. *Asia's Computer Challenge*. New York: Oxford University Press, 1998.

Dedrick, Jason, Kenneth L. Kraemer, and Juan Palacios. "Impacts of Liberalization and Economic Integration on Mexico's Computer Sector." *Information Society: An International Journal* 17, no. 2 (2001): 119–32.

De la Garza Toledo, Enrique. "Free Trade and Labor Relations in Mexico." Paper presented at the International Labor Standards Conference, Stanford Law School, Stanford, CA, May 19–21, 2002.

De la O Martínez, María Eugenia. "La transformación de las relaciones laborales y la contratación colectiva en Jalisco." In *Cambios en las relaciones laborales. Enfoque sectorial y regional*, vol. 1, edited by Enrique de la Garza and José Afonso Bouzas, 187–247. México D.F.: UNAM, 1999.

———. "Las maquiladoras en Jalisco: ¿el nuevo Silicon Valley?" In *Globalización, trabajo y maquilas: Las nuevas y viejas fronteras en México*, edited by María Eugenia De la O Martínez and Cirila Quintero Ramírez, 277–309. México D.F.: Plaza y Valdés, 2001.

De la Paz Hernández Águila, Elena. "Hacia una nueva cultura empresarial." In *Jalisco antes y después de 1995*, edited by Jorge Regalado Santillán, Ramírez Sáinz, and Juan Manuel, 129–47. Guadalajara: University of Guadalajara, 2002.

Dombois, Rainer. "The North American Agreement on Labor Cooperation: Designed to Fail?" *Perspectives on Work* 6, no. 1 (2002): 19–21.

Dombois, Rainer, and Ludger Pries. *Neue Arbeitsregimes im Transformationsprozess Lateinamerikas: Arbeitsbeziehungen zwischen Markt und Staat*. Münster: Westfälisches Dampfboot, 1999.

Dörre, Klaus. "Das flexibel-marktzentrierte Produktionsmodell—Gravitationszentrumeines neuen Kapitalismus?" In *Das neue Marktregime*, edited by Klaus Dörre and Bernd Röttger, 7–34. Hamburg: VSA Verlag, 2003.

Dussel Peters, Enrique. "Características del sector manufacturero Mexicano, recientes medidas comerciales y retos de la política empresarial." Paper prepared for a joint seminar by the Division of Production, Productivity and Management, ECLAC and the Department of

Research, IDB, 2001. http://www.cepal.org/noticias/noticias/9/6139/tapadussellok.pdf (accessed April 15, 2001).

———. "Ser o no ser maquila, ¿es esa la pregunta?" *Revista de Comercio Exterior* 53, no. 4 (2004): 328–36.

———. *Economic Opportunities and Challenges Posed by China for Mexico and Central America.* DIE Studies, vol. 8. Bonn: Deutsches Institut für Entwicklungspolitik, 2005.

Edwards, Chris. "Skilled and Unskilled Foreign Labour in Malayasian Development—A Strategic Shift?" In *Technology, Competitiveness and the State: Malaysia's Industrial Technology Policies*, edited by Greg Felker and K. S. Jomo, 235–66. London: Routledge, 1999.

Edwards, Richard. *Herrschaft im modernen Produktionsprozeß.* Frankfurt am Main: Campus, 1981.

EIRO (European Industrial Relations Observatory). "2004 Annual Review for Romania." EIROnline, http://www.eurofound.europa.eu/eiro/2005/01/feature/ro0501103f.htm, 2005.

EMSNow. "Sanmina-SCI Guadalajara Recognized as an International Contributor with Key Export Programs." EMSNow, December 6, 2005. http://www.emsnow.com/newsarchives/archivedetails.cfm?ID=11495 (accessed October 6, 2006).

Ernst, Dieter. *The Global Race in Microelectronics.* Frankfurt am Main: Campus, 1983.

———. "What Are the Limits to the Korean Model? The Korean Electronics Industry under Pressure." Working paper, Berkeley Roundtable on the International Economy, University of California, Berkeley, 1994.

———. "What Permits David to Grow in the Shadow of Goliath? The Taiwanese Industry Model in the Computer Industry." In *International Production Networks in Asia: Rivalry or Riches?* edited by Michael Borrus, Dieter Ernst, and Stephan Haggard, 110–40. London: Routledge, 2000.

———. "The Economics of Electronics Industry: Competitive Dynamics and Industrial Organization." In *The International Encyclopedia of Business and Management (IEBM): Handbook of Economics*, edited by William Lazonick. London: International Thomson Business Press, 2002a.

———. "Global Production Networks in East Asia's Electronics Industry and Upgrading Perspectives in Malaysia." Working Paper 44, East-West Center Economics Series, East-West Center, Honolulu, 2002b.

———. "The New Mobility of Knowledge: Digital Information Systems and Global Flagship Networks." In *Digital Connections in a Connected World*, edited by Robert Latham and Saskia Sassen, 89–114. Princeton: Princeton University Press, Social Science Research Council, 2003a.

———. "Internationalization of Innovation: Why Is Chip Design Moving to Asia?" Working Paper 64, East-West Center Economic Series, East-West Center, Honolulu, 2003b.

———. "How Sustainable Are Benefits from Global Production Networks? Malaysia's Upgrading Prospects in the Electronics Industry." Working Paper 57, East-West Center Economics Series, East-West Center, Honolulu, 2003c.

———. "Limits to Modularity: A Review of the Literature and Evidence from Chip Design." Working Paper 71, East-West Center Economics Series, East-West Center, Honolulu, 2004.

———. "Limits to Modularity: Reflections on Recent Developments in Chip Design." *Industry and Innovation* 12, no. 3 (2005a): 303–35.

———. "Searching for a New Role in East Asian Regionalization: Japanese Production Networks in the Electronics Industry." In *Beyond Japan: The Dynamics of East Asian Regionalism*, edited by Peter J. Katzenstein and Takashi Shiraishi, 161–87. Ithaca: Cornell University Press, 2005b.

———. "Innovation Offshoring: Asia's Emerging Role in Global Innovation Networks." Special Report 10, East-West Center, Honolulu, 2006a.

———. "Can Chinese IT Firms Develop Innovative Capabilities within Global Knowledge Networks?" Paper presented at the Stanford and Tsinghua University workshop on Greater China's Innovative Capacities: Progress and Challenges, Beijing, May 20–21, 2006b.

———. "Upgrading through Innovation in a Small Network Economy: Insights from Taiwan's IT Industry." Paper presented at the workshop on High Tech Regions 2.0—Sustainability and Reinvention, Stanford Project on Regions of Innovation and Entrepreneurship, Stanford University, November 13–14, 2006c.

Ernst, Dieter, and Boy Lüthje. "Global Production Networks, Innovation, and Work: Why Chip and System Design in the IT-Industry Are Moving to Asia." Working Paper 63, East-West Center Economics Series, East-West Center, Honolulu, 2003.

Ernst, Dieter, and Barry Naughton. "China's Emerging Industrial Economy: Insights from the IT Industry." In *China's Emergent Political Economy: Capitalism in the Dragon's Lair*, edited by Christopher A. McNally, 39–59. London: Routledge, 2007.

Ernst, Dieter, and David O'Connor. *Competing in the Electronics Industry: The Experience of Newly Industrializing Economies*. Paris: OECD, 1992.

Esser, Josef, Boy Lüthje, and Roland Noppe. *Europäische Telekommunikation im Zeitalter der Deregulierung: Infrastruktur im Umbruch*. Münster: Westfälisches Dampfboot, 1997.

Evertiq. "Sanmina Opens New Enclosure Plant." Evertiq, June 21, 2006. http://www.evertiq.com/news/4233 (accessed October 6, 2006).

Faust, Michael, Ulrich Voskamp, and Volker Wittke. "Globalization and the Future of National Systems: Exploring Patterns of Industrial Reorganization and Relocation in Enlarged Europe." In *European Industrial Restructuring in a Global Economy: Fragmentation and Relocation of Value Chains*, edited by Michael Faust, Ulrich Voskamp, and Volker Wittke, 19–84. Göttingen: SOFI-Berichte, 2004.

Felker, Greg, and Kwame Sundaram Jomo. "Introduction." In *Technology, Competitiveness, and the State: Malaysia's Industrial Technology Policies*, edited by Kwame Sundaram Jomo and Greg Felker, 1–36. London: Routledge, 1999.

Feng, Tongqing. "Wal-Mart Zhongguo jianli gonghui: Zhongguo de laodong zhengzhi, huiyu-an shehui shenfen bianhua jiqi dui gonghui de qishi (Building the Trade Union at Wal-Mart: China's Labor Politics, the Changing Social Status of Employees and Their Attitude towards Trade Unions)." Paper prepared for workshop on Wal-Mart in China, Beijing University, Department of Sociology, June 30, 2007.

Ferguson, Charles H., and Charles R. Morris. *Computer Wars: How the West Can Win in a Post-IBM World*. New York: Times Books, 1993.

Flextronics. *Corporate Fact Sheet Asia*. CD-ROM file. Singapore, 2003.

Flores Robles, Manuel. "Sindicalismo en Jalisco: Nuevos procesos." In *Jalisco antes y después de 1995: transformaciones sociales y políticas*, edited by Regalado Santillán and Juan Manuel Ramírez Sáinz, 169–91. Guadalajara: Universidad de Guadalajara, Centro Universitario de Ciencias Sociales y Humanidades, División de Estudios de Estado y Sociedad, Depto. de Estudios sobre Movimientos Sociales, 2002.

Florida, Richard, and Martin Kenney. *The Breakthrough Illusion: Corporate America's Failure to Move from Innovation to Mass Production*. New York: Basic, 1990.

Fressmann, Rebecca. *Leiharbeit in Mexiko: Rechtliche Bestimmungen und sozialpolitische Realität*. Survey commissioned by the Friedrich Ebert Foundation, Mexico City, 2004.

Fröbel, Folker, Jürgen Heinrichs, and Otto Kreye. *Die neue internationale Arbeitsteilung*. Reinbek: Rowohlt, 1977.

Gardawski, Juliusz. "Industrial Relations and Work in Foreign Hypermarket Chains." EIROnline, 2002. http://www.eurofound.europa.eu/eiro/2002/11/feature/pl0211104f.html (accessed May 28, 2007).

Gereffi, Gary, and Miguel Korzeniewicz, eds. *Commodity Chains and Global Capitalism*. London: Praeger, 1994.

Grace, Elizabeth. *Shortcircuiting Labour: Unionising Electronic Workers in Malaysia*. Petaling Jaya: INSAN, 1990.

Grove, Andrew S. *Only the Paranoid Survive: How to Exploit the Crisis Points That Challenge Every Company and Career*. New York: Currency Doubleday, 1996.

Guangdong Sheng Tongji Nianshu. *Statistical Yearbook of Guangdong Province*. Guangzhou: Guangdong Sheng Zhengfu, 2006.

Guangdong Sheng Tongji Yu. *Guangdong tongji nianjian*. Beijing: Zhongguo tongji chuban-she, 2002.

Hainzl, Margit, and Emil Wimmer. "Freihandel um jeden Preis: NAFTA und die Folgen für Mexiko." OE1-Orf.at web radio, 2006. http://oe1.orf.at/highlights/55254.html (accessed October 6, 2006).

Hardt, Michael, and Antonio Negri. *Empire*. Cambridge, MA: Harvard University Press, 2000.

Harwit, Eric. *China's Telecommunications Revolution*. Oxford: Oxford University Press, 2008.

Havas, Attila. "Entry Strategies of Foreign Firms: The Case of Telecom Equipment Manufacturing in Hungary." Paper presented at the CEES-Workshop of the Copenhagen Business School, 1998.

Henderson, Jeffrey. *The Globalisation of High-Technology Production*. London: Routledge, 1989.

Hilpert, Markus. "Schottland: High-Tech am Rande Europas." *High-Tech-Regionen: GeoPoint*, no. 7 (2002): 15–34. http://www.geo.uniaugsburg.de/sozgeo/gp/gp7/schottland.htm (accessed November 11, 2004).

Hobday, Michael. "Understanding Innovation in Electronics in Malaysia." In *Industrial Technology Development in Malaysia: Industry and Firm Studies*, edited by Kwame Sundaram Jomo, Greg Felker, and Rajah Rasiah, 76–105. London: Routledge, 1999.

Holdcroft, Jenny. "Creating Conditions for Collective Labour Relations to Improve Labour Rights in the Electronics Industry." Discussion paper. International Metalworkers' Federation, Geneva, 2009.

Hopkins, Terence, and Immanuel Wallerstein. "Commodity Chains in the World Economy Prior to 1800." *Review* 10, no. 1 (Summer 1986): 157–70.

Hsing, You-tien. *Making Capitalism in China: The Taiwan Connection*. Oxford: Oxford University Press, 1998.

———. "Land and Territorial Politics in Urban China." *China Quarterly* 187 (September 2006): 575–91.

Hungary Department of the Economy. *Szécheny Plan: National Development Plan*, 2000. http://www.ikm.iif.hu/deutsch/szechenyi.htm (accessed November 4, 2003).

Hürtgen, Stefanie. "Der ganz normale Weltmarkt: Kontraktfertigung als 'Unterseite' der New Economy und Formen gewerkschaftlicher Interessenartikulation in Osteuropa." *Mitteilungen des Instituts für Sozialforschung* 14 (2003): 45–72.

INEGI (Instituto Nacional de Estadística y Geografía). *Las mujeres en Jalisco, Estadísticas sobre desigualdad de género y violencia contra las mujeres*, http://www.inegi.org.mx/prod_serv/contenidos/espanol/bvinegi/productos/estudios/sociodemografico/mujeres_en/La_Mujer_Jal.pdf (accessed May 14, 2013).

International Labour Organization (ILO). *The production of electronic components for the IT industries: Changing labour force requirements in a global economy*. Geneva: International Labour Office, 2007.

Ismail, Mohd N. "Foreign Firms and National Technological Upgrading: The Electronics Industry in Malaysia." In *Industrial Technology Development in Malaysia: Industry and Firm Studies*, edited by Greg Felker and K. S. Jomo, 21–37. London: Routledge, 1999.

Jomo, Kwame Sundaram, Greg Felker, and Rajah Rasiah, eds. *Industrial Technology Development in Malaysia: Industry and Firm Studies*. London: Routledge, 1999.

Jomo, Kwame Sundaram, and Patricia Todd. *Trade Unions and the State in Peninsular Malaysia*. Kuala Lumpur: Oxford University Press, 1994.

Jorgenson, Barbara. "EMS Prepares for Its Next Phase." *Electronic Business*, January 12, 2004.

Jürgens, Ulrich, and Rolf Rehbehn. "China's Changing Role in Industrial Value Chains and Reverberations on Industrial Actors in Germany." In *Emerging Multiplicity: Integration and Responsiveness in Asian Business Development*, edited by Sten Söderman, 181–201. New York: Palgrave Macmillan, 2006.

Jürgens, Ulrich, and Thomas Sablowski. "A New Model of Industrial Governance? Wintelism in the InfoCom Industry." In *European Industrial Restructuring in a Global Economy: Fragmentation and Relocation of Value Chains*, edited by Michael Faust, Ulrich Voskamp, and Volker Wittke, 221–40. Göttingen: SOFI, 2004.

Kern, Horst, and Michael Schumann. *Das Ende der Arbeitsteilung? Rationalisierung in der industriellen Produktion*. München: Beck, 1984.

Kiduckel, David A. "Winning the Battles, Losing the War: Contradictions of Romanian Labor in the Postcommunist Transformation." In *Workers after Workers' State: Labor and Politics in Postcommunist Eastern Europe*, edited by Stephen Crowley and David Ost, 97–120. Lanham, MD: Rowman & Littlefield, 2001.

Kluge, Norbert, and Eckhard Voss. "Managementstile und Arbeitnehmerbeteiligung bei auslän-dischen Unternehmen in Polen, Tschechien und Ungarn." *WSI-Mitteilungen* 1 (2003): 66–69.

Krätke, Michael. "Hat das europäische Sozialmodell noch eine Zukunft?" *Widerspruch: Beiträge zu sozialistischer Politik* 25, no. 48 (2005): 85–94.

Kurz, Constanze, and Volker Wittke. "Die Nutzung industrieller Kapazitäten in Mittelosteuropa durch westliche Unternehmen. Entwicklungspfade einer neuen industriellen Arbeitsteilung." *SOFI-Mitteilungen* 26 (1998).

Kwon, Seung-Ho, Dong-Kee Rhee, and Chung-Sok Suh. "Globalization Strategies of South Korean Electronics Companies after the 1997 Asian Financial Crisis." *Asia Pacific Business Review* 10, no. 3–4 (Spring 2004): 422–40.

Langlois, Richard N. "The Vanishing Hand: The Modular Revolution in American Business." Paper presented at conference in honor of Richard R. Nelson and Sidney Winter, Danish Research Unit on Industrial Dynamics (DRUID), Aalborg, Denmark, 2001.

Lee, Ching Kwan. *Gender and the South China Miracle*. Berkeley: University of California Press, 1998.

———. "From the Specter of Mao to the Spirit of Law: Labor Insurgency in China." *Theory and Society* 31, no. 2 (April 2002): 189–228.

———. *Against the Law: Labor Protests in China's Rustbelt and Sunbelt*. Berkeley: University of California Press, 2007.

Leng, Tse-Kang. "State and Business in the Era of Globalization: The Case of Cross-Strait Linkages in the Computer Industry." *China Journal* 53 (January 2005): 63–79.

Lester, Richard K., and Michael J. Piore. *Innovation: The Missing Dimension*. Cambridge, MA: Harvard University Press, 2004.

Li, Hanlin. *Research on the Chinese Work Unit Society*. Frankfurt am Main: Lang, 1996.

Lichtenstein, Nelson. *Walter Reuther: The Most Dangerous Man in Detroit*. Urbana: University of Illinois Press, 1995.

Lin, George C. S. *Red Capitalism in South China: Growth and Development of the Pearl River Delta*. Vancouver: University of British Columbia Press, 1997.

Linden, Greg. "Building Production Networks in Central Europe: The Case of the Electronics Industry." Working Paper 126, Berkeley Roundtable on the International Economy, University of California, Berkeley, 1998.

Linden, Greg, Clair Brown, and Melissa Appleyard. "The Net World Order's Influence on Global Leadership in the Semiconductor Industry." In *Locating Global Advantage: Industry Dynamics in the International Economy*, edited by Martin Kenney with Richard Florida, 232–57. Stanford: Stanford University Press, 2004.

Lipietz, Alain. "Akkumulation, Krise und Auswege aus der Krise: Einige methodische Überlegungen zum Begriff der Regulation." *Prokla* 58 (March 1985): 109–37.

———. *Mirages and Miracles: The Crisis of Global Fordism*. London: Verson, 1987.

Liu, Xielin, Boy Lüthje, and Peter Pawlicki. "China: Nationales Innovationssystem und marktwirtschaftliche Transformation." In *Innovationospolitik: Wie kann Deutschland von anderen lernen?* edited by Frank Gerlach and Astrid Ziegler. Marburg: Schüren, 2007.

Lung, Yannick, and Rob van Tulder. "Introduction: In Search of a Viable Automobile Space." In *Cars, Carriers of Regionalism?* edited by Jorge Carillo, Yannick Lung, and Rob van Tulder, 1–20. Houndmills: Palgrave Macmillan, 2004.

Lüthje, Boy. *Die Neuordnung der Telekommunikationsindustrie in den USA: Krise fordistischer Akkumulation, Deregulierung und Gewerkschaften*. Wiesbaden: Deutscher Universitätsverlag, 1993.

———. *Standort Silicon Valley: Ökonomie und Politik der vernetzten Massenproduktion*. Frankfurt am Main: Campus, 2001.

————. "Electronics Contract Manufacturing: Global Production and the International Division of Labor in the Age of the Internet." *Industry and Innovation* 9, no. 3 (December 2002): 227–47.

————. "Kehrt der Fordismus zurück? Globale Produktionsnetze und Industriearbeit in der 'New Economy.'" *Berliner Debatte—Initial* 15, no. 1 (2004a): 62–73.

————. "High-Tech Industrie." In *Historisch-Kritisches Wörterbuch des Marxismus*, edited by Wolfgang Fritz Haug, vol. 5. Berlin: Argument-Verlag, 2004b.

————. "Electronics Contract Manufacturing, Work and Industrial Upgrading in Malaysia." Working paper, Institut für Sozialforschung, Frankfurt am Main, 2005.

————. "Global Production, Industrial Development, and New Labor Regimes in China: The Case of Electronics Contract Manufacturing." Unpublished manuscript, Institut für Sozialforschung, Frankfurt am Main, 2006.

————. "Making Moore's Law Affordable—Modularisierung und vertikale Re-Integration in der Chip-Entwicklung." In *Gesellschaft und die Macht der Technik: Sozioökonomischer und institutioneller Wandel durch Technisierung*, edited by Ulrich Dolata and Raymund Werle, 179–200. Frankfurt am Main: Campus, 2007a.

————. "The Rise and Fall of 'Wintelism': Manufacturing Strategies and Transnational Production Networks of U.S. Information Electronics Firms in the Pacific Rim." In *Competitiveness of New Industries: Institutional Framework and Learning in Information Technology in Japan, the U.S. and Germany*, edited by Andreas Moerke and Cornelia Storz, 180–209. London: Routledge, 2007b.

————. *Arbeitspolitik in der chinesischen IT-Industrie—neue Perspektiven in der Diskussion um internationale Arbeitsstandards*. Survey commissioned by Hans Böckler Foundation, Düsseldorf, 2008.

Lüthje, Boy, and Christoph Scherrer, eds. *Zwischen Rassismus and Solidarität Diskriminierung, Einwanderung und Gewerkschaften in den USA*. Münster: Westfälisches Dampfboot, 1997.

Lüthje, Boy, Wilhelm Schumm, and Martina Sproll. *Contract Manufacturing: Transnationale Produktion und Industriearbeit im IT-Sektor*. Frankfurt am Main: Campus, 2002.

Lüthje, Boy, and Martina Sproll. "Produktion als Dienstleistung: Kontraktfertigung in der IT-Industrie als gewerkschaftspolitische Herausforderung." *Das Argument* 44, no. 248 (2002): 739–51.

————. "Electronics Contract Manufacturing: Networks of Transnational Mass Production in Eastern Europe." In *European Industrial Restructuring in a Global Economy: Fragmentation and Relocation of Value Chains*, edited by Michael Faust, Ulrich Voskamp, and Volker Wittke, 249–66. Göttingen: SOFI, 2003.

Mahathir, Mohamad. *Regional Cooperation and the Digital Economy: Selected Speeches of Dr Mahathir Mohamad, Prime Minister of Malaysia*. Subang Jaya: Pelanduk Publications, 2000.

Martínez, Gustavo. "Celestica cierra plantas en EU." Electronicos Online, April 14, 2005. http://www.electronicosonline.com/2005/04/14/Celestica-cierra-plantas-en-EU/?imprimir=true.

Mazurek, Jan. *Making Microchips: Policy, Globalization, and Economic Restructuring in the Semiconductor Industry*. Cambridge, MA: MIT Press, 1999.

McGee, Terence G. "Joining the Global Assembly Line: Malaysia's Role in the International Semiconductor Industry." In *Industrialisation and Labour Force Processes: A Case Study of Peninsular Malaysia*, edited by Terence G. McGee, 34–67. Canberra: Australian National University, 1986.

McKendrick, David, Richard F. Doner, and Stephen Haggard. *From Silicon Valley to Singapore: Location and Competitive Advantage in the Hard Disk Drive Industry*. Stanford: Stanford University Press, 2000.

MIDA (Malaysian Industrial Development Authority). *The Cost of Doing Business in Malaysia*. Kuala Lumpur: MIDA, 2002.

Miller, Max. *Welten des Kapitalismus*. Frankfurt am Main: Campus, 2005.

Moreno-Brid, Juan Carlos, Juan Carlos Rivas Valdivia, and Jesús Santamaría. "Mexico: Economic Growth: Exports and Industrial Performance after NAFTA." Research Paper 42, Serie estudios y perspectivas, CEPAL, Economic Development Unit, México D.F., 2005.

Müller, Wolfgang. "Am Ganges und am Jangtse sprießen die IT-Jobs." *Frankfurter Rundschau*, September 4, 2003.

———. *Die großen Wirtschaftlügen: Raffgier mit System*. München: Droemer/Knaur, 2009.

Naughton, Barry. *The China Circle: Economics and Technology in the PRC, Taiwan and Hong Kong*. Washington, DC: Brookings Institution Press, 1997.

Nee, Victor, and Shijin Su. "Institutions, Social Ties, and Commitment in China's Corporatist Transformation." In *Reforming Asian Socialism*, edited by John McMillan and Barry Naughton, 70–103. Ann Arbor: University of Michigan Press, 1996.

Neuenhöffer, Gisela, and Anne Schüttelpelz. "'Offene' und 'geschlossene' Transformation: Von peripheren und noch periphereren Kapitalismen in Osteuropa." *Prokla* 128 (June 2002): 377–98.

Nuttall, Chris. "Sony Sets 150m Sales Target for PlayStation 3." *Financial Times*, July 21, 2008.

O'Connor, David. "Electronics and Industrialization: Approaching the 21st Century." In *Industrialising Malaysia: Policy, Performance, and Prospects*, edited by Kwame Sundaram, 210–33. London: Routledge, 1993.

OECD (Organisation for Economic Co-operation and Development). "Estudio territorial de México, 2002." *Sinopsis de Política*, 2002. http://www.oecd.org/regional/regional-policy/1957257.pdf.

Ong, Aihwa. *Spirits of Resistance and Capitalist Discipline: Factory Women in Malaysia*. Albany: SUNY Press, 1987.

Ong, Anna. *Penang's Manufacturing Competitiveness*. Penang: Socio-Economic and Environmental Research Institute, 2000.

PAIZ (Polish Information and Foreign Investment Agency). *Poland—Electronic Industry*. Warsaw: PAIZ, 2001.

Palacios, Juan J. *Production Networks and Industrial Clustering in Developing Regions: Electronics Manufacturing in Guadalajara Mexico*. Guadalajara: Universidad de Guadalajara, 2001.

Parker, Mike, and Jane Slaughter. "Management-by-Stress: Die dunkle Seite des Team-Konzepts." In *Jenseits des Sozialpaktes: Neue Managementstrategien, Arbeitskämpfe und Gewerkschaften in den USA*, edited by Boy Lüthje and Christoph Scherrer, 50–61. Münster: Westfälisches Dampfboot, 1993.

Partida Rocha, Edith Raquel. "Las instituciones empresariales, educativas y laborales en el cluster de la electrónica en Jalisco." In *La industria maquiladora mexicana: aprendizajes tecnológicos, impactos regionales y entornos institucionales*, edited by Jorge Carrillo and Raquel Partida, 331–66. Guadalajara: El Colegio de la Frontera Norte, 2004.

Pawlicki, Peter. "Consumer Electronics Chains—The Case of Microsoft's Xbox." Paper presented at the WZB workshop On the Governance of Value Chains by Retailers, Berlin, September 16–17, 2005.

———. "Beyond Wintelism—Vertical Integration and Modular Chip Design in the Game Console Industry." Paper presented at the JDZB workshop on Path Dependency and Path Plasticity: Innovation Processes in the Software Sector, Berlin, January 28, 2008.

Pechová, Eva. "A Meeting in Kolín—Vietnamese Workers in the Czech Republic." MigrationOnline.cz, June 2, 2009. http://www.migrationonline.cz/e-library/?x=2146802 (accessed March 23, 2010).

Pellegrin, Julie. "German Production Networks in Central/Eastern Europe: Between Dependency and Globalization." Discussion Paper FS 99-304, Wissenschaftszentrum Berlin für Sozialforschung, Berlin, 1998.

Pick, Adam. "Survival of the Fittest?" EMSNow, October 14, 2004. http://www.emsnow.com/newsarchives/archivedetails.cfm?ID=6633 (accessed October 10, 2006).

Plank, Leonhard, Cornelia Staritz, and Karin Lukas. "Labour Rights in Global Production Networks: An Analysis of the Apparel and Electronics Sector in Romania." Position paper, Kammer für Arbeiter und Angestellte für Wien, Vienna, 2009.

Pohlmann, Markus. *Der Kapitalismus in Ostasien: Südkoreas und Taiwans Weg ins Zentrum der Weltwirtschaft.* Münster: Westfälisches Dampfboot, 2002.

Polanyi, Karl. *The Great Transformation.* New York: Rinehart and Co., 1944.

———. *The Great Transformation.* Frankfurt am Main: Suhrkamp, 1978.

Poschmann, Hartmut. "Die Elektronik-Industrie Osteuropas steht vor einer wirtschaftlichen Wiedergeburt." FED, October 2004. www.fed.de (accessed October 21, 2004).

Preda, Diana. "New Labour Minister Plans to Amend Labour Code." EIROnline, http://www.eurofound.europa.eu/eiro/2004/08/inbrief/ro0408101n.htm, 2004.

Pun, Ngai. *Made in China: Factory Workers in a Global Workplace.* Hong Kong: Hong Kong University Press, 2005.

Purvis, David. "New Approach to Design Partnerships: Solectron's Design Approach Preserves Customer's Valuable Intellectual Property." *Solectron World* 4, no. 1 (2004): 1–3.

Radosevic, Slavo. "The Electronic Industry in Central and Eastern Europe: An Emerging Production Location in the Alignment of Network Perspective." Working Paper 21, University College London School of Slavonic and East European Studies, 2002.

———. "The Electronic Industry in Central and Eastern Europe: A New Global Production Location." Paper for the University College London School of Slavonic and East European Studies, 2004. https://revistas.ucm.es/index.php/PAPE/article/view/PAPE0505120009A/25775 (accessed March 2, 2013).

Rasiah, Rajah. *Foreign Capital and Industrialization in Malaysia.* Basingstoke: Macmillan, 1995.

———. "Regional Dynamics and Production Networks: The Development of Electronics Clusters in Malaysia." Paper presented at Conference on Global Networks, Innovation, and Regional Development, University of California, Santa Cruz, November 11, 1999a.

———. "Malaysia's National Innovation System." In *Technology, Competitiveness and the State: Malaysia's Industrial Technology Policies,* edited by Kwame Sundaram Jomo and Greg Felker, 180–98. London: Routledge, 1999b.

———. "Systemic Coordination and the Knowledge Economy: Human Capital Development in Malaysia's TNC-Driven Electronics Clusters." Working paper, United Nations University/INTECH, Maastricht, 2003.

Rowen, Chris. *Engineering the Complex SoC: Fast, Flexible Design with Configurable Processors.* Upper Saddle River, NJ: Prentice Hall, 2004.

Ruiz Chávez, María del Rocío. "Competitividad de la Industria Electrónica y de Alta Tecnología." Secretaría de Economía, Subsecretaría de Industria y Comercio, México D.F., 2005.

Salzinger, Leslie. "From High Heels to Swathed Bodies: Gendered Meanings under Production in Mexico's Export-Processing Industry." *Feminist Studies* 23, no. 3 (Fall 1997): 549–74.

Sauer, Dieter, and Volker Döhl. "Arbeit an der Kette: Systemische Rationalisierung unternehmensübergreifender Produktion." *Soziale Welt* 45, no. 2 (1994): 197–215.

Saxenian, AnnaLee. *Regional Advantage: Culture and Competition in Silicon Valley and Route 128.* Cambridge, MA: Harvard University Press, 1994.

———. "Transnational Communities and the Evolution of Global Production Networks: The Cases of Taiwan, India and China." *Industry and Innovation* 9, no. 3 (December 2002): 183–202.

———. "Taiwan's Hsinchu Region: Imitator and Partner for Silicon Valley." In *Building High Tech Clusters: Silicon Valley and Beyond,* edited by Timothy Bresnahan and Alfonso Gambardella, 190–228. Cambridge: Cambridge University Press, 2004.

Sayer, Andrew, and Richard Walker. *The New Social Economy: Reworking the Division of Labor.* Cambridge, MA: Blackwell, 1992.

Schiemenz, Carolin. "Auswirkungen der Maquiladora-Industrie in Mexiko" (blog). *Perspektive* 89, 2006. http://perspektive89.com/arbeitsmarkt/01-04-2006/auswirkungen_der_maquiladora_industrie_in_mexiko (accessed April 4, 2013).

Schirm, Stefan A. "Indirekte Macht: Zum Einfluss der USA auf den wirtschaftspolitischen Paradigmenwechsel in Mexiko 1982–1992." In *Ausländische Unternehmen und einheimische Eliten in Lateinamerika,* edited by Thomas Fischer, 231–49. Frankfurt am Main, 2001.

Schumann, Michael. "Das Ende der kritischen Industriesoziologie?" In *Metamorphosen von Industriearbeit und Arbeiterbewußtsein: Kritische Industriesoziologie zwischen Taylorismusanalyse und Mitgestaltung innovativer Arbeitspolitik*, 157–75. Hamburg: VSA Verlag, 2003.

Schumm, Wilhelm. "Technologiegeneseforschung und der Wandel des Rationalisierungsparadigmas." In *Formen und Felder politischer Intervention: Zur Relevanz von Staat und Steuerung: Festschrift für Josef Esser*, edited by Sonja Buckel, Regina-Maria Dackweiler, and Roland Noppe, 188–207. Münster: Westfälisches Dampfboot, 2003.

Seibert, Anita. "Gender Aspects: Production of Next-Generation Electronics in Poland." Report for makeITfair campaign. Warsaw: Karat Coalition, 2007.

Sepp, Jüri, and Ralph M. Wrobel. "Die aktuelle Position Estlands im internationalen Steuerwettbewerb: Empirische Ergebnisse." In *Eesti majanduspoliitika teel Euroopa Liitu: XI majanduspoliitika converents*, Tartu-Värska, Eesti, June 26–28. Berlin: Berliner Wissenchafts-Verlag, Mattimar, 2003, 281–89. Available at http://www.mattimar.ee/publikatsioonid/majanduspoliitika/2003/2003/3_Majanduskasvupol/27_SeppJ_Wrobel.pdf (accessed June 8, 2013).

SERI (Socio-Economic and Environmental Research Institute). *Penang Statistics*. Penang: SERI, 2002.

Shaiken, Harley. "Advanced Manufacturing and Mexico: A New International Division of Labor?" *Latin America Research Review* 29 (1994): 39–71.

Shilov, Anton. "Microsoft's Xbox Business Finally Becomes Profitable." Xbitlabs, 2005. http://www.xbitlabs.com/news/multimedia/display/20050130063954.html (accessed July 30, 2005).

Siegel, Lenny, and John Markoff. *The High Cost of High Tech: The Dark Side of the Chip*. New York: Harper & Row, 1985.

Silver, Beverly J. *Forces of Labor: Workers' Movement and Globalization since 1870*. Cambridge: Cambridge University Press, 2003.

Silver, Beverly J., and Lu Zhang."China as an Emerging Epicenter of World Labor Unrest." In *China and the Transformation of Global Capitalism*, edited by Ho-Fung Hung, 174–88. Baltimore: Johns Hopkins University Press, 2009.

Solinger, Dorothy J. *Contesting Citizenship in Urban China: Peasant Migrants, the State, and the Logic of the Market*. Berkeley: University of California Press, 1999.

Soskice, David. "Divergent Production Regimes: Coordinated and Uncoordinated Market Economies in the 1980s and 1990s." In *Continuity and Changes in Contemporary Capitalism*, edited by Herbert Kitschelt, Peter Lange, Gary Marks, and John Stephens, 101–34. Cambridge: Cambridge University Press, 1999.

Spiegel, Rob. "Taking on the Supply-Chain Mess." EDN Network, January 1, 2002. http://www.edn.com/electronics-news/4342012/Taking-on-the-Supply-Chain-Mess (accessed October 10, 2006).

———. "Manufacturing Trending Away from China." *Electronic Business*, October 13, 2009.

Sproll, Martina. "Unternehmensverantwortung." In *ABC der Globalisierung*, 196–97. Hamburg: VSA Verlag, 2005.

———. *High-Tech für Niedriglohn: Neotayloristische Produktionsregimes in der IT-Industrie in Brasilien und Mexiko*. Münster: Westfälisches Dampfboot, 2010.

Standing, Guy. "Global Feminisation through Flexible Labour: A Theme Revisited." *World Development* 27, no. 3 (March 1999): 583–602.

Studnicna, Lucie. "The Czech IT Sector: Its Role in the Global Value Chain of IT Production and Local Working Conditions." Presentation at the International Workshop of the ProcureITfair Network—Sustainable Procurement of Computers—Perspectives for Implementation, Prague, Czech Republic, June 25, 2009.

Sturgeon, Timothy J. "Turnkey Production Networks: A New American Model of Manufacturing?" Working Paper 92A, Berkeley Roundtable on the International Economy, University of California, Berkeley, 1997.

———. "Turn-Key Production Networks: Industry Organization, Economic Development, and the Globalization of Electronics Contract Manufacturing." PhD diss., University of California, Berkeley, 1999.

————. "How Silicon Valley Came to Be." In *Understanding Silicon Valley: The Anatomy of an Entrepreneurial Region*, edited by Martin Kenney. Palo Alto: Stanford Business Books, 2000.

————. "Modular Production Networks: A New American Model of Industrial Organization," *Industrial and Corporate Change* 11, no. 3 (2002): 451–96

————. "Modular Production's Impact on Japan's Electronics Industry." In *Recovering from Success: Innovation and Technology Management in Japan*, edited by Hugh Whittaker and Robert Cole, 47–69. New York: Oxford University Press, 2006.

————. "From Commodity Chains to Value Chains: Interdisciplinary Theory Building in an Age of Globalization." In *Frontiers of Commodity Chain Research*, edited by Jennifer Bair. Stanford: Stanford University Press, 2009: 110–35.

Sturgeon, Timothy J., and Ji-Ren Lee. "Industry Co-evolution: A Comparison of Taiwan and North American Electronics Contract Manufacturers." In *Global Taiwan: Building Competitive Strengths in a New International Economy*, edited by Suzanne Berger and Richard K. Lester, 33–75. Armonk, NY: M.E. Sharpe, 2005.

Sturgeon, Timothy J., and Richard K. Lester. "Upgrading East Asian Industries: New Challenges for Local Suppliers." Working paper, MIT Industrial Performance Center, Cambridge, MA, 2002.

Sullivan, Laurie. "Motorola wirft Auftragsfertiger aus Preisverhandlungen." *EETimes.de*, November 11, 2003.

Sun, Wen-bin. "Labour Disputes in Shenzhen: The Origin, Pattern and Settlement of Workplace Conflicts." In *Guangdong in the Twenty-first Century: Stagnation of Second Take-off?* edited by Joseph Y. S. Cheng. Hong Kong: City University of Hong Kong Press, 2000.

Szalavetz, Andrea. "The Role of FDI in Fostering Agglomeration and Regional Structural Change in Hungary." Working paper, EURECO, 2004. http://www.zei.de/eurec/WP4_Hungary.pdf (accessed February 1, 2004).

Takahashi, Dean. "Back from the Brink." *EE Times*, October 10, 2004. http://eetimes.com/electronics-news/4179793/Back-from-the-brink?pageNumber=1 (accessed April 3, 2013).

————. *The Xbox 360 Uncloaked: The Real Story behind Microsoft's Next-Generation Video Game Console*. Napa, CA: Lulu Press, 2006.

Tatur, Melanie. "Ökonomische Transformation, Staat und moralische Ressourcen in den postsozialistischen Gesellschaften." *Prokla* 112 (September 1998): 339–74.

Taylor, Bill, Kai Chang, and Qi Li. *Industrial Relations in China*. Cheltenham: Edward Elgar, 2003.

Ten Brink, Tobias. *Geopolitik: Geschichte und Gegenwart kapitalistischer Staatenkonkurrenz*. Münster: Westfälisches Dampfboot, 2008.

TLIEA (Taiwan Labor Information and Education Association). "Suzhou diqu xinyi dianziye taishang de juji jingji jiqi tedian" (Cluster Economics of Taiwanese IT Investments in the Suzhou Area and its Characteristics). Paper presented at Suzhou International IT and Labor Standards Conference, Kenneth Wang Law School, Suzhou University, November 26–28, 2006.

Toh, Kin Woon. "The Political Economy of Industrialization in Penang." Unpublished manuscript, 2002.

Tubilewicz, Czeslaw. *Taiwan and Post-Communist Europe: Shopping for Allies*. New York: Routledge, 2007.

UNCTAD (United Nations Conference on Trade and Development). *World Investment Report 2004: The Shift towards Services*. New York: United Nations, 2004.

Van der Pijl, Kees. *Global Rivalries from the Cold War to Iraq*. London: Pluto Press, 2006.

Verseck, Keno. "Vom Auszug der Multis aus Ungarn." *Die Tageszeitung*, June 26, 2003.

Voskamp, Ulrich, and Volker Wittke. "Hochlohnstandorte werden aufgegeben." *Die Mitbestimmung* 3 (April 2008a): 40–44.

————. "Chancen fuer Hochlohnstandorte in globalen Produktions- und Innovationsnetzwerken der High-Tech Elektronik: das Beispiel der Handy-Produktion." Draft report. Göttingen: SOFI/Hans-Böckler-Stiftung, 2008b.

Wangel, Arne. "Manufacturing Growth with Social Deficits: Environmental and Labour Issues in the High Tech Industry of Penang, Malaysia." Technical report, Technical University of Denmark, 2001.

Whitley, Richard. "The Social Regulation of Work Systems: Institutions, Interest Groups and Varieties of Work Organisation in Capitalist Societies." In *Governance at Work: The Social Regulation of Economic Relations*, edited by Richard Whitley and Peer Hull Kristensen, 227–60. Oxford: Oxford University Press, 1997.

Wittmütz, Kerstin. *Die "Contratos de Protección" im Gewerkschaftssystem Mexikos: Rechtliche Hintergründe und sozialpolitische Bedeutung*. Survey commissioned by Friedrich Ebert Foundation. http://fesmex.org/common/Documentos/Ponencias/Studie%20Contratos%20de%20Proteccion.pdf, 2004 (accessed August 6, 2013).

Wolf, Martin. "Struggling with a Great Contraction." *Financial Times*, August 30, 2011.

Wong, Poh-Kam. "Technological Capability Development by Firms from East Asian NIEs." In *Technology, Competitiveness and the State: Malaysia's Industrial Technology Policies*, edited by Greg Felker and Kwame Sundaram Jomo. London: Routledge, 1999.

———. "Riding the Waves: Technological Change, Competing US-Japan Production Networks, and the Growth of Singapore's Electronics Industry." In *International Production Networks in Asia: Rivalry or Riches?* edited by Michael Borrus, Dieter Ernst, and Stephen Haggard, 179–97 London: Routledge, 2000.

Woo, Guillermo. "Hacia la integración de pequeñas empresas en la industria electrónica en Jalisco: Dos casos de estudio." In *Claroscuros: Integración exitosa de las pequeñas y medianas empresas en México*, edited by Enrique Dussel Peters, 107–56. México D.F.: Jus, 2001.

World Bank. *Malaysia Economic Monitor: Repositioning for Growth*. Washington, DC: World Bank, November 2009.

Yeung, Henri Wai-chung, and Kris Olds, eds. *Globalization of Chinese Business Firms*. Houndmills: St. Martin's, 2000.

Zapata, Francisco. "Transición entre modelos de desarrollo y nuevas instituciones laborales en América Latina." In *El sindicalismo en México ante el nuevo milenio: una perspectiva global*, edited by Raquel Partida, Alfonso Bouzas, Patricia Ravelo, and Óscar Contreras, 31–52. Zapopan: University of Guadalajara, 2001.

———. "NAFTA: Few Gains for Mexican's Workers." *Perspectives on Work* 6, no. 1 (2002): 22–24.

Ziltener, Patrick. "Hat der EU-Binnenmarkt Wachstum und Beschäftigung gebracht?" *WSI-Mitteilungen* 56, no. 4 (2003): 221–27.

Index

About the Authors

Boy Lüthje is senior research fellow at the Institute of Social Research in Frankfurt and a visiting professor at the School of Government, Sun Yat-Sen University, Guangzhou. He holds a PhD in sociology from Frankfurt University. He has held various visiting scholar appointments at the University of California, Berkeley; the East-West Center, Honolulu, Hawaii; and China Renmin University, Beijing. He has also been a labor educator for German trade unions since the 1980s. His main research area is global production, innovation, and work in advanced manufacturing industries. In recent years, industrial relations in China have become a major topic of his work.

Stefanie Hürtgen is research fellow at the Institute of Social Research (IfS) in Frankfurt. Originally from and employed in East Berlin, after reunification she studied political science at Free University, Berlin, and worked in different European countries owing to scientific and also labor-education commitments. Previously she was assistant and lecturer at the European Academy of Labour in Frankfurt. Her main research topic is the social, political, and economic impact of the current European integration and transformation processes. Her latest article is "Labour as a Transnational Actor, and Labour's National and Cultural Diversity as an Important Frame of Today's Transnationality," in *Capital & Class* 37, no. 2 (forthcoming).

Peter Pawlicki has been a research fellow at the Institute of Social Research in Frankfurt since 2003. In 2006 he was a professional associate at the East-West Center in Honolulu, Hawaii. Since 2001 he has been working on several international research projects on globalization and work in the electronics industry. He received his PhD from Frankfurt University, where he focused on engineering work in the semiconductor industry. He now works as a staff researcher for IG Metall, Germany's largest trade union.

Martina Sproll was a research fellow at the Institute of Social Research in Frankfurt from 2001 to 2008. She is currently a postdoctoral researcher at "desiguALdades.net" (Research Network on Interdependent Inequalities in Latin America), Free University, Berlin. Research areas include labor sociology, gender relations, transnationalization of production and services, sociology and economy of Latin America, and social inequalities. Among her recent publications are "Precarization, Genderization and Neotaylorist Work: How Global Value Chain Restructuring Affects Banking Sector Workers in Brazil," desiguALdades Working Paper Series (April 2013); and *Symbolische Gewalt und Leistungsregime: Geschlechterungleichheit in der betrieblichen Arbeitspolitik* (2012, with M. Funder).